The Girl in the Show

The Girl in the Show

Three Generations of Comedy, Culture, and Feminism

Anna Fields

Arcade Publishing • New York

First Edition

Arcade Publishing books may be purchased in bulk at special discounts for sales promotion, corporate gifts, fund-raising, or educational purposes. Special editions can also be created to specifications. For details, contact the Special Sales Department, Arcade Publishing, 307 West 36th Street, 11th Floor, New York, NY 10018 or arcade@skyhorsepublishing.com.

Arcade Publishing® is a registered trademark of Skyhorse Publishing, Inc.®, a Delaware corporation.

Visit our website at www.arcadepub.com.

10 9 8 7 6 5 4 3 2 1

Library of Congress Cataloging-in-Publication Data is available on file.

Cover design by Brian Peterson

Print ISBN: 978-1-5107-1836-4
Ebook ISBN: 978-1-5107-1837-1

Printed in the United States of America.

I dedicate this to you, my one and only You.

contents

part four
LOOKISM

part five
"YES, AND-ING" THE F-WORD

introduction

Being a "female comedian" is like bicycling in heavy traffic. You can ride on the same roads as cars, but they weren't built for you. You spend way more time avoiding collisions and trying not to get hurt than navigating with ease.

If you doubt this, try a little sidewalk exercise: As you're moving along, minding your own business, try *not* stepping out of a man's way as he walks toward you. Let me know if he notices you're there. If not, let the inevitable collision happen. And then let me know if he gets confused as to *how* it happened.

I'm reminded of this kind of collision of consciousness whenever I see photos of the Not Ready for Prime Time Players, many of whom later became the first cast of *Saturday Night Live*. Watching the show's 1975 pilot episode, I first learned of the male Players' decision to harness Gilda Radner's gender as a publicity technique, hoping to get butts into seats by announcing "and there's a *girl* in the show!" Two decades after Elaine May arguably invented the form, live, televised sketch comedy in 1975 was apparently still as much a novelty as having a girl in an improv troupe. Based on this realization, I began to research all the other girls who helped to first make, then change, and eventually control what we now refer to collectively as "improv," "stand-up," and serialized, nationally broadcast "comedies."

I wondered about the power of comedy to shape society. I wondered whether women* find the same things humorous today as we did yesterday. I wondered about the past's influence on the present: Has humor *itself* changed, or has change only permeated the surface, going no further than the language we're using? Some of my interviewees insisted that entertainment's largely censored, racially segregated, and highly misogynistic beginnings paved the way for our current actively inclusive, revealing-to-the-point-of-raw comedy landscape; others felt little connection to these women or to liberation itself. I asked them to share their experiences in an industry where they're expected to simultaneously be both masculine and feminine and to shock the audience with explicitly sexual jokes while avoiding "gross topics" like tampons, periods, and pregnancy; a profession where bookers continually judge all women based on a single woman's performance, and where comics who draw inspiration from their everyday, gendered experiences are often dismissed as "blue" and relegated to the second-class category of "women's comedy." Club owners routinely offer no more than two performance slots in every show for "the girls" in this category, and because all of "the girls" are presumed to make the same jokes, unspoken rules

---

* As 50.8 percent of the American population. (Gallup Poll 2011)

dictate that they must *always* be broken up, buffered by male comics who, due to their genitalia alone, are presumed to have a much wider range of perspectives.

I asked each woman whether, in her opinion, much has changed since Gilda was first introduced as "the girl" in the show. I hoped that telling her story along with many others' would help us reach an answer.

First, however, I had to learn everything I could about Gilda herself. I took a detour through Detroit to pay a visit to her tombstone, which read:

COMEDIENNE—BALLERINA, 1946 . . . 1989

In 1986, Phyllis Diller gave an interview for *Fresh Air*, wherein she defined what a "comedienne-ballerina" is, as opposed to a comic or a comedian. According to Phyllis, a "comedienne-ballerina" was a performer with an investment in creating new worlds, filled with characters. Lucille Ball was an actress because she reacted to comic situations, and Phyllis Diller and Joan Rivers were comics because they spent their careers "standing on stage with a microphone, making quips," Phyllis said. Regardless of the distinctions, their collective job was to help their audiences relax and release some of their own personal pain. It's nearly biblical in scope, the catharsis of laughter, and has been known to become a spiritual, detoxifying experience for performers and audiences alike. *Here's my heart in my hand, and here's my soul,* the performer says. *There are moldy, ugly parts, but it's still quite beautiful, don't you think?*

Today, however, "comedienne-ballerina," "female comic," and "women's comedy" are no longer welcome terms. They have gone the way of "lady doctor," "female reporter," "woman writer," and others terms commonly used to refer to all non-male professionals during and immediately after

World War II, from roughly 1941 until the mid-1960s—a period of radical social change, during which many ambitious women were caught in an awkward catch-22, working outside the home and building nascent careers without the hard-won benefits that working women currently enjoy. This period fed into the commonly understood Second Wave Feminist movement and corresponding sexual revolution, which didn't get into full swing until Betty Friedan's *The Feminine Mystique* seemed to clarify its purposes.

To most modern, educated persons, referring to a physician or a professor (who also happens to be a woman) as "lady doctor" sounds ridiculous. Yet performers, their audiences, and the general media persistently use terms like "female comic" and "women's comedy" to refer to either humorists (who happen to be female) or their craft. It denotes a confining subcategory, segregating women into their own special lane of comedy. This gender-based segregation implies that while comedians who happen to be male fall under the default standard of "comedy," women who happen to be comedians are a specialty. A niche. A nonstandard deviation from "normal." This idea—that male comedians are normal while female comedians are special exceptions—perpetuates not only discrimination against women in comedy but also gender-based segregation against us all. It promotes the sexist illusion that the lingering question "Are Women Funny?" is still valid and remains up for debate—despite countless articles, documentaries, and other media that have already provided the obvious answer: Yes. They are. What century are you from again?

Rather than indirectly reopening this debate by using the segregationist terms "female comic," "female comedian," or even "comedienne" on their own (the continued existence of which perfectly illustrates our extremely pressing and continued need for a strong, unified Feminism), this book will use the specialized term "comedienne-ballerina." In so doing, I hope that we can all finally agree to use Patriarchy's own language to disprove its presumption, moving the verb to second place and replacing that annoying question mark with a firm period: Women Are Funny.

Personally, when I see the word "ballerina" in isolation, I think of someone very skinny with busted toes who has made sacrifices in her life to do a job that doesn't pay particularly well, and who was tormented in some way. But brought out of isolation and combined with "comedienne," this definition no longer suffices. The juxtaposition of a "comedienne-ballerina" evokes an image of duality: fragility supported by strength, darkness deepened by light, speaking and staying silent, both color and its absence.

In this way, I imagine Gilda *reaching* for everything there was to grasp inside each moment. Did she reach it? I don't know. I have no idea how she inherited that instinct to be both at once. But this revolutionary need to be everything, all at once; to simultaneously inhabit two seemingly mutually exclusive roles—funny yet truthful, light tinged with dark, masculine but still feminine, comedically irreverent while artistically grounded—now permeates our society. I refer to this modern (and, in my opinion, extremely positive) need as "Both-ness," and as I'll detail throughout the remainder of our discussion: It has come to define what it means to be a woman, a Feminist, a millennial, and a comedienne-ballerina.

When we experience "Both-ness," we feel Gilda's and Lucy's need to express their whole selves in one lifetime. We sense their fingers reaching over some invisible line, and then drawing back in hesitation, fearful of the message they've silently absorbed: No woman can reasonably (or happily) exist in more than one sphere. Do Not Enter. And yet their very way of life as comedienne-ballerinas has already countered this message and urged them forward.

Today, when we embrace "Both-ness," we reach back to Gilda and Lucy. We touch them when we laugh. When we laugh, we are our truest selves. And laughter, like violence, is also how we re-create ourselves. How we reject society's harmful messages. How we recognize our instincts apart from what we've been taught. How we unlearn in order to *know*. In this way, each generation must discover itself anew, and through that self, discover its mission. Then it must decide whether to fulfill or betray that mission.

Gilda's mission was to reach; ours is to grasp. We discovered we were revolutionaries when we discovered what's funny. When we see that politics is war without bloodshed and war is politics with bloodshed. When we grasp how many other humorists have changed our world, and how their histories can help us to change ourselves. They reached forward into the future, clasping our hands as we reach back. A million, billion amazing women most people will never know. Whom most of us will never even get the chance to know.

After leaving Gilda's tombstone in Detroit, I spent the better part of three years attempting such fundamentally life-altering movement. I forced myself out of my self-imposed safe space (my head) to replace it with an ever-unsafe one: real life. I traveled to various cities and spent countless hours engaging in real life, offline, *in-person* conversations. I sought out living, breathing humans and asked them all sorts of uncomfortable, nosy, sometimes intentionally offensive questions—and I recorded their answers. I walked around inside traditionally unsafe (meaning Patriarchy-controlled) spaces: comedy clubs and improv theaters all over the country, from Los Angeles to

Chicago to Austin to New York. I studied every comedian who also happened to be a woman from 1920 to the present.

By the end, I had a better idea of the exact intersectional relationship between comedy and Feminism; how one created the possibility of the other, and how *both* are necessary for the future of comedy. *The Girl in the Show* seeks to illustrate the direct links between past and present by juxtaposing three generations of comedienne-ballerinas against three waves of intersectional Feminism. Early Feminists like Lucille Ball (who didn't necessarily use the term "Feminist," since she was born before women could vote and women's liberation was still in its infancy) paved the way for performers like Gilda, who in turn created opportunities for today's current comedienne-ballerinas, who have gone on to know themselves in vastly new ways. Together, these three generations have arguably done more to further gender equality as a whole than any piece of legislation since the Nineteenth Amendment and the Civil Rights Act of 1964.

Our ignorance of women's history and the resulting mirror effect between equality and comedy is growing. We rarely read, talk, hear about, or even recognize our own historical figures, and yet our generation is deeply connected to women like Sarah Silverman, Amy Schumer, Lena Dunham, Wanda Sykes, Mindy Kaling, and Issa Rae, among many others, who admittedly owe their successes to the radically progressive liberationists of the nineteenth and twentieth centuries. Unfortunately, we tend to view our present as entirely disconnected from their past. Some of us suspect that few traces of inequality persist outside the obvious wage gap, and we refuse to consider any noneconomic injustice.

For others, this extends to our relationships with other women. We see ourselves as [BLANK] first and women second.

The first blank is usually our race, our class, our sexual orientation, or our marital status. These distinctions, for many women, are far more important in defining our sense of self than the first thing most people notice about us: our gender. For this reason, and many others, we sometimes treat other women as our enemies, fierce competitors rather than potential collaborators. We focus on our differences and dismiss our similarities, forgetting (or ignoring) the fact that if *anyone* understands what we're going through, *she* does. Instead, we compartmentalize. We rationalize away another woman's suffering as somehow different from our own. If it's not *our* problem, it's not *a* problem. This mindset allows the age-old divide-and-conquer strategy to divide and conquer us.

Sometimes, we compartmentalize the *severity* of the problem rather than the problem itself or whom it affects. When we do this, we're insisting that sexism must be both open and obvious in order to exist at all, which suggests that anything less glaring than a male chasing a female around his desk in an episode of *Mad Men* is just "boys being boys." Still others absorb these tendencies and *become* the boys. You'll find them ordering their fellow females to "smile more" and "stop dressing like you're asking for it," ignoring (or even instigating) the most obvious misogyny. We refuse to believe anything that departs from our preapproved image of "harmless" locker-room talk as a default setting for how men are.

I refer to this setting as Stella Kowalski Syndrome. It's akin to Stockholm Syndrome—wherein a victim is so deeply brainwashed by her captor that she becomes his defender—but like the character of Stella Kowalski from Tennessee Williams's 1947 play *A Streetcar Named Desire*, this victim defends the Patriarchy because, like any victim of kidnapping, her existence depends on survival. To survive, she must adapt. Sometimes we find ourselves adapting with her—once both of us have forgotten to feel for the invisible bars within our cages. Our eyes adjust to the half light. Our fingers lose feeling. We get used to feeling sick. It's contagious. So it's no longer enough. It's no longer enough, in the twenty-first century, to fight the Patriarchy. Today, we must learn to fight the Patriarchy within *us*.

Confronting the subconscious sexism of our age is exhausting. If we *really* stopped to consider how fucking terrifyingly vulnerable we feel, minute-to-minute, even life within the safety of a box would seem unlivable. So we just . . . don't. We stop feeling. Or talking. Or thinking. We'd rather zone out. We'd prefer another glass of wine, thanks. As Gilda once said, "Women are lucky because we can give up." And most of us, most of the time . . . do.

I do it too. I am totally with you, right here inside the box. I'll be honest and admit that I binge-watch *Crazy Ex-Girlfriend*.

Somehow, shows about women who proclaim themselves to be "bad Feminists," illustrating the continued gap between what society tells us we should want (physical perfection, marriage, children) and what Feminism has tried to instill (the notion that we can choose all or none of those things), make me feel less alone. (This is one of the main purposes of comedy.)

As Claire Fallon wrote about *Crazy Ex-Girlfriend* in the *Huffington Post*, "It can be uncomfortable to watch a show about a troubled woman who drastically alters her entire life for a man she barely knows. It feels un-feminist. But frowning on all TV show characters who paint women as something other than strong, girl-power icons only limits what women in comedy can do."

Fallon's description of the show's main character, Rebecca Bunch, as "strong because she's weird, self-centered, insecure and deeply in denial" sounds like a mirror image of Lucy Ricardo's neurotic, grasping, wannabe actress character. Just like Lucy, Rebecca "probably looks very little like most, or all, women we know. But she reveals more about us than we'd like to admit. Some women fully embrace traditional womanhood, and others fully embrace radical independence, but most of us are caught in a limbo somewhere between." Lucy mirrored women's struggle against dual expectations in a conservative society, just as Rebecca continues to do today. The generations are just alike, both before and after the full-blown Feminist movement of the late 1960s and 1970s. Only today, as Fallon notes, "like Rebecca, we conceive of ourselves as strong, independent and far too cool to sacrifice ourselves for male attention, but also like Rebecca, we weren't exactly raised in a world that fostered those qualities. Instead, here we are, caught between what we've been trained to want and what we're not embarrassed to say we want . . . it's held up a dark mirror to the empowered image Feminists present to the world, and the suppressed, internalized sexism we can't all banish."

So are we all "bad Feminists," or has Feminism become a bad word? Is it even possible to fully participate in the world today and *not* be a Feminist?

I don't know about you, but I'm so personally steeped in the benefits of Feminism that I catch myself wondering if it even exists. Like air or gravity, it remains unseen while surrounding me, anchoring me to the earth and keeping me alive. I wonder if inequality is something of the past, as so many conservative women and Fox News pundits insist. Part of a dark place we'd rather forget all about, since it obviously no longer pertains to real life anymore—kind of like medieval England, where peasants "cured" their diseases by bleeding the sick and "cleaned" their food by making the sign of the cross. That nonsense is over, and *so is sexism, right*? Right.

Inequality is something that we smart women have gotten over. What are we still complaining about, anyway? We can vote and work now, and abortion is technically legal now (even though almost everyone who's had one—like your dermatologist or your landlady or your *mom*—is too ashamed to tell you).

As Fallon indirectly points out, we often fail to recognize the insidious nature of sexism. My gut instinct that some sexist bullshit may be afoot has been rationalized and minimized until it's shrunk to almost nothing. And so I miss the subliminal nature of each message as it screams, *shut up already so we don't have to hear/see/acknowledge you*. I'm busy counting calories and posting to Twitter as it floods my subconscious. Like so many others, it took me *years* to wake up to what was happening. When my eyes finally opened, I saw then what I'd become: an unwitting champion for my own suffering, a loyal defender of silence and secrets, an enthusiastic cheerleader for my lifelong captors.

But when I forced myself to be honest, to take a hard look at my language and mindset, the truth became clear: I had re-victimized myself and all those I loved by believing the old, seductive lies: I'm "bad." I should feel sorry and apologize for my choices. I'm either/or. I can't have it all, and I shouldn't try or I'll be unhappy. Instead, I should really just try lowering my expectations. And, above all, I should be smart about it, because there's nothing less attractive than a dumb bitch who tries too hard.

Don't I realize how *lucky* I am?

Shouldn't I go ahead and get in line and choose the *one* [BLANK] that will define the rest of my life?

Wouldn't I be happier that way?

Unfortunately, some of us defend the Patriarchy even when doing so threatens our lives. Feminist philosophies created every civil right we've ever won, and the basic idea that women are (and should be treated as) equals to men forms the basis for everything we enjoy about modern life. We openly profess this belief and yet, paradoxically, reject Feminism—which is like eating an apple while asking, "Why do we still need apple trees?"

Some of us defend the Patriarchy because we're simply ignorant. We don't know any history but men's history. We have been groomed to remember and celebrate what Patriarchy wants us to remember and celebrate: men's accomplishments. For this reason, for example, most of us can't name even a single current female senator, let alone explain Madame Curie's mind-blowing contributions to science. The origins of entertainment—and especially comedy—are no exception. We immediately recognize valuable works of Charlie Chaplin and Jerry Seinfeld, but we've never even heard of Moms Mabley, who was arguably the first American stand-up comedian, or Anita Loos, the very first staff writer of *any* television show or feature film *of any kind*.

Today, many of us still don't understand the connection between women's liberation and the comedy we enjoy. We have an idea, but we're still not exactly sure how Feminism made "women's comedy" possible, or how "women's comedy" has broadened, expanded, and illuminated our need for Feminism. The history behind this symbiotic "chicken and egg" relationship is generally unknown—which is supremely dangerous for anyone who enjoys the freedom both to laugh and to control her own vagina. When we fail to study the history, we can forget it. When we forget something, its value can be lost. And anything that isn't valuable becomes easier to discard.

I recently had a conversation with a comedy writer who happened to be female.

Comedy writer: "So. What's your book about?"

Me: "The relationship between women's liberation and 'women's comedy.'"

"There are *women* in *comedy*?" *

That being said, certainly not all women are Feminists simply by virtue of their reproductive organs, any more than all men are sexists by virtue of theirs. If all women were Feminists and believed in their own inherent self-worth as equals to men, #WomenForTrump wouldn't have propelled blatantly anti-woman politicians to positions of power, and the Equal Rights Amendment would have passed into law in 1979 instead of being defeated time and again—in large part by self-proclaimed anti-Feminists like Phyllis Schlafly and Anita Bryant. If all women were Feminists, we wouldn't suffer so much. We wouldn't be making anywhere from 21 to 66 percent less than our male colleagues. We wouldn't have to laugh at sexist jokes that we don't find all that funny just to make men comfortable. We wouldn't have to buy rape-resistant underwear or go to self-defense classes or buy mace or teach our daughters not to accept drinks from strangers. We wouldn't immediately question all rape victims' motives. We'd have finally admitted, along with the Guttmacher Institute, that nearly one in three women has *at least* one abortion by the time she reaches menopause (including, as a reminder: your mom, landlady, and/or dermatologist). We wouldn't quit a job we liked and

---

* She wasn't kidding.

worked really hard to get simply because we got pregnant. We wouldn't take a job (if we could avoid it) that didn't provide maternity leave and daycare benefits. We wouldn't expect to lower *our* standards; we'd expect our employers, elected officials, friends, family, partners, and all current and future Internet advice-writers to raise *theirs*.

So why don't we?

Because we're asleep. Or we've been shamed into silence by stigma and fear. Or because we're just trying to survive our captivity. Or because we're still stubbornly [BLANK] first and women second. Because we don't do what we should, which is to shout from the rooftops that the whole of society benefits when motherhood is voluntary. To yell at the top of our lungs: "I don't care if Planned Parenthood *only* offers abortions! I don't care if they operate an entire abortion theme park, complete with abortion cotton candy, abortion roller coasters, and abortion water slides! Abortion is a legal, necessary medical service that has freed billions of women from reproductive oppression and saved billions more from death at the hands of back-alley, hanger-carrying quacks!"

If we were all Feminists, we *would* do what we *should*. We would all be out, away from our self-imposed safe spaces, in the dangerously real world, interacting face to face with employers, elected officials, friends, family, partners, and all current and future Internet advice-writers, and calling that shit out. We would all, in unison, point out how incredibly fortunate some men are that their gender (and, in some cases, their wealth and/or race) protects them from the consequences of their decisions, their policies, and their choice of president. We'll keep in mind how happy they are to work with us on the "real issues" while we're enduring all of the horrors they never have and never will.

The Girl in the Show is intended to help us do what we should by showing us how far we've come and how far we still have left to go. To help us shake off our resignation and get to work. To help us see and remember (or learn, if we never knew) precisely how the ebbs and flows of three generations of comedienne-ballerinas starring in, writing, and running the show have gone hand in hand with the progressive steps that Feminists and Feminism have taken to liberate our 51 percent from not only (quite literal) physical, legal, and financial bondage, but also a deeply subconscious self-loathing that has long enslaved our minds. The latter is arguably far more destructive that the former, since it so often leads to we, the prisoners, voluntarily throwing away the keys. The notion that women's voices should be heard at all is often deemed "radical," but it is this longstanding, symbiotic relationship between comedy and Feminism that has given women everywhere a collective voice and the many comedians who now celebrate that voice a platform. Despite attempts to persuade us otherwise, the histories of women like Lucille Ball, Moms Mabley, Gilda Radner, and Ellen DeGeneres teach us that comedy itself is a powerful tool in this "humorless" fight toward equality. Through seeing, remembering, or learning these things, *The Girl in the Show* attempts to guide our 51 percent toward embracing our duality as both [BLANK] *and* women, and to offer us all some much-needed medicine within a spoonful of sugar.

Over the course of my research, I quickly found that while humor has long been a well-documented weapon for rebellion, offering a nonviolent mouthpiece to the oppressed and discontent, women were rarely afforded the opportunity to speak. Before 1940, standout females rarely appeared in comedy, and those who did usually became the butt of the joke: wide-eyed damsels on the run from the Marx Brothers; tools to be used in Chaplin's riotous machinations; or the childlike, borderline incompetent half of a coed duo ("Say goodnight, Gracie!"). Alternately, they became props—attractive bimbos, nagging wives, neurotic mothers, or needy daughters— vehicles through which the "take my wife, please" generation drove home their brand of humor. With few exceptions (Pert Kelton, Sophie Tucker, and a few others whom we'll explore at length), early film, radio, and vaudevillian actresses conformed their characters to appease hardline, misogynist gender expectations: the number one requirement for remaining in the show. Feminism helped to change all this, creating the impetus for women to enter male-dominated stages, radio waves, and eventually television networks as more than the passive objects of comic affection.

Because Lucille Ball and writer Madelyn Pugh Davis were the first females to successfully transition from stage to screen, and the first to exercise creative control over the content of "the show"—both onscreen and off—they will serve as our historical through line, binding earlier generations to today's well-known comedic voices. Many decades later, Lucy and Madelyn remain Feminist icons for comic actresses and writers, spurring on the first generation of women's involvement in televised comedy and inspiring some of the most prolific performers we see today.

But several questions remain: Which came first, liberation or comedy? Would one have been possible without the other? Can either continue alone? And how has today's pushback against gender labels furthered, sustained, or changed "women's comedy" for better or worse?

Using Lucy as a touchstone, *The Girl in the Show* will travel from 1920 to the present, wrapping multigenerational comedienne-ballerinas in their own particular social, historical, and political context, illustrating the changes women have made in the wake of full-blown liberation, including greater participation in new forms of comedy and the impact of a rapidly changing landscape. "Women's comedy" and women's liberation have evolved together—each expanding upon the other to create new avenues for diversity and opportunity, empowerment and humor. After the era of Moms Mabley, Lucille Ball, Anita Loos, Joan Rivers, Phyllis Diller, Totie Fields, Dorothy Parker, and so many others, a Second Wave of comedic Feminism was arguably kick-started by Gilda Radner, Laraine Newman, and Jane Curtin, who captivated audiences from the moment they appeared on *Saturday Night Live*, the first women to shepherd in the era of nationally televised improv—a more democratic type of comedy in which performers create their own characters, giving them the opportunity to take control of the truths told in jest. Another powerful threesome—Rosie Shuster, Anne Beatts, and Marilyn Suzanne Miller, the first female writers in *SNL* history—aided Gilda, Jane, and Laraine. Together, this group changed the show, creating sketches that spoke specifically to women viewers—a huge departure from the boundaries first imposed on and then internalized by Lucy and Maddy.

While the generation before *SNL* contributed to liberating women from the domestic sphere, this new wave of comics and "sketch" comedy writers raised our collective awareness of sexism's negative effects on women's emotional, financial, and physical well-being. Because they came of age at the height of the women's liberation movement, their influences on *SNL* became a turning point in our historical, political, and cultural timeline. By the 1970s, Feminism was in full swing, bringing millions more women into the workplace at the same time as television sets were rapidly established as the dominant sources of entertainment in the home (replacing the radio comedies, which had, for many years, provided outlets for "Funny Girl" Fanny Brice and other notable female voices). For the first time since *I Love Lucy*, female-driven content came directly into American homes—but this time, the girls in the show weren't married. They weren't mothers. They weren't downtrodden sidekicks or beautiful plus-ones to leading men. They were just themselves. And they were funny. Even as the girls became immersed in a well-known boys' club, their work spoke for itself. The result was a nationwide consciousness raising, both for that era's audiences and future generations seeking inspiration.

Their combined contributions—and the similarities between their work and that of Feminist activists—go largely unnoticed today in large part because the industry continues to be male dominated. This history has been largely overlooked—and not just by men. While many people of both genders recognize the names Bob Hope, George Burns, Jerry Stiller, Jackie Gleason, Charlie Chaplin, and others, few know anything about the efforts of women like Pert Kelton, Elayne Boosler, Moms Mabley, Marlo Thomas, and so many others who used humor to liberate both men and women from misogynist mindsets. The Second Wave of girls in the show balked at the idea that the male gaze should determine who and what made it on air, and yet the network still paraded these performers' gender as a way to "hook" an audience. This parade put gender at the forefront, implying that audiences were watching these women because they were women and not necessarily because they were funny. Such implicit, subconscious segregation ("Here we have the women, and here we have the actual 'funny people'") forced these groundbreakers—like so many who came before them—to make the best of their situation, using television as a platform for promoting Feminism: the movement that made their careers possible.

Finally, *The Girl in the Show* is a synthesis of interviews—either directly transcribed or paraphrased—with present-day comics, writers, executives, performers, and showrunners whose work you'll likely recognize (even if their names aren't yet as famous as their comedy and their eventual influences have yet to be determined). Their words form part of the collective conversation about women's current roles in humor, in life, and in the public eye, seeking to celebrate the present by teaching us about the past. They also seek to reinforce the positive empowerment that so many women feel today by educating them about the need for further liberation in the future. Often, during interviews, performers were unaware of how much they—and their audiences—owed to the women who came before them, and how they might be subconsciously perpetuating many of the harmful stereotypes and assumptions that these women worked so hard to overcome. Still, the number of performers, writers, and executives who are committed to addressing their own shortcomings in order to promote Feminism and women's empowerment through comedy is growing, and as a result, the potential for social impact is truly substantial.

In this ever-shifting landscape of cable, online, and social media–driven entertainment, many of us may be unaware of the ties between the past and present underlying the comedy we enjoy. By comparing these current comedienne-ballerinas to their predecessors, *The Girl in the Show* shows us how far we've come and how far we have yet to go.

part one

A SPOONFUL OF SUGAR

"A smile is a curve that sets everything straight."
—Phyllis Diller

truth *plus*

THE OPENING MONOLOGUE OF GILDA Radner's filmed Broadway show *Gilda Live* begins with a thirty-four-year-old woman with overalls and red ribbons in her hair approaching the end of the stage to explain her dreams. She grew up in Detroit, she says, where her dad used to take her to shows. They'd sit in the third row. She'd look up at the people on stage and marvel at how happy they seemed. What a good time they were having! She'd want that good time, too. *That's what I want to do*, she thought. *That's who I want to be.* And when the performers would come down to the end of the stage and look out, she was always sure "that they were looking at me—at little Gilda Radner. And now that I'm finally up here, I can't see a thing!"

This was 1980, when she and a Canadian television producer named Lorne Michaels turned many of her most famous *Saturday Night Live* characters into a Broadway show. I wasn't there, of course. I hadn't yet been born. But when I saw it, years later, I thought she was looking down at me, too. Our consciousnesses seemed to collide.

Beyond her political and cultural achievements, Gilda Radner's childhood tragedy, estrangement from her mother, and devotion to Biddy, her childhood caretaker—the three forces that inspired Emily Litella, the first of her most famous characters—have always resonated with me on an emotional level. I also grew up with a mother who took to her bed with severe depression. To get her to come out of her room, I developed the same comedic routines that had worked for Gilda: I did impressions. I reenacted scenes from her favorite television shows. But while Gilda was impersonating Elaine May and Phyllis Diller, I was impersonating Gilda and Lily Tomlin. My mother's favorite characters were Roseanne Roseannadanna, Gilda's brashly crude television news reporter, and Ernestine, Lily's evil phone operator. Her second favorite was "Fish Face," which required me to stretch my mouth into a straight line while flapping my hands on either side of my face to create gills. It was uncomfortable but far less so than watching my mother suffer—and besides, it always worked. She always laughed.

In my mind, Gilda and I were both funny girls who developed our comedy around our early experiences with tragedy. We both used the latter to create the former, and our childhoods were inextricably linked to our art. We also shared pain, a deep desire to make our mothers proud, and the ambition to become everything the women before us somehow couldn't. In many ways, Gilda's story is my story, too. I've yet to meet an artist in any age group who can't say the same.

In 1978, during episode 304 of *The Muppet Show*, Gilda appeared as a hapless tap dancer who just couldn't catch a break. She banged her head, nearly fell over in her unbuckled patent leather shoes, and flailed around in her red satin shorts and characteristic frizzy pigtails, all while singing to her audience to "*tap your troubles away!*" In order to tap her own troubles away, Gilda performed. She never spoke directly about her problems with her mother, her father's sudden death, or her rampant bulimia. She was considered a "personal" performer because she created characters from the people she'd known or with whom she'd personally interacted, and then used them to make a new world on stage.

That was her job, really—dancing when it was raining. To achieve this, some comedians are deeply personal, digging through "their own crap," as they often call it, and making it festive. Their job is "to help audiences lose themselves and to have an epic night out," as UK solo artist Luisa Omielan says. "To deliver my show in the best way I can, every night, as if I'd just thought it up on the spot—like it's a new show, just for them—and make them rest easy that the show is built for them to do so."

Comic actress Molly Shannon agrees. "I like making people laugh and making people feel good, maybe forget their trouble for a little while. That's a great feeling, when people come up and ask, 'Can I give you a hug?' because they associate you with a feeling of warmth and joy. There's something about being on television that makes me accessible to them. They feel, because I'm in their living room, like I'm like their friend. It's very sweet. Bringing joy and happiness and helping people forget their troubles for a little while is a comedian's job, I think. Hopefully people will laugh if they relate to it, and hopefully they will laugh even if they don't relate to it. And then you cover it up with other shtick, just in case."

In return, the performer gets to be honest. She earns an outlet for sharing how distraught and devastated she is, and how much she hates those same feelings. She actually gets to talk. And to reward her for turning lead into gold—pain into tap dancing—the audience laughs. It's a beautiful transaction where the currency may change, but the value stays the same.

"At my lowest point, I was my most beautiful on stage," Luisa Omielan said when we spoke by phone during her comedy tour in Australia. "Every time, without fail, every time that I've had horrendous feelings about myself, or thought, 'shit you're worthless, you're bad,' then my issues are coming up my face to confront me, the second I can go on stage and go, 'blah here it all is,' it turns it into something beautiful. I go, 'oh, thank God, that's not my life.' Otherwise you'd die, I think."

Luisa now uses this currency to teach people how to seek help for mental illnesses. "When you talk about that, and how there's a male member in my family who took an overdose and tried to kill himself a few years ago, you realize: it's not only bullshit, it's failed mental health. I struggled then to go on antidepressants. To talk to the doctor and be like, 'I'm not homeless, I'm not a smack head, and I'm not some old man who's just been dropped from his job of forty years. Why am I struggling so much?' And yet I was afraid of antidepressants. They were something that felt so ugly to me, something I so didn't want to be associated with. Thank God I got the help that I needed. Because you know what? It's totally normal! *I'm totally normal!* And I like going on stage and being like, 'Guys, you don't have to agree, but I think I'm cool. I'm funny, I'm normal. Look, it's a party, here's your meds. Some wonderful people have been on them, too, so it's okay if you need them. Go out and get the help that's out there! And now, here's some more jokes.'"

Other comics disagree that there's so much beneath the surface. To them, a joke is a joke is a joke. For stand-up comic

Brandie Posey, the job is "to be a funny idiot, and that's it. That's all I want to do. I don't speak for other women. I speak only for myself."

In keeping with this idea, comedian and writer Naomi Ekperigin said that while she'd always thought of entertainment as a means of educating people, "there's not always something to teach." Meaning that the funny *is* the thing (much like, for writers, "the play is the thing"). If people are laughing, they're listening. It's a spoonful of sugar that can help the medicine go down, but not every single show or every single episode of every show should taste medicinal. And not everyone is able to understand the lesson, anyway, as Tina Fey pointed out in *Bossypants*: "You can tell how smart someone is by what they laugh at."

Perhaps this is why comic actress Mo Collins believes that her job is to "play as hard and often as we can. If we're playing, we're schooling other people on how to play and take life less seriously. Literally our job is to play. If we're not having fun, how can you expect to accomplish being funny? It's got to be light; it's got to be fun; it's got to be play."

One of a comedian's jobs is obviously to make people laugh, but I don't think that's her sole job, and I'm not entirely certain that it's her main job. So many struggle for a long time to even call themselves comedians. Others do *one* open mic and feel confident enough to proclaim, "I'm a comedian!" It took most of the women in this book many years to be able to say, "I'm a comedian; that's my only job," because, unlike Gilda, who came from wealth and whose father had supplied her with a trust fund, most comedians have to work (sometimes several) *other* jobs in order to survive. They spend years working in bagel shops, or sweeping the hair off the floor after a drunk girl gets a scalp tattoo, or walking dogs in the rain, or raising rich people's test-tube babies. When they can move on from that and focus solely on their humor, it's a triumph.

As a well-known stand-up comic who requested anonymity recently said, "I had jokes about all of my boring, weirdo side jobs, until some older, wiser comedian was like, 'Eventually, you're not gonna want to joke about your job, because your job is supposed to be telling jokes. When people pay money to see you, they don't want to know that you have another job.' Not everyone takes that advice. I think some people continue to be like, 'I'm also a teacher, and I tell jokes at night . . .' But it stuck with me. Eventually I wanted to talk about the past in a past tense. Comedy *is* my job."

Still others are comedians with delusions of grandeur that I think any good performer has to possess. To them, their role in society is to make existence tolerable and fun and exciting. To open people up, allow them to feel vulnerable by *being* vulnerable, and let them escape. It's all about getting into people's heads and exploding that outward, as Steve Martin described early *SNL*: "I do remember when I first saw the show. I was living in Aspen, and it came on and I thought, they've done it! They did the *zeitgeist!* They did what was out there, what we all had in our heads, this kind of new comedy!"

Most comedians of any gender do feel the need to "explode outward" whatever they—or others they know—are feeling. It might be part of a healing process, or simply a way to process healing, but comedy has always proved a balm to wounds, and as they grow into comedy, many comedians eventually take control of their words' own healing powers. Some feel an inherent responsibility, in all kinds of transactions, to crack jokes. To provide a release valve for others. To light up even the darkest events.

Mo Collins describes this often overwhelming responsibility to care for and provide catharsis to others as a blessing in disguise: "I have this need to potentially make somebody's day better. It can be just, you know, cashing a check at the bank. Going to the doctor's office. Oh, I'm the best patient, because it's like I'm always trying to make a joke even when it's horrible. That is my responsibility, and I take it quite seriously."

Sometimes, that need to heal others' wounds comes from childhood memories. Gilda wrote that her father, Herman, was consciously funny—a bubbly, slightly overweight man who'd tell silly jokes like, "Don't suck your thumb because it's got a nail in it." He loved life and had a great spirit, and each joke he told was the funniest he'd ever heard. He loved to watch her perform and called her his "little ham." Her mother, on the other hand, was harder to reach. She had a great sense of humor, Gilda insisted in her 1989 autobiography, written before Henrietta passed away. "Almost the only thing that gets through to her is to make her laugh. She has an infectious response to humor so it was a way of getting to her when nothing else worked." Based on this, it's rumored that Jane Curtin's portrayal of Mrs. Loopner in the *SNL* sketch "The Nerds"— with Gilda playing her whiny teenage daughter, Lisa, and Bill Murray as Lisa's horny boyfriend—was based on Henrietta. When Mrs. Loopner reaches a point of ultimate frustration, she growls at Lisa, "I begrudge you every breath you ever took!" It's rumored that this, too, was based on Henrietta's way with words toward her daughter.

In 1958, Gilda lost her father over the course of forty-eight hours. Herman Radner finally went to the hospital about his headaches. They were terrible, and he'd been suffering them for years with little improvement. The doctors had already changed his glasses many times and put him on various medications, but the headaches always came back. At the hospital, he was supposed to have routine tests but ended up in surgery. When the doctors opened him up, they found a malignant brain tumor that was so advanced they couldn't do anything but close him back up. He then had a stroke that paralyzed the left side of his body, so when twelve-year-old Gilda came to visit him two days later, instead of the happy sixty-five-year-old who'd left the house, she found a bald, weak, confused old man whose appearance froze her with fear and confusion. He held her hand as she stood next to his bed and spoke to her, but he was a shell of who he'd been. His personality was changed. To Gilda, it seemed, losing someone altogether and suddenly would have been less painful than interacting with what was left over after that person disappeared.

Chemotherapy didn't exist in 1958, so Herman underwent radiation that left him nauseated. He stayed in the hospital for another few months, relearning how to use the left side of his body through combinations of exercise and concentration. When Gilda visited, everyone pretended that he was normal, living that fantasy for two years, and leaving Gilda without any explanation at all. She'd hear ambulances coming to their house every night, and men coming up the stairs with a stretcher and talking to Herman like he was a little boy. She'd lie in her bed feeling angry and resentful because she didn't understand what had happened or why, and because no one would ever tell her the truth.

When she was fourteen and away at camp, he died in the middle of the night. Someone tapped her on the shoulder at camp, and she boarded a small plane back to Detroit, where her brother held her hand and her mother seemed almost relieved. The three remaining Radners sat shiva, and then Gilda went back to camp because she wanted to. But she never got an appropriate mourning period and spent years of her adult life mourning her father's death through therapy and analysis. Her family, she wrote, could've used some help processing his illness. Even thirty years later, they were still living with the cancer that killed Herman.

Five years after Herman's death, Henrietta got breast cancer. Her mother, Golda, and Golda's sister eventually died of stomach cancer. Then, at eighteen, Gilda had a lump removed from her own right breast, which turned out to be a benign cyst. The surgeon (who later lost his license for performing unnecessary surgeries on women) made an incision that left Gilda with an ugly scar, keeping the fear of cancer marked on her body and her mind but leaving her with a sense of humor about the transient nature of life. Motivated to heal herself from the inside out, despite (or perhaps because of) her enduring scars, she endeavored to laugh, and this endeavor gradually extended to include others. Gilda entertained her family members, friends, and eventually audiences—creating a feedback loop of mutually beneficial healing.

This outward progression binds many comedians both before and after Gilda. Their collective need to heal others' wounds can often be traced back to their own. Sometimes those wounds are physical, as in the case of comedians like Tig Notaro, who famously used her very real struggle with cancer to help audiences remember to laugh. Sometimes the wounds are mental and emotional.

Sarah Silverman has spent decades opening up to her audiences about her battles with depression, which she's experienced since she was thirteen, but in *I Smile Back*, an independent drama from 2016, she showed a side of herself and her comedy that audiences rarely glimpse in any but the bravest performers. In the film, Silverman's character willfully goes off her meds, choosing instead to self-medicate with cocaine, pills, and wine. Drugs and depression create a self-destructive cocktail that ultimately poisons her relationship with her husband and children. Silverman is honest about her real-life feelings of serious depression, which she likened to coming down with a sudden flu.

She'd been an extremely social child, with best friends and a clowning attitude in class, but all of that changed suddenly with the onset of her illness. She no longer saw any reason to maintain friendships; spending time with other people was nothing more than a burden. When the depression came over her, she'd experience a frustrating sea change: a radical emotional shift that she likened to feeling terribly, insatiably homesick while still at home. The feeling lasted for three long years. Finally, Sarah told Terry Gross of NPR, "I was sent to a psychiatrist who said, 'I'm going to give you a prescription for something called Xanax, and whenever you feel bad, you take one.'" By the time she was fourteen, Sarah was taking sixteen of them a day. She kept the empty medication bottles in a shoebox so that, if she were to overdose, the person who found her would understand what happened.

Another doctor weaned her off Xanax, but the depression came roaring back in her early twenties. She recognized it as recurrent mental illness rather than temporary homesickness, but the fear that it would last another three years was terrifying. She had paralyzing panic attacks while trying to hold down her new job at *Saturday Night Live*. All she kept thinking was how much she wanted to go home to New Hampshire and avoid anything frightening. Eventually she met a new doctor who introduced her to Klonopin, a medication that specifically blocks panic attacks. "It saved my life. I was able to go to work at *Saturday Night Live* and exist through each day while I was figuring this out."

Like Sarah, longtime stand-up comic Paula Poundstone has joked about her own mental illness—and her alcoholism in particular—by admitting, "I was in the thirty-day program for 180 days. I can't even sit in a chair unless it's in a circle anymore," and revealing in an interview with Neal Conan for *Talk of the Nation* that she was court-ordered to Alcoholics Anonymous on broadcast television. "That pretty much blows the hell out of the second 'A,' wouldn't you say?" She admits that whereas most people would recognize red flags, she was too drunk to do so. "They're kind of blurry and they zip on by." She makes light of her disease by claiming that she once mistook it for an ice cream addiction and then a predilection for adopting animals. "I should have known. About three weeks before I went into rehab I got really drunk, went into a pet store, and bought a dog. It would have been no big deal, but we had nine cats. Believe me, the cats started hiding the alcohol after that. We now have ten cats, a big stupid dog, two tadpoles, a bearded dragon lizard, and a bunny. I'm going to be honest with you. I'd been drunk in that pet store before, and I don't want to play the victim here, but I believe they knew and I believe they took advantage. Does anybody else's pet store have a wine section? It seems unusual to me." Though she expertly adds sugar to her medicine, Paula's main source of pain seems to stem from the fact that her alcoholism affected her children's lives.

Like Paula's children, the beloved comedian and actress Carol Burnett grew up witnessing similar events due to her own parents' alcoholism. Carol in particular was shaped by a history of emotional instability that finally resulted in her raising her younger sister, Chrissie, when addiction overtook their mother's life. She wrote extensively about the years leading up to the event—first in Depression-era San Antonio and then in Hollywood—when she and her grandmother, "Nanny," moved into a studio apartment down the hall from her starstruck mother, "Mama." Mama had married her high school sweetheart, a kind but downtrodden salesman, but then divorced him when he too became an alcoholic. As a result, Carol grew extremely attached to Nanny, the least tumultuous, most reliable, and the only consistently sober adult in her life. Nanny was steady and devoted, but she suffered from addiction, too. As a hoarder, Nanny routinely stole silverware from restaurants and had been married, divorced, and widowed six times as a means of financial support. Nanny often fought with Mama over Mama's drinking, her dreams of becoming a writer in Hollywood, and Mama's unwillingness to marry a man so she could use him as "a meal ticket," as Nanny had so many times. Despite all of their arguments, Nanny was a stable parental figure, and Carol responded with an intense, lifelong loyalty, signaling good night to Nanny at the end of every episode of *The Carol Burnett Show* by pulling fondly at her ear.

Like so many comedienne-ballerinas, Gilda's, Sarah's, Paula's, and Carol's comedy all sprouted from a common psychological seed: disease. But a tragic childhood isn't necessarily the rule. Comedy writer Alison Flierl of *BoJack Horseman* and *School of Rock* had a pretty good one.

"My parents were actually very sweet. My mom is a breast cancer survivor, and she used to make jokes about leaving her fake boob around. This was back in the early eighties when people didn't talk about breast cancer and women were ashamed to have it, and yet she didn't give a shit. I'm sure it was hard for her, but she just put it all out there. I think that's been good for me. Living in LA, as a girl, we *all* have our issues, but I do think having a mom who didn't give that much of a shit about losing a boob helped me to remember not to get too caught up in physical flaws. People will love you *with* them, not in spite of them. That was a good lesson."

For Alison and her mother, comedy served less as a healing method and more as a survival tactic, a brilliant way of getting through something that might otherwise destroy both the performer and her audience.

But this tactic requires staying tethered to the same painful reality that comedians—and audiences—so often wish to escape: the status quo. Our current reality's invisible bars, behind which both performer and audience are so fully imprisoned that they can think only of *what is* and *what will always be*. The tactic requires them both to feel around and regain their senses; to first recognize that the cage exists, that the bars surround them, and then break through. It requires a kind of "truth *plus*," as many performers call it, wherein the comedian heightens our collective reality in order to help us not only survive the status quo but face its flaws, and in so doing, begin the process of changing *what is* into *what should be*. As if staring into a mirror, it is only when we face ourselves that we can grow, and so a comedienne-ballerina must begin by facing her audience, transforming them into that mirror, and using their laughter as a reflection. This transformation goes beyond mutual healing, and well beyond survival, to create truth. Once established, truth promotes safety. And once both performer and audience feel safe, they can, together, break through to true freedom through forgiveness.

the mockingbird

A LOT OF PEOPLE DON'T KNOW what it is that makes a good person; what it is that makes you feel proud of yourself at the end of the day," LA-based comedian Eliza Skinner said, crossing her legs on the couch in her Hollywood apartment, not far from where Carol Burnett once worked as an usher at the old Warner Brothers theater. "There are voices in our society that say, 'A way to be a good person is to tell everybody else that they're shitty.' But that's definitely not it. Respect where other people are coming from. The biggest asshole in the world wants to be doing a good job. They want to be right. Life isn't a video game where you can just kill them, and their little spaceship goes out of the sky. You *want* them on your side. You *want* them agreeing with you. You want them going, 'Oh yeah, that makes so much sense. I get it now.' You don't want to shut them down; you want to change their minds."

"So how would you respond to the quote, 'Everybody thinks that he's the hero of the story—especially the bad guy'?" I asked. Her eyes grew bright.

"I think that's exactly true. Everyone does think he's the hero. So if you can use that and tap into that and tell them, 'Yeah, you *are* the hero. And you know what would be a really heroic thing to do in this situation, or given this topic? Help other people. Get out of the way so that someone with actual experience can speak about it.'"

Eliza's words reveal an underlying truth about life in the twenty-first century: We all need forgiving. Everyone's having a hard time. *Everybody.* Women are having a hard time. Men are having a hard time. At its very core, compassion, paired with the sincere belief that human beings can truly change, is the cornerstone of all the great religions. This compassion and belief encourages us to embrace mutual respect and forgiveness in order to bring people together in shared experience, rather than allowing our pride to force us apart, so that we work against each other or view each other as separate and divided individuals, competing over the respective size of our wounds to make ourselves feel special.

This compassionate understanding is yet another of so many ties that bind Gilda's comedy to Carol's, Sarah's, Paula's, and countless others'. By making light of their own scars, inside and out, they imply that goodness, safety, forgiveness, and truth are all possible within one performance. It also acknowledges that while everybody wants to be a good person, and everybody wants to do the right thing . . . we don't truly know what "the right thing" is. We don't know how to find or follow it. So we don't. We're bad. Sometimes, for some of us, badness lasts a lifetime. But when (if) we grow tired of either treating others badly or others treating us much the same way, we start to change. We forgive. We let go of our own badness and of others', too. This heals the wounds that made us bad in the first place.

The world is so full of wounds, and there is real medicine available, but it needs a little sugar to best take effect. For some, even the sweetest medicine is difficult to swallow, but over time, it works, and its effects are arguably universal. Forgiving others—and through our forgiveness, demonstrating compassion—is the only way to avoid dying an early emotional death. In a world where you can be anything you want, why be anything but kind? Still, it's hard—not to forgive an act, but to forgive a person who doesn't believe or even know she needs forgiveness.

On a segment of *This American Life* entitled "Ask Not for Whom the Bell Trolls; It Trolls for Thee," comic and author Lindy West recounted her experience with comedy's healing effects:

"In the summer of 2013, in certain circles of the Internet, comedians and feminists were at war over rape jokes. Being both a comedy writer and a committed feminist killjoy, I weighed in with an article in which I said that I think a lot of male comedians are careless with the subject of rape. Here's just a sample of the responses I got on social media: *'I love how the bitch complaining about rape is the exact kind of bitch that would never be raped.' 'Holes like this make me want to commit rape out of anger.' 'I just want to rape her with a traffic cone.' 'No one would want to rape that fat disgusting mess.' 'Kill yourself.' 'I want to put an apple into that mouth of yours and take a huge stick and slide it through your body and roast you.' 'That big bitch is bitter that no one wants to rape her.'*"

Lindy's harassment "went on for weeks. It's something I'm used to. I have to be. Being insulted and threatened online is part of my job, which is not to say it doesn't hurt. It does. It feels—well, exactly like you would imagine it would feel to have someone call you a fat cunt every day of your life.

"When I got that message from my 'dad,' it was well into 'rape joke summer.' I was eating thirty rape threats for breakfast at that point, or more accurately, 'you're fatter than the girls I usually rape' threats. And I thought I was coping. But if you get a blade sharp enough, it'll cut through anything.

"The account was called Paul West Donezo—Paul West, because his name was Paul West, and Donezo, because I guess he was done. He was—done being alive, done doing crossword puzzles, done forcing me to sing duets at dinner parties, done writing little poems on the back of every receipt, done being my dad.

"The little bio on Twitter read 'embarrassed father of an idiot—other two kids are fine, though.' His location: 'dirt hole in Seattle.' The profile photo was a familiar picture of him. He's sitting at his piano smiling in the living room of the house where I grew up. The day they sold that house—when I was twenty-five—I sat on the stairs and sobbed harder than I ever had before, because a place is kind of like a person, you know? It felt like a death. I wouldn't cry that hard again until December 12, 2011 when I'd learned that a place is not like a person at all. Only a person is a person. Only a death is really a death.

"My dad lost consciousness on a Saturday night. That afternoon, when we could feel his lucidity slipping, we called my brother in Boston. 'You were such a special little boy,' he said. 'I love you very much.' He didn't say very many things after that. I would give anything for one more sentence. I would give anything for 140 more characters.

"The person who made the Paul West Donezo account clearly put some time into it. They'd researched my father and

19

my family. They'd found out his name, and then they figured out which Paul West he was among all the Paul Wests on the Internet. They knew that I have a brother and sister. And if they knew all that, they must have known how recently we'd lost my dad. Conventional wisdom says never feed the trolls. Don't respond. It's what they want. I do that. It doesn't help.

"I could just stop reading comments altogether, but sometimes I get threatening ones, like the other day someone said I should get Charlie Hebdoed. Colleagues of mine have had their addresses published online, had trolls actually show up in person at their public events. If I don't read comments, how will I know when they've crossed the line?

"I could just stop writing altogether. I've thought about it. But it seems to me that our silence is what the trolls want."

Lindy is, sadly, correct. And other Feminists, comedians, and comedy writers have also felt these effects, running scared into the safety of Internet-free anonymity, "going off the grid" to save their lives and livelihoods (or at least their sanity). The threats usually go further than their seeming targets. Acclaimed writer Jessica Valenti quit social media entirely after receiving rape threats aimed at her five-year-old daughter.

"Faced with Paul West Donezo," Lindy continued, "I was struck with the question, what should I do? If I respond, I'm a sucker. But if I don't respond, I'm a punching bag. So I did what you're not supposed to do. I fed the troll.

"I wrote about Paul West Donezo in an article for *Jezebel.com*. I wrote sadly, candidly, angrily about how much it hurt, how much that troll had succeeded. And then something amazing happened.

"The morning after that post went up, I got an email. 'Hey Lindy, I don't know why or even when I started trolling you. It wasn't because of your stance on rape jokes. I don't find them funny either. I think my anger toward you stems from your happiness with your own being. It offended me because it served to highlight my unhappiness with my own self. I have emailed you through two other Gmail accounts just to send you idiotic insults. I apologize for that. I created the paulwestdonezo@ gmail.com account and Twitter account. I have deleted both. I can't say sorry enough. It was the lowest thing I had ever done. When you included it in your latest *Jezebel* article, it finally hit me. There is a living, breathing human being who's reading this shit. I'm attacking someone who never harmed me in any way and for no reason whatsoever. I'm done being a troll. Again, I apologize. I made a donation in memory to your dad. I wish you the best.'

"They attached a receipt for a fifty dollar donation to Seattle Cancer Care Alliance where my dad was treated. I guess he found that out in his research, too. It was designated Memorial Paul West. I didn't know what to say. I wrote, 'Is this real? If so, thank you.' The troll wrote back one more time, apologized again, and this time he gave me his real name. I could have posted it online, which he knew. But I didn't. And I'm not going to be saying it here either. That was almost eighteen months ago, but I still think about it all the time because I still get trolled every day. If I could get through to one troll, the meanest one I ever had, couldn't I feasibly get through to any of them, all of them? Was he special? Or did I do something right? I wonder how he would tell me to respond to the people trolling me today. I wish I could ask him. But then I realized, I could."

So she called him. She actually called this guy and had a full-on, live, ear-to-ear conversation with her meanest troll.

TROLL: "Hello."
LINDY: "Hi . . . How are you?"

A few awkward seconds later:

TROLL: "I got to tell you, I'm really nervous at the moment."
LINDY: "I'm a little nervous also."
TROLL: "At least I'm not alone."
LINDY: "No, no, not at all."

Even after such an understandably awkward beginning, over the course of their long conversation, miracles happened. Change occurs from the inside out. According to Lindy, "he says he doesn't troll anymore and that he's really changed. He tells me that period of time when he was trolling me for being loud and fat was a low point for him. He hated his body. His girlfriend dumped him. He spent every day in front of a computer at an unfulfilling job. A passionless life, he called it. And then gradually, he changed. He enrolled in graduate school. He found a new relationship. He started teaching little kids. He had a purpose. Slowly, his interest in trolling dried up. We verified nearly everything that he told us about himself. Except, did he really stop trolling? I have no way of knowing, but I believe him. It felt true. And if this was all a con, it's one that cost him a fifty dollar charity donation. We talked for over two hours, and I spent a lot of time trying to get him to walk me through his transgressions in detail—the actual physical and mental steps and how he justified it all to himself. I felt like if I could just get the specifics, gather them up and hold them in my hands, then maybe I could start to understand all of the people who are still trolling me."

Charlene Conley of Portland's iconic All Jane Comedy Festival echoes this concept of changing through understanding. "This is where my opinion is going to differ from a lot of people on this, I know . . . but in the comedy community in Portland, there's a lot of talk about unsafe spaces, and a lot of talk about whether we should censor people on stage—usually the guy who's telling an offensive joke that makes the audience feel less connected to him and less interested in what he has to say next. I just look at it from the standpoint of opportunity. This is an opportunity to have a conversation with that person and say something like, 'Hey, I noticed that when you told this joke, it did not hit, and here's why it didn't hit. Maybe you should think about a different topic next time or changing how you handle this topic so that other people can get on board.' And if that person acts like a real asshat afterwards, then that person's an asshat, right? And *then* you can get mad at him. But not while he's still learning."

"Or unlearning," I point out.

"Right. *Unlearning*, exactly. But without having any kind of conversation, we create this dynamic of contrast, where everything becomes a fight. I don't think everything is a fight. I think we can ignore a lot of idiocy that happens and just let it go and focus on the really important things: Are women getting enough stage time? Are they being recognized for their skills or are they being demeaned because they are women? And how can we fix that problem? And it doesn't have to be every tiny little thing. We can look at the bigger picture."

LA-based stand-up comic Brandie Posey does exactly this through her Rube Goldberg Machine joke. The machine itself was originally created by American cartoonist and inventor Rube Goldberg, who drew hilarious images of regular people accomplishing something simple through complicated means—for example, his 1931 drawing of "Professor Butts and the Self-Operating Napkin," which depicted a man eating soup at a table, wearing a gigantic contraption on his head that, through an immense series of levers and wheels, raised his napkin to his lips for him to wipe. Today, describing something as a "Rube Goldberg Machine" implies that it performs a simple task in an overly and unnecessarily complicated way. Brandie's joke replaces the "self-operating napkin" with a baby, and uses this baby to comment on society's overly and unnecessarily complicated expectations of women. "Instead of trapping a man using a hole in the ground covered by sticks, I trap him using a *baby*—which is in reference to a female stereotype that supposedly *all* women do but only, like, five women *actually* do. It's funny. But when I tell the joke, some people respond with, 'Oh my God, is she for real? She would actually trap a man by having a baby?' And then, of course, the misdirect is my saying, 'Oh, no. Don't worry. I didn't actually *have* the baby—I found it, killed it, and then covered it up with sticks to trap him!' Which somehow makes them feel better. Which is exactly the problem. They'll find a joke about my killing a baby funny, so long as I'm not using it to trap a man—because *that's* apparently the unfunny, horrifying detail that ruins the humor."

Yet another form of truth *plus*. Lacing societal medicine with just enough sugar to feel its healing effects. There's that contradiction, that misdirect that Brandie referred to, underneath it all. That glimmer in her eye that makes it necessary. It's a truth-telling tactic that made comedians like Lisa Lampanelli famous: She says something awful, but her audience thinks it's wonderful. They all go home and put it on the Internet and share it everywhere.

I had the good fortune to see Lisa perform a couple of years ago in a Planned Parenthood fundraiser. I wouldn't have necessarily chosen to see her live because of the way I felt at the time about her material, but she blew me away. It was so interesting, feeling myself change both in the way I viewed her and in the way I *viewed myself* viewing her. Listening to her speak, watching her interact, I realized that I'd never seen a better live performer—ever. She was electrifying. She had so much energy, so much warmth, and so much love. She wanted her audience to laugh. She cared deeply about the experience that they were having right then, in that moment with her, and she brought her all to the stage. It changed the way I watched comedy, and it forced me to face my own preconceived notions about performers whose healing warmth sometimes fails to permeate through screens. Much like watching a fire on TV versus warming yourself with the real thing, you don't truly get to experience Lisa's energy until you've seen her live. Only then does it become obvious that her "awfulness" is in reality true love, and her outward "badness" an expression of her innermost good.

Stand-up and comedy writer Laura House says that, for performers, this combination of what—in your mind—makes you "awful" can also make both you and your audience feel a deep sense of relief. When Laura started doing comedy, she was obsessed with it. She did it constantly. She taught seventh grade during the day, came home and took a nap, and did stand-up at night. During the day, between periods, she would write her act. It's all she wanted to do and it helped her to succeed—she was on television, on *Austin Stories*, on MTV, and she started a show, all at once. Then her constant revelations reached a point of unsustainability. She reached the point of, "Wait, what's it all about? What am I doing up here—helping you or myself?" During this time, she got married and then got divorced. She had a whole life that she had to break apart and put back together, and these secret pains kept her off the stage. "For a while I didn't perform a lot. There are definitely performers that are going to bring that to the stage, but I didn't feel like I had the right to do that."

But, eventually, Laura started sharing those secret moments as a way to be both funny and authentic, and it helped her to move past the past—a process that helped her come up with an entirely new act. "I'm interested in people saying, 'Oh my God—me, too!' That's the best kind of comedy. That's my sole aspiration now. There's a healing there on some level, because you surprise yourself by revealing what you'd been holding in darkness. And when you do, the audience reacts with something like, 'I never would have said that, but I'm so glad she did!' Even if it's something silly, you know what I mean? It's a joy to let that go, and to just ask yourself, 'What can I say that will help *us*?' Because it's not *just* you or *just* them at that point. Instead, you're asking yourself, 'What can I expose or share for *our* sake?'"

In this same way—sharing her guiltiest, darkest parts for a mutual benefit—Brandie Posey agrees that writing and speaking honestly is the only way to create healing. "When I write bits, I honestly picture myself as a defense attorney for a murderer. I ask myself, 'What is the most airtight way to make everybody have to get on board with this joke or else they become the enemy?' Because it's important to ask yourself, 'who are you helping right now? Who are you up here for? Who are you interpreting and what are you repeating in order for other people to hear? What are you putting out there? Does it say anything? Does it have any content at all? What are you tethered to? Where is your responsibility? It's such a gift to be in this world of comedy. *Such* a gift. Hold it dear. Take responsibility for it. We heal people when they don't feel well, you know."

Today, comedians share their feelings on stage—and, through sharing, heal people with humor—in ways that earlier women never could. In 2007, Barbara Walters interviewed Ellen DeGeneres, showing clips of Ellen—much like Gilda and Lucy before her—dancing in a silly way to warm up the audience. "She's not a great dancer; she's not a bad dancer. She's simply enormously entertaining. [She's] built a career as the 'girl next door.' Of course, there's a twist. She grew up near New Orleans, in a middle-class family. Her parents divorced when she was thirteen, and she went with her mom to a small town in East Texas. Ellen was different. She didn't like dresses. And although she dated boys, something was missing. At nineteen, she came out—first to her father, and then to her mother. Both were supportive, and she soon found companionship in gay bars. Ellen's new friends thought she was funny, and they pushed her to perform." In one of her earliest performances at the Improv Station, home of "America's original comedy showcase," Ellen tells the audience, "A friend of mine said, 'Ellen, listen. Having sex is kind of like riding a bicycle. You know what I mean?' And I know it's been a while, but I don't ever remember pedaling."

By thirty-six, Barbara explains, this kind of humor landed Ellen her own sitcom—but she was playing a straight woman. It wasn't really her revealing her darkest secrets . . . yet. Ellen was playing *Ellen*, of course—not on stage, for a live audience, but under the umbrella of a network, which broadcast to a national audience—and so there was far less intimacy and very little outlet for her to either heal or help others to heal. Maybe this is partly why her 1996 film, *Mr. Wrong*, immediately flopped. Again, she'd played a straight woman, but unlike Lily Tomlin, Ellen wasn't able to convince audiences that she sexually desired men. She finally came out onscreen in 1997 in a seminal, game-changing moment of release that many millennials still remember as an integral part of their generation's acceptance of homosexuality as a biological necessity. No doubt the moment when Ellen announces to actress Laura Dern—over an airport loudspeaker, of course, to lend the moment comedy—"I'm gay!"—the real Ellen was able to express her feelings and heal from years of pretending. But her confession was ahead of its time (for network executives, anyway), and her show was soon cancelled. These kinds of growing pains indicate actual *growth*. Change. Internal and external revolution. Comedy became the sugar in the industry's reactionary medicine. "What would bug the Taliban more than seeing a gay woman in a suit surrounded by Jews?" she later asked at the Academy Awards.

Even though the networks clearly treated Ellen and so many other women like her as disposable, they ultimately found that they needed these women desperately. They needed their voices and their edginess to survive. Embracing and promoting women who also happened to be comedians became, at some point, the only true way to grow with the times.

When we sat down to talk at Second City Hollywood, comic actress Mo Collins said, "When you think about it, in some ways, we made it a bit easier for them. Having a woman up there, pushing those boundaries forward, makes it easier for some audiences to take. It's a kind of gentler nation that way, isn't it? It's a bit more forgiving somehow, you know? Women and children first, right? Have the women and children do the jokes about cross-dressing. Transgender identity. Lopping off somebody's dick. Whatever it is. Is there a certain softness there that makes it easier . . . ?" and then she stopped, and thought, and in one seamless transition did as all brilliant comedienne-ballerinas always have: she discovered the truth for both of us. "Maybe we're scapegoats? Fuck. Were we scapegoats for the edge?"

Transgender comedian Riley Silverman answered, "Yes! I remember the first night that I did come out on stage . . . I was still saying at the time that I was a cross-dresser because I hadn't fully realized my identity as transgender. I remember that night, when I said cross-dresser, I got off stage and my hand was shaking because I'm, like, 'I can't believe I just did this.' It was one of those things where, if I could walk on a stage in front of a room full of people who do not know me and aren't ready to see this, and I can turn them around and get them to actually *listen* to me and *laugh* . . . then I can handle anything."

At forty-nine, Ellen went further, telling Barbara about the true source of her comedy—her childhood. Her mother's deep depression after the divorce could be cured only by Ellen's antics. So, like Gilda and so many others before her, teenage Ellen made her mother laugh: "It was the first time I realized what kind of power humor has. She's crying one minute, and the next minute, she's laughing hysterically. It was amazing to be able to do that for people."

"So it's almost like truth *plus*," I said to Eliza Skinner, back in her apartment. "Is that your job? To tell the truth and use it to heal others *and* yourself?"

"Oh God. That feels like so much work."

"You've got a lot of responsibility!" I said, and then we laughed together.

"Yeah, we do have a lot of responsibility. It's hard to, for me at least, to think about the enormity of it . . . otherwise I get so wrapped up in what I'm trying to say that I can't say anything. I can't get to the jokes. I think there are certainly comedians who do take that on and do it really well, though."

When I asked Abbi Jacobson of Comedy Central's *Broad City* to define how her real life affects her job as a comedienne-ballerina, she answered, "I have a half hour a week for ten weeks of the year to bring people out of whatever's going on in their lives, so they can either laugh at what these characters are going through, or how they're reacting to situations. I hope it mirrors real life for the people at home—either because Abbi and Ilana are doing things that the people at home would love to do, or because they get to live vicariously through our characters, or because we remind them of their younger selves, or because, through us, they get to be wild for a night . . . all while also commenting on issues I think are important and issues I think are ridiculous. This is a complicated job!"

On a grander scale, sometimes the need to heal others' wounds comes from shared trauma on a national or even international scale. Brandie Posey used comedy as a way to heal from the collective shock and horror that reverberated through America in September of 2001. "I did a show at a college in Santa Monica, and they had a chalk mural of 9/11 on the wall right next to where I was performing. I kind of made fun of it because it was weird that there was a comedy show happening next to a 9/11 mural. It was like, 'Is this weird to anybody else?' See, I'm from DC, so 9/11 was really weird for us. Everyone that I went to school with has at least one spy in their family, so that day, most of my friends did not know where their family members were . . . so obviously that day is really intense for us, which means that I make a lot of jokes about it because it's just like really a crazy thing we all dealt with. It's my way of pairing comedy with tragedy."

Mo Collins says comedians should embrace that level of responsibility. "People YouTube our stuff to feel better because they're having a shitty day or because they haven't been able to get out of bed for three months. *Take responsibility.* What do you want to pass along? What do you want to say? What do you want to reflect? You're the mirror; you're the mockingbird. What are you putting back out there? Let's tether it to *real* stuff . . . If you look, the successful comedians are doing that. And that's why. That's why. They're not here today, gone tomorrow; they have legs because they're staying tethered to things that are real and human."

Perhaps most often for today's comedienne-ballerinas, the need to heal others' wounds is less about either the audience's experience or the performer's memories and more a combination of both. A conversation between two people—an individual and a group that represents a single whole—that creates a special relationship between them. A give and take. The kind of cathartic, therapeutic, group healing environment that comes from confessing painful secrets in public—and in so doing, relieving the sickness that is both their cause and effect—is not unlike the intimate communication between writers and readers, painters and collectors, parishioners and priests, or actors and fans. I asked NYC stand-up comic Kaileigh McCrea whether she agrees that comedians have that sort of medicinal relationship with their audiences.

"Very much. Sometimes it's dissociative. Sometimes you've got to emotionally leave the room when you're bombing so hard, so irretrievably hard. I definitely had experiences like that where, 'Oh they don't like me and there's nothing I can do about that. I'm not going to spend the next five minutes trying to make these people like me.' But you do want that, you do want to build a bond and let them get to know you and see something about yourself. For most of us, the material, whether we necessarily realize it or not, is very personal. It's stuff we wouldn't tell people, normally, outside of comedy. And then we'll get out on stage and tell a hundred people about it. As many people as possible about it."

"What are some of your tools that you use to reveal things to people?"

"I love to talk about my family background. It's the sort of thing where, if anyone else were to [make] fun of them, I would kick their butts. I would not accept that. But it's okay for me to do it because I love them."

"Because the love is there?"

"Exactly. It's that sort of talking about the flaws and accepting them and embracing them and that's something I try to bring when I talk about myself. And when I talk about myself it's usually just the contradictions that I find in my own beliefs and logic. And I think, just the stupid things I've done over the years. The mistakes I never thought I would make. Comedy relieves that kind of pain. Comedy based on truth makes you forget pain entirely."

As an example:

The only man whom I really, truly loved before my husband—and the only person to ever, and might I add cruelly, twist my heart to the point of breaking—promptly gained seventy-five pounds, married a presumably less agoraphobic version of his agoraphobic mother, and moved to the middle of the desert to grow "medicinal plants" for "religious ceremonies." Which I guess is a kind of retirement plan from selling cocaine in college.

This is the person who first said, "I love you."

This is the person who fingered me in crowded limousines.

This is the person who wrote me love letters ten pages long.

This is the person who rubbed his head against me like a pillow because I was his favorite thing.

This is the person who matched his cummerbund to my baby-blue evening gown, and who shook with eagerness when he held my hand.

This is the person who told me that "new lovers are nervous and tender, but they smash everything, for their heart is an organ of fire."

This is the person who told me that I had fat on my upper arms and needed to lose some weight when I was five foot seven and 115 pounds.

This is the person who slow-danced with his ex-girlfriend right in front of me.

This is the person whose aunt called me "that girl" because I wasn't Jewish.

This is the person who told my mother, after she'd traveled a thousand miles to celebrate *his* graduation, that he was apparently dating other people. While we still lived together.

This is the person who hid rolls of quarters in the knuckles of his boxing gloves during a charity match . . . to try to knock out his *best friend.*

This is the person who left me for being too needy, but then called every weekend to ask, "Are you still mine?"

This is the person who told me that my stomach was looking concave and I needed to gain some weight when I was still five foot seven and 115 pounds.

This is the person who abandoned me at a bus terminal in Boston after I'd traveled all through the night to see him.

This is the person who asked if I'd "ever dated a black guy," and when I paused for a moment in shock, he took that as a no and answered, "Good."

This is the person who cried into his hands when I tried to leave.

This is the person who never said, "I'm sorry."

I am the person who finally said, "I forgive you."

Dear Reader, I hope this helps you to remember: it could be worse. May I wish you the same good fortune in dodging such an obvious bullet.

. . . See? Forgot whatever bullshit preceded this little journey, didn't you?

Comedy's so beautiful that way—especially satire, riding the middle line, the light and the dark. And when that stuff is brought out, then all of us perhaps sitting isolated in our own worlds within the world, go, "Oh my God, that's me." And the other person goes, "Oh wow, that's me, too." There's a ripple effect. The more time we spend listening, the more we're able to forgive, the better we are at talking, the more we care for each other and ourselves. The less alone we all are in clinging to the stubborn belief that no one else ever could or ever has felt our brand of pain.

Naomi Ekperigin calls this "the laughter of knowing." For her, when she talks about her interracial relationship with her Jewish fiancé, whom she lovingly calls her "Jew Boo," and the audience laughs, "it's like they get what you're saying. So if you get what I'm saying, that means what I'm saying is not so crazy. The thought I had isn't so ridiculous—or rather, it *can* be ridiculous, but I'm not alone in that thought. That can feel so good sometimes: saying certain things. Feeling less alone and not so insane."

"We're probably all far less unique than we think," I told her.

"Right! We're not all special snowflakes."

Thank goodness for that. If we were, we'd all melt separately. At the same time, we sometimes cling to our pain because it sets us apart. It belongs uniquely to us. Those things that have left scars are the things we own.

"Do you feel like there's anything in your past that's still uniquely painful?" I asked comedian and actress Mo Collins. "Anything secret, or simply private—since there is, of course, a difference—that you really don't want to bring into your comedy because it's still a source of sickness?"

"Personally, I have yet to really embrace—" She stops short, on the verge of tears. "Oh, I can't even believe I'm going to say this . . . I steer clear of talking about my mother because that is my toxic place. So I won't . . . it's like my best material, but I haven't been able to do it yet. Does she influence stuff? *Absolutely.* Look at me! I don't want to get in trouble . . ."

As she says this, her husband Alex chimes in, encouraging her to tell her story. "If it's true, it's true."

She looks at me again with her wet eyes, and I'm reminded of the late comedy writer Nora Ephron. In her autobiography *I Feel Bad About My Neck*, Nora described her own wonderful, lively mother (also a well-known screenwriter, like her then teenage daughter would someday become), who morphed into an unbearable albatross around Nora's neck when, seemingly overnight, she became an alcoholic. This is likely unrealistic, but this rapid-fire descent is how Nora remembered it. Her mother would visit Nora at college and moan in her bed like a banshee. At the time, Nora was ashamed of the sudden change. Years later, she mourned her final memories—both of the mother she'd had as a child and the mother that woman eventually became. As the child of an addict, Nora struggled with the past, but that's the thing about being the child of an alcoholic. The person she was holds enormous power over you; the person she is has no power at all.

Nora seemed to love her mother more than anyone. She also seemed to hate her mother more than anyone. Most of all, perhaps, she hated her mother for not loving herself as much as Nora loved her. Ultimately, her mother's spiraling descent from addiction to death left her the most simultaneously beautiful and terrible person that Nora had ever met. A mother collected of genius, diluted by fear, fueled by hatred. Perhaps she didn't know how else to reconcile the three, save drowning them in alcohol.

All of us are like this, though we may not know or admit it. As Karen Armstrong, a former Catholic nun turned British author and commentator known for her books on comparative religion, once said, "we're addicted to our pet hatreds. We don't know quite what we'd do without the people we dislike. We meditate on their bad qualities, and they become almost our alter egos, everything that we are not. We define ourselves in this way. And when we say something unpleasant about somebody, we can get a sort of horrible buzz of pleasure, rather like the first drink of the evening. So we have to wean ourselves away from our addictions to annoyance and having pet grudges and hatreds, but it's a project for a lifetime."

I suspect what's true about addicts is therefore true about all of us: We cling to our drug of choice because what's underneath is so much worse. Without a fix, the fear, and the *fear* of the fear, is all that's left. The only question remaining for comedienne-ballerinas is what to do with your own power, how to use it to grow your compassion and channel your truest, boldest, most fearless self. This is why the key to being remembered is to remember.

But a lot of people don't want to remember others' brilliance, just their own. Which doesn't make any sense at all, if you think about it. If you never bother to remember the past, why would the future remember you? Ego is, as always, the death of everything.

A lot more people just don't *want* to be compassionate. They prefer anger to healing, and they'd rather be righteous than well. But as Armstrong reminds us, compassion is the source of our greatest comedy because they both originally developed (and continue to grow) out of conflict. All of this is why the most brilliant lights, the strongest voices, the most thrillingly funny comedienne-ballerinas choose to bend their art toward more rather than less. Not to water it down, not to try to make it logical, not to edit their own souls according to the fashion—rather, they choose to follow their most intense obsessions mercilessly.* Your obsessions reveal your soul. They can either grow or hinder your compassion. They can change you. They can save your life.

In the late 1980s, years after gleefully ordering her audience to tap away its troubles, Gilda was facing ovarian cancer. She spent a few years from 1986 to 1989 moving in and out of hospitals—kind of like her father Herman, thirty years before. "Throughout my career I felt like the girl in Rumpelstiltskin, spinning straw into gold . . . my job was to find what was funny about whatever was going on. So I began to think that I should do the same thing with cancer. It needed me badly because it has such a terrible reputation. I decided, 'Well, if I'm gonna have it, I've gotta find out what could be funny about it.' I'm a comedienne-ballerina. My life has made me funny and cancer wasn't going to change that. Cancer, I decided, needed a comedienne-ballerina to come in there and lighten it up."

---

* An ode to Franz Kafka.

She told stories to her wellness groups about weekly checkups and blood work. About the numbness in her hands and feet. She called them "The Adventures of the Independent, Baldheaded Chemo Patient." "Between chemos seven and eight, I totaled Gene [Wilder]'s car at an intersection in Santa Monica," she wrote. "I stopped. I looked both ways. I entered the intersection at three miles an hour, and almost in slow-motion, I was colliding with the cutest blue-eyed guy in a Triumph convertible. I turned into Imogene Coca and Lucille Ball. I kept repeating, 'My husband's gonna kill me!'"

Her stories grew bolder and more personal, and much as it had during her painful childhood, truth-based comedy kept Gilda afloat even during the hardest times. "I bought three pairs of funny slippers: ones that looked like puffy running shoes, my ballet shoes with watermelons on them, and the pair I bought in England that only grannies wear and cost a dollar. This was all to make the night nurse laugh. Can you imagine me trying to entertain the person in the room when I was asleep?"

Others tried to entertain her, too. The healing offered by strangers somehow felt mutual.

"When I called the young guy with the Triumph to exchange insurance information, he'd changed his answering machine message to his impersonation of Roseanne Roseannadanna ranting about car accidents, and ending with, 'It's always something.' He made me laugh."

Eliza Skinner claims this new sense of mutualism—of comedians making audiences laugh, and audiences making comedians laugh, too—is a new direction for comedy and for comedienne-ballerinas in particular, who have long held an informal patent on such sugary medicine. "One-sided, absurdist humor, ironic humor, non sequiturs, all that stuff—it's starting to die off. I think people are getting really bored with jokes that are just funny. With humor that is just there to be wacky and crazy and nothing deeper. People want catharsis. People want it to be emotional, honest, political . . . it needs to be something *more*. People want *more* with their comedy."

"Why do you think they need this?" I asked.

"Because all the ironic stuff is cold. It's isolating. The underlying message seems to be, 'Isn't it stupid that somebody cared about something? Isn't it stupid that someone tried?' And that gets very grating on individuals and society, and eventually everyone's like, 'Oh wait, I *want* to care about things. I *want* to have feelings. I *want* to make a difference. I want to try! And I *am* angry about things. And I *am* sad about things. And I want that to be discussed.'"

She's right. Comedy has always been at the forefront of what we're willing to talk about and which boundaries we want to push. Sympathy, empathy, and compassion are what we've been missing, and now we're coming to a place where comedy can unite people. It reminds them that we've all had similar experiences, that we all have similar pains and successes and frustrations. That there is something worse than loneliness, and that is the fear of loneliness. Fear will make our decisions for us and, if we let it, end our lives before they've begun.

Comedy is now embracing a kinder, gentler, more mutually inclusive sensibility, which embodies our need for healing through compassion. This is the same kind of humor that made Carol and Gilda talk to their audiences and expect their audiences to talk back. It's the same kind of laughter that made many comedians want to go into the business in the first place. It's becoming less cynical. Instead, it's becoming truth *plus*. Comedians are expected to still point out the painful truths about what's wrong with the world, but now we're expecting them to follow that up with something *more*. Something that will help us all to come together and feel safe so that we can forgive, heal, and move forward. As Eliza put it, "You can tell us about the darkness . . . but then what? I mean, we get it: things are really shitty in a lot of areas. But instead of just being like 'Everything sucks, right? Okay, bye!' we want our comedy to give us hope for something better. We want comics to embrace the idea of 'Okay, these things are all really bad . . . but it's so easy for them to get better!'"

Comedienne-ballerinas want the same. They want laughter based on truthful emotions. Laughter that makes them feel loved and validated and powerful—and found.

"I love it when somebody makes me laugh," LA-based stand-up and comedy writer Laurie Kilmartin says. "And it's a little harder now because I've either written comedy or performed it for so long that I know what you're doing. I see your tricks. But when somebody still gets me, I'm like, 'Fuck! *This* is why I love comedy!' It's great. It feels so great. And if it feels great for me, it's got to feel even better for an audience member, hearing your truth and thinking, 'Me, too! That's what *I* think! And I didn't know how to say it in that way. And you made me laugh at it.'

"Your circumstances made them feel better about their circumstances?" I asked.

"Yes. And in that way, I guess I'm always talking to a version of myself in the audience. I know I said before I was trying to dominate . . . but maybe that's not the whole truth. Maybe the person I'm trying to make laugh is somebody who's just like me in the crowd. And when she does, and I hear her, I know neither of us is alone. Maybe that's why I think everything is pretty much fair game. I think again that goes back to the responsibility of comedy. I think that what we're finding out these days—and I like this trend—is that people are being more honest and coming out about perhaps the dark things that have happened to them. Using those things as a service to other people through comedy is an especially great way to heal. We're only as sick as our secrets, and like Gilda (quoting Mr. Rogers) once said, 'if it's mentionable, it's manageable.'"

Gilda died in 1989, at the age of forty-three. "One night, during a quiet walk along a California beach," *SNL* writer Alan Zweibel later wrote, "She told me she would have preferred to be a ballerina; that comedy was about what was wrong with the world—people laughed because something was too big, or too small, or too much, or not enough. Quirks and exaggerations were the essence of parody. Irony and discomfort the grist for humor. But ballet was about harmony. Poetry in controlled motion. A finely tuned, musically carried body at peace with all that surrounds it." Which reminded me of the simple yet beautiful fact that darkness can't exist in the light; that sadness and sickness are driven out by a comedienne-ballerina's spotlight.

Because sometimes, in the middle of the saddest opus, you stop to look up at the sky. And that is when you wonder:

"Were the birds always singing?"

part two

THE SOMEBODY

"I'm not funny at all. What I am is brave."
—Lucille Ball

lucy/lucille

S OMEWHERE OFF THE RED LINE in Boston, I found myself walking into the Berklee College of Music and taking the stairs up to the doctor's office. A professor of cultural studies who teaches courses on the lasting feministic effects stemming from *I Love Lucy*, Dr. Lori Landay has written and spoken about Lucille Ball for years, and her friends still routinely gift her with Lucy-inspired trinkets. Her walls were bright and covered with shelves of memorabilia: *I Love Lucy* lunchboxes and picture books and faux vitamins and figurines. Lucy as a ballerina, all in pink, clipped to the side of a bookcase. I pushed it with my finger to make it wiggle on its spring-loaded pirouette in a kind of hula dance. It was fragile. Feminine. To me, these are vastly different adjectives, since I believe that femininity implies enormous strength, but somehow Lucy's figurine captured both. It also connected Lucy's mindset and motivations to Gilda: the former had quite deliberately departed from everything her mother had (or could have) been, while the latter spent most of her life subconsciously following in her mother's footsteps.

While the sole career choice available to women born in the late nineteenth century—like Lucy's mother, Desiree ("DeDe") Evelyn Hunt—was that of wife and mother, Henrietta Radner faced a seemingly opposite limitation. She had once been—or had very much wanted to be—a professional ballerina, but she chose to give up that career ambition to become a wife and mother. She did so in order to marry Herman Radner and raise their two children, Gilda and Michael. When Gilda grew up, however, she always thought of herself as a pale comparison to her mother; in her own estimation, Gilda was a terrible dancer, and so, instead of actually dancing or taking herself seriously, she intentionally exaggerated her self-perceived flaw. She often turned herself into the funniest, craziest, least serious dancer in the world. This is evident in many of her *Saturday Night Lives* sketches, but perhaps most acutely in 1978's "Dancing in the Dark," where Gilda and Steve Martin parody Fred Astaire and Ginger Rogers, breaking the elegant waltz every few seconds to either disco or jiggle wildly. The question of how much strength it takes to appear that fragile—how much talent it takes to appear untalented—permeates her performance. It also recalls *I Love Lucy*'s iconic nineteenth episode, "The Ballet."

In 1952, *I Love Lucy* was still in its first season. Episode 19 was devoted to the idea of Lucy attempting to manipulate her way onto Ricky's show, even though, he claims, she has no talent *and* (as if that weren't enough) there are apparently only two openings: a ballerina and a burlesque dancer (which, at that time, referred to a male comedian performing a vaudeville routine). To this Lucy insists she'll become the *best* ballerina he's ever seen. She leaves the room and reappears in a child's silk and crinoline tutu, fairy wings pinned to the straps, and a hat shaped like an upside-down rose. (Lucille Ball was forty-one at the time.) She lifts her arms above her head and waves her star-shaped wand, swaying to music that only she can hear. Later in the episode, Lucy attends a ballet class with Madame Le Mond, where she ultimately ruins every position by turning it into modern jazz.

"Then the ballet mistress makes her stop, and by the end, the mistress has put Lucy through a hundred pliés and all these other things, and her body literally gets hung up on the barre, where she gets stuck," Dr. Landay said, explaining the scene. "She is trying to obey the mistress's commands, but her leg gets caught, and she can't control it. And that whole interaction perfectly mirrors women's performance: the ideal of the feminine performer as the ballerina, who seems weightless, as if she exerts no effort at all, and just glides and almost flies and floats."

"She's supposed to be perfect," I added.

"She *is* perfect. Of course, if we think about it, or if we have any experience with dance, we realize that the reality behind maintaining that expected level of perfection—the truth behind a ballerina's performance—is entirely different. If we were to *really* watch closely and consider everything that Lucy's voluntarily putting herself through in this scene, we'd realize that there's an enormous amount of strength and training—and *pain*—in her performance. It's a *very* exacting art that demands a lot of self-sacrifice and treats both the female body and psyche harshly—and because of all this, it appears lighter than air, but is quite the opposite. The seeming is far removed from the being. Just like simply existing as a woman in the world. All of a ballerina's seemingly effortless perfection is, in reality, an unattainable ideal—both for Lucy in this episode and for all of us who identify as female while watching her."

At home, over Lucy and Ricky's bed, we see a picture of a ballerina. This remains the indelible image of her as a female performer, as a feminine being, and as the symbol of ideal womanhood. In this particular episode, however, Lucy doesn't try to live up to some crazy standard. She says being a ballerina is just too tiring and far too much work, so she gives up. It's just too hard to be both incredibly strong and yet appear incredibly weak, so instead she turns to vaudeville.

A performer attempts to teach her a routine entitled "Slowly I Turned," but here she fails again and ends up cast as the "straight man" who gets hit by the performer's whoopee cushion and is squirted in the face with seltzer. Then she gets a pie in the face. Lucy gives up on this, too—but not on the act itself, only on her designated role. Being purely feminine doesn't work and neither does her attempt to be purely masculine.

Later, however, Ethel calls to tell Lucy that she's needed in the show after all. Lucy gets ready to perform the routine she learned as a male comic, but it's really the ballerina the show has requested. Lucy appears on stage in the comic's baggy pants, hat, and tie with her seltzer water and whoopee cushion; she's ready to perform a routine that came straight from traditionally male-dominated vaudeville—a routine that involves inflicting pain on other people's bodies—as opposed to performing the ballerina's embodiment of passive feminine perfection.

Lucy starts hitting the male dancers with the whoopee cushion and squirting the ballerinas in the face with seltzer, generally creating havoc in a wonderful synthesis of both masculine and feminine performance, and of course, in the end, putting a pie in Ricky's face.

This was the 1952 version of Gilda's breaking up the fourth-wall waltz with spurts of disco. In both "The Ballet" and "Dancing in the Dark," the new suddenly overtakes the old. Tradition is disrupted. Fragility breaks down and explodes away any serious pretense of strength. Preconceived notions of proper dancing are called into question, even as Madame Le Mond orders Lucy to fix her posture, keep her legs straight, hips forward, stomach in, chin up, and shoulders back. To all this, we realize, Lucy must add a gracefulness to hide her discomfort. She must raise her legs flawlessly above the barre . . . five hundred times.

"To be a ballerina is using your body to show what's right with the world, and to be a comedian is using your voice to show what's wrong," Kristen Bartlett, a writer for *Saturday Night Live*, told me. "There's something lighter than air about that, don't you think?"

In an unintended answer to this question, Kaye Ballard tells the story of Lucy versus the mad dog. This was in the mid-1940s, before Lucy was *Loved*, and she would come over to Kaye's house for some company. They'd go for a bike ride. One day as they were riding down Sunset and Gower, by Hollywood Boulevard—back then, apparently, there were no houses or businesses or crazy traffic, only palm trees—a mad dog came out of the woods and starting growling. It bared its teeth. It foamed at the mouth. Kaye got so scared that she fell off her bike, but not Lucy. She screamed, "Get the hell out of here!" And the dog obeyed.

"That's why you'll be the queen of the world someday," Kaye said. Yet Lucy herself refused to ally with Kaye's allusions to emergent Feminism or, many years later—with the sexual revolution in full swing—to support the women's liberationists she'd inspired through comedy. Lucy, like many of her time and today, had to some degree internalized the sexism she'd been brought up to believe. According to Dr. Lori

Landay, "someone once asked her about 'women's lib,' and [Lucy] responded, 'I've been so liberated, it hurts.'"

Indeed, the historical, social, and political context of the 1950s illuminates her statement. For Lucille Ball, Feminism didn't exist. It was called "women's liberation" back then, and it didn't mean what it does now, since in those days the idea that women should enjoy the same rights, freedoms, and privileges as men was still a radical notion. She was a proto-Feminist. But she certainly did things in her everyday life and in her career that actively worked toward women being recognized equally for their contributions, which is an inherent part of what it means to be a Feminist today: Someone who advocates, whether in practice or in their speech, for women's equality. Lucy didn't yet have the vocabulary for her actions and instincts, but she undoubtedly felt the injustice behind the gender expectations put upon her. The exact articulation of those feelings was left to Madelyn Pugh Davis, Lucy's head writer and close friend, when she later described writing the original pilot episode for *I Love Lucy* and the premise for Ricky's character:

"We wrote, 'Ricky says, "I want a wife who is just a wife."'" And I don't know what we were thinking, except that Lucy and I didn't know any better."

For 1950s American audiences, and certainly for Lucy and Madelyn, Ricky's sentiment, though deeply unfair, was not considered unusual. In fact, it was completely typical.

I'm abruptly reminded of this normalizing whenever a friend of mine insists that her husband or partner "might be willing to babysit" for fifteen minutes, once every three years, while we enjoy a single cup of coffee together before she returns to her regularly scheduled duties as "just" a wife. Or that he's helping much more than other men traditionally have to take care of the responsibilities they created together and now supposedly share.

We rarely if ever acknowledge the fact that many heterosexual men have, for generations, been raised to "have it all," *all at once.* They assume that their heterosexual female partners will help them to achieve both a family and a career simultaneously. They've never had to stop doing one until little Whatshername goes to kindergarten in order to go back to taking care of the other. Putting their careers on hold to stay home and raise children has never even crossed their minds, nor has the idea that their ambitions might affect their fertility.

Meanwhile, many heterosexual women assume the exact opposite. They grow up with the nagging—but often undiscussed—suspicion that they *won't* receive this same kind of assistance from their male partners. And so, because few of us ever talk about our fears until they become our realities, we're far too often terrified to even *ask.* We self-sabotage. We are Lucy and Ethel, working away in the candy factory, doing everything on our own and pretending everything's okay. The pressure builds, and the candy comes and comes, and the machine eventually drives us nuts . . . yet too often we say nothing, turning our frustrations back onto ourselves (or worse, our children), finally proclaiming that "women *can't* have it all!" while our male partners somehow manage to do so. The assembly line continues. Our self-sabotaging cycle is complete.

The problem isn't our inability to have it all. The problem is our inability to *expect* it all. Because our expectations are so low and our inferiority so high, we make choices to ensure we never get what we're convinced we don't deserve.

Again, I'm with you—here, inside the box. I am equally unable to open my eyes wide enough to see myself. I'm just as susceptible to the false belief that *any* choice—even one that restricts my own free and equal participation in society—is inherently Feminist. I sleepily accept that I am "just." After a while, it starts to feel—though deeply unfair—not unusual. In fact, it almost seems . . . completely typical.

But was it normal for Gilda? Or had gender expectations evolved from the premiere of *I Love Lucy* to the premiere of *SNL*?

Gilda grew up idolizing Lucy during the 1950s and 1960s in much the same way that so many of today's comedians grew up idolizing Gilda during the 1970s and 1980s—LA-based author and longtime stand-up comic Judy Carter in particular.

"I was just starting in stand-up. *SNL* had just hit, and I got a gig at the Bottom Line. I'm from LA, so this is a big deal. I fly out to New York, and I invite all my relatives to come to the show. I'm opening for a band then called the Roaches. They were on *SNL* a lot, and it's an industry audience, so they don't care about the opening act. If the show's writers are in the audience, this is how they'll go: 'Yeah, that's funny. Let me write that down for next week.' They're listening to poach. They aren't even looking at me. And no matter what I did, I couldn't get their attention.

"So I finish my set, and I go to see my relatives—only I find them not in the audience but standing outside, in the snow! My Aunt Edith, my orthodox Jewish relatives, they wouldn't even let them in! So I come backstage and I just start to sob. But then somebody takes my hand and pulls me into a toilet. Let me tell you about the back stage of places like the Bottom Line. They're not filled with Jacuzzis and spas. You have a toilet, and you're sharing it with cockroaches. This woman pulls me down and sits me on her lap—we're both on the toilet. I'm sobbing. She's holding me in her lap, and she says, 'What happened?' So I answered, 'They wouldn't let my relatives in and nobody looked.' And I start crying again, and she goes, 'Oh, it's okay,' and I look up and realize, 'Oh my God, you're Gilda Radner!' I'm sitting backstage with Gilda Radner, who was my hero . . . *on a toilet.*

"Anyway, from that moment on, Gilda taught me something. You see it's tough being a comic—just *being* a comic. Add the adjective—*female* comic—and you're dissed even more. But she taught me that even (and maybe *especially*) when I got more successful, I should remember to look out for my opening act. I should take care of that person, the way she took care of me, and I should try to help that person to be less afraid. It was Gilda, and that night, that I'll never forget. She made me see who she really was."

Today, on Hollywood Boulevard near the corner of Wilcox, you'll find Gilda's name surrounded by others of an even earlier era: John Forsythe, Helen Hayes, Basil Rathbone, Stu Nahan, Penny Singleton, Martha Raye, Jack Warner, Mickey Rooney, Bob Hope, Leslie Nielsen, and more. You'll also find another branch location of the Second City, where Gilda first discovered improv and where new generations of comedienne-ballerinas still go to discover Gilda. But who *first* discovered her?

Rosie Shuster, one of the original writers for *Saturday Night Live*, told me her version of this origin story. It was 1973, before *Saturday Night Live* hit, and Rosie had just gotten a call from a friend who'd gone to high school with Rosie and her then husband, Lorne Michaels. The friend was raving about some girl from his old summer camp, who was apparently *super* talented and funny and Rosie should meet her.

"Then I saw her in *Godspell*, and her whole presence was so galvanizing. She had this little *teeny* face and this massive amount of hair. She stood out, even among all the talent on that stage—and there was a lot. Marty Short was in that cast and Eugene Levy, too . . . everyone was very impressive, but Gilda still commanded *so much attention*."

Gilda started her career performing for children rather than adults, clowning around in fairy princess costumes for youth theater shows. Later, she trained at Second City Toronto and became the only girl in the Not Ready for Prime Time Players' rep company, where she honed the comedy chops that galvanized Rosie. And yet, apparently, Gilda had never even heard of *Godspell* until she happened to see a flyer for an open call and then showed up with her own unique version of "Zip-a-Dee-Doo-Dah." Still, she'd spent years crafting her take for children, and so her performance proved perfect for the director's uniquely childlike vision: a character dressed as Raggedy Ann in clown's makeup and pigtails. The show made her—like many of the cast members—an almost instant star.

Saturday Night Live began in 1974, when Johnny Carson told NBC that he wanted the network to stop airing reruns of *The Tonight Show* on weekends by the following summer. NBC president Herbert Schlosser hired Dick Ebersol away from ABC Sports and gave him one year to create an original program to run at eleven thirty p.m. on Saturday nights. Ebersol met Michaels, then a twenty-eight-year-old Canadian television writer who had worked on *Laugh-In* and Lily Tomlin's specials for CBS. Michaels won Ebersol over with his idea for a show that would assail the tired conventions of variety television and reflect the language and attitudes of America's youth. Schlosser proposed that it be broadcast live from Studio 8-H in Rockefeller Center.

Rosie, who had been writing jokes for Lorne's straight man/funny man duo on *The Hart and Lorne Terrific Hour,* came along as a package deal. She, Anne Beatts, and Marilyn Suzanne Miller became the first "girl writers" for *Saturday Night Live,* and they created many of Gilda's most memorable characters.

New York–based author and columnist Mary Elizabeth Williams told me all about staying up late and watching Gilda on *SNL*: "I'd never seen anybody like that who was so physical, weird, and nerdy. It made being nerdy funny! And I think that's another aspect of it: She let herself *be*. She *became* that weirdo character again and again and again and found the heart."

LA-based Second City performer Lyndsay Hailey recalled that when she was taking classes at Second City in Chicago, she and her boyfriend traveled to Noblesville, Indiana, to do a benefit show that his parents were hosting. She and four other comedians stayed at their home. "After they'd watched our set, his father said, 'You know, you remind me a lot of Gilda Radner,' which I knew to take as an instant compliment. I'd seen just enough of her work from *SNL* to fall in love, but I'd never seen anything else. So, the next day, we sat down and watched *Gilda Live* and I felt like I was like seeing a part of myself."

"What part of yourself were you seeing?" I asked.

"The kid. The child. The one inside, who wants to play. I felt like with her work, she gave herself permission to be that girl, and you could feel that she didn't judge herself. That's so powerful . . . watching Gilda's work, she channeled that vivaciousness, that uninhibited joy. It's just beautiful. It's something that I can still look at and go, '*That's* what I want to do when I grow up!'"

For others, comedy was more the result of a sudden impulse than the fulfillment of a childhood dream. Lizz Winstead, longtime stand-up comic and co-creator of *The Daily*

Show, first got on stage not because she idolized comedians but because "somebody dared me when I was in college, during the early '80s. The Equal Rights Amendment had just failed to pass, and so I was waxing wise and observing how crappy the world was working, anyway—and so it was just the right time to start pointing things out and asking people, 'This is nuts, right?' But what I find most interesting, looking back, was how stand-up was presented to me in a time before the Internet. Before we could google comedians' names. The 'female comedians' presented to me at that time were Phyllis Diller and Joan Rivers—and that was basically it. And those people were great and smart, but they didn't have the same life experiences that I'd had, so my first reaction to the dare was literally like, *I don't know if I'm allowed or supposed to do this.*"

Though she began her career two decades later, in the 2000s, LA-based comedienne-ballerina Riley Silverman's coming of age as a transgender female (whose onstage "look" has also progressed from masculine to feminine) still echoes this universal feeling of seeking permission to be funny.

"For a long time, I didn't let myself come out and identify as being female and ask for female pronouns because I didn't think that I was allowed to. I'd been taught that if I didn't fit the 'female comic' mold, I couldn't be a 'female comic,' and if I didn't fit the 'hyper feminine' role, I couldn't be a 'female' at all. There's a lot of really harmful information out there for young trans people that stems from previous generations' psychological gatekeeping, outdated gender terms, and harmful binary gender roles. For example, this very strict idea of what a 'woman' should be. Most people think a woman should be silent, obedient, agreeable, thin, young looking, breeding, and available to her man—and, unfortunately, many of the resources for transsexual women, and transgender people in general, promote this idea, which originally made me (like many others) believe that if I didn't fit this hyper feminine role then I probably wasn't really trans. And because I didn't look or sound the way a 'female comic' should look or sound like, I thought I probably couldn't really *do* comedy. But watching the *real* thing, and not just absorbing the harmful messages, changed my mind."

While Riley credits her fellow comedienne-ballerinas for guiding her eventual self-actualization, Lizz credits her family—specifically, her father—for not only inspiring her sense of humor but also instilling her with an enduring sense of self-worth. For many performers, such inner confidence is invaluable. It can become an antidote to the anxiety, fear, and insecurities that so often tempt them to seek permission from gatekeepers rather than follow their own comedic instincts. For Riley, this antidote came in the form of friends from her comedy circles; for Lizz, it seems, the antidote was inherited much earlier.

"There are five kids in my family. Before he died, my dad sent all of us a card that read, on the outside, 'Don't open this until I'm dead.' So, of course, I opened the card, and inside he'd written: 'I love you. You're my favorite. Don't tell the others.' I was *floored*. I was so happy that I carried it around with me. I even felt kind of guilty that I'd opened it—especially later, at his deathbed. We were all there, and my mom was sitting beside him, holding his dead hand . . . and suddenly, she goes, 'Did you all get cards from your dad?' And we all looked around and were like, 'yeah.' So then she goes, 'I want to hear what they said.' Then we were all like, 'Well, we weren't supposed to open them 'til he died.' And she's like, 'I *know* y'all opened them. I want y'all to read them.'

"I kept thinking, *I'm a total jerk. I can't read a card in front of all my siblings that says 'you're my favorite, don't tell the others.' I'll sound like an asshole! I can't read this card! What do I do? Do I change the words while I'm reading aloud or . . . ?* Whatever. And so, she goes, 'Lizz, you start.' And I was like, 'Why the fuck do *I* have to start? This is the worst thing ever! Like, he's not even cold, and he's dead, and this is awful!' And she calmly goes, 'Just read.' So I finally open the card and start reading, 'I love you, you're my favorite . . . ' and that's when everyone cracked up and said, in unison, 'Don't tell the others!'

"Turns out my mom and dad had sent that card to *everyone*, knowing that we would all open it before he was dead, and knowing that we would read it and have some sort of bullshit satisfaction, thinking, *I knew I was the favorite!* It was brilliant! He'd wanted us all to do that. And for the two of them to coordinate the whole joke, together, and for my mom to actually carry it out was crazy. We all laughed and laughed. But that's what he'd wanted: To have the last laugh. That was the whole point: 'I'm having the last laugh at my own death.' That was *it*, and it was an amazing experience. In many ways, I think those kinds of experiences become—if not the literal source of actual jokes—doors that open up the world of comedy."

LA-based stand-up and television writer Shelby Fero experienced a different kind of "coming to comedy." Instead of drawing on her own family, she was inspired almost entirely by TV. And yet, even separated from Lizz by thirty years of experience, Shelby, too, felt she "got lucky," not because someone dared her to go on stage in college or because she grew up in a funny family but because she was fortunate to grow up "in the Tina Fey, Amy Poehler, Chelsea Peretti era."

"Do you feel like your comedy is a reflection of theirs?" I asked.

"I would say that the way I operate within the industry is a reflection."

"How so?"

"Well, I started out, from the very beginning, thinking, *I can do this.* A woman can helm her own show, and write about her own opinions and experiences, and be just as much of a perfectionist and a workaholic as any man."

"Do you think this mindset is different from that of earlier generations?"

"Yes. I get the impression that mainstream entertainment in the '40s and '50s, before Feminism really got started, would pretty much summarily dismiss women for thinking that way—especially if they tried to act on it. They were basically blacklisted for displaying that level of self-awareness."

LA stand-up Brandie Posey came of age from the late 1980s and 1990s, when *SNL* and *Seinfeld* were "the biggest things on TV. All my girlfriends and I religiously watched *Seinfeld* on Thursday nights (mostly for Elaine because Julia Louis-Dreyfus is the funniest human being on earth), and *SNL* on Saturday nights . . . So my favorite comics growing up were Molly Shannon, Cheri Oteri, Ana Gasteyer, and my girlfriends from middle school. All of those girls were equal heroes to me. I saw Molly Shannon one time in a Starbucks and was totally starstruck. I couldn't say anything. I just stared at her and thought, *you're real! Look at you!* She's amazing. Even if there was nothing going on in a sketch, she'd still make amazing things come out of it. And Molly Shannon probably grew up in the era where she was watching Gilda, you know? I think the people that you laugh with when you're a child will forever be your rock stars. They're always going to be larger than life."

Molly Shannon's decision to get into comedy was never formalized in the traditional sense. "I never even thought about it at all. I was just an actress—and I was actually more attracted to dramas. So I consider myself a dramatic comedian, in many ways. I treat comedy very seriously—almost the same way I would perform a dramatic scene. I weigh the emotional stakes. I really think about what my character wants.

"I think that's why a lot of the characters, like the Joyologist, and Sally O'Malley, were versions of my father, re-created as women. He was a very influential personality on me, growing up, because of what he'd experienced in his life. Sometimes I think of my characters as my various different imitations of him. For example, when Sally O'Malley walks out with a limp when she first comes on—that's my dad. During a car accident he was very badly injured, and that's his limp. When she says 'Don't be fooled by this brace on my leg, 'cause I can kick! Hit and kick!' she's so strong, she kicks the brace off. That was always my wish for my father: to move faster and to be stronger, like Sally."

Molly's wanting to become an actress came from him. He loved classic Hollywood stars like Elizabeth Taylor, Judy Garland, and Liza Minnelli, and after her mother died, they watched movies like *Easter Parade* and *Butterfield 8* together. She didn't grow up in a comedic household or as part of a funny family, either; she just loved watching old movies with her dad. "He was like the Mama Rose to my Gypsy. He tasted that life through me, which made me so proud, and certainly gave me the get up and go to keep hustling in show business when there was a lot of rejection."

"Do you feel like the characters based on your dad empowered you? That *they* made you stronger?"

"Definitely. But you know, the truth is I never thought about that at the time," she said. "Like Mary Katherine Gallagher. I was basically writing an exaggerated version of myself and reenacting how I felt when I was little. I was nervous and accident prone. My mom died when I was four in a terrible car accident, and so I felt like I'd been through a war by the time I got to kindergarten . . . I was just trying to survive my childhood and doing the best I could to try to keep my chin up."

Her performances turned comedic once she saw *Saturday Night Live*. As a sixth-grade babysitter, she would put the kids to bed, and then stay up to watch Gilda and Bill Murray play the Nerds: "brace face" Lisa Loopner and her pocket-protected boyfriend, Todd. "I remember thinking, *Oh my God, this is so fantastic*! I thought they were so sweet. I thought she was so sweet and endearing and real. She had such warmth in her characters. There are some comedians today who guard against that, who don't want to reveal their own human vulnerability. They're defensive. They've allowed themselves to be hardened by their experiences instead of sharing them. But what was so great about Gilda is that she left her heart open."

After she first performed Mary Katherine Gallagher on *SNL*, the crew came up to tell her that the character felt equally real—and so familiar that, for a second, a few forgot that Mary was actually Molly. She still thanks Gilda for this lifelong gift.

Similarly, Abbi Jacobson of Comedy Central's *Broad City* and the Upright Citizens Brigade explained that her parents exposed her to the first *SNL* cast. She was immediately attracted to Gilda, and "in eighth grade I read her book. I was very into it. I focused on visual art in high school, where we had to make these huge cutouts of a historical figure, and I chose to make a life-sized cutout of Gilda as Roseanne Rose-annadanna. It was in my school's library with historical figures, and I think she was the only actor. It was all, like, kings and Benjamin Franklin and whoever . . . and then my Gilda. She was a *huge* influence. I had obviously seen people that I could kind of relate to on TV and movies, but her humor just really stuck with me."

In a touching speech given in 2015, another UCB (Upright Citizens Brigade) alum and *SNL* groundbreaker, Amy Poehler, also thanked Gilda for being the person whose voice filled her childhood home and made Amy's mother laugh, eventually inspiring Amy to pursue her own career in improv. Once she became a household name, people began to ask, "What's the secret to your success?" and Amy answered, "Just copy what your heroes do, and no one will notice!" During her years on *SNL*, during the late '90s and early 2000s, when Amy created a working relationship with uber-talented comedy writer Emily Spivey, they endeavored to do exactly that: copy their heroes—especially when it came to fearlessness. For both women, it seems, Gilda lit a fuse that "turned into a fire and now is this blaze that I get to stand next to," Amy said. "I commend all of you who are doing the same thing: rubbing two sticks together and waiting for a spark to catch. Stay warm, stay strong."

Millennials have now inherited this same inspirational spark. Gilda inherited it, too—from First Wave comedians, whose comedy either directly or subliminally encouraged the Feminist fight to secure citizenship and voting rights for *all* colors of women. The great pride they must have felt when universal suffrage became law planted the seeds for our current belief that we can accomplish even the seemingly impossible.

Generations later, women like Laurie Kilmartin would venture into comedy because "it was the only thing that felt right.

I wanted to be an actress, I definitely [knew] that, but I found out that I didn't like auditioning. I didn't like being judged by [the] casting director. I felt very uncomfortable. So I went to see some stand-up in San Francisco, and it made me think, 'I bet I could do that.'"

This very concept—*I bet I could do that*—is an entirely modern privilege that only began to take political, legal, and financial shape in 1920. These six words have sprung triumphant from centuries of all the things that no woman of any color, creed, religion, or culture could ever be, think, or feel—let alone *do*. They represent a huge, mind-altering shift in perspective that earlier Feminists fought first to create, then instill, and then pass down through three generations—from Moms Mabley and Lucille Ball to Phyllis Diller to Joan Rivers to Molly Shannon to Amy Poehler and, finally, to us.

But the pendulum swings both ways. How lucky are we?

Maybe *too* lucky?

Have we finally become the victims of our own hard-won success? Are we so liberated today that it's starting to hurt? Has the pendulum swung so far that we've found ourselves stuck in the same unfair, catch-22, either/or reality of having to choose between being "just" wives (and therefore remaining *outside* the show), like Lucy Ricardo, or "just" performers (and therefore getting to be *in* the show), like Lucille Ball?

the pit and the pendulum

THE BETTER ARGUMENT ABOUT LUCY is that she rode the pendulum as it swung, hoping for the best but planning for the worst. She agreed to this gender-based pigeonholing so long as it opened doors, playing the character of an incompetent wife so long as it got her laughs. This character was her currency, just as women's sexuality has always been our currency, for better or worse. If playing along, riding the pendulum, ensured that she remained "the somebody" rather than just "the girl" in the show, so be it. To Lucy, the ends (making something by, for, and about women's experiences) likely justified her means. As *Vanity Fair* pointed out, she "would wear almost anything—Carmen Miranda dresses, muumuus, and crazy hats—to transform herself into the childish and braying Lucy Ricardo." In this way, playing the incompetent and lying about her age worked for Lucy until it became her turn to take over and make the decisions. And so, for a time, she played right into something that her (mostly) male audiences clearly sought out. But it was not without backlash for her and for the women who would come after her.

Dr. Landay explained the motivations behind Lucy's approach: "First, as she said in a lot of interviews, she didn't feel confident, so I think there was a part of her that maybe it appealed to. Second, it played into so many ideas that people already had about women. So while incompetence and not being able to do things is always funny in both genders—after all, it's funnier when somebody *can't* do something than when they can because it plays into our foibles and our fears and our anxieties, and so we release our tension—when a male character can't do something, nobody watches that and thinks, *Right, of course he can't, because he's a man. All men are as incompetent as that guy.* However, when a woman can't do something, especially during that time period, many people laugh because they think it's more true than funny. They view it as a commentary on reality and the failures of womanhood as opposed to the incompetency of a single, individual, fictional character. And especially during that time, when people were far less aware of their own underlying sexism, audience members and executives would watch an episode where Lucy and Ethel try to get jobs as factory workers and they would watch them fail in the funniest of ways—but instead of understanding that this is a joke, they would actually believe that women can't have real jobs. Their thought process would be, 'We can't put women on as assembly line, because look: They can't do it. Or we can't have women do whatever it is that Lucy is doing, because women can't do any of these things.'"

In essence, the pre-Feminists of the 1950s—much like anti-Feminists of today—willfully mistook Lucy's self-deprecating character for her *actual self*. They fell into the pit of self-sabotaging misperception.

"Unfortunately," Dr. Landay said, "there's a way in which Lucy's humor played into those stereotypes, and those really negative, belittling, demeaning ideas about women's competence. It really comes down to whether someone's comedy is intended to be conciliatory, emancipatory, or demeaning. For example, she did Chaplin impersonations later on in her career, and you can see all the ways in which she was similar to Chaplin—they both had this amazing facility with props that is not easy for most people, and they both also played the incompetent, although his incompetence is *really* different from hers. They both did these roller-skating routines, for example, only in Lucy's, her incompetence is the butt of the joke whereas in Chaplin's, he's only a victim of circumstance.

"Back then—and, to a large degree, [in] mainstream comedy today—jokes are geared toward teenage boys. This continues to be the most highly-sought-after demographic for all larger-budget, studio-made films. In television, comics and sitcoms feature jokes that writers and executives think that men (and women who enjoy laughing *at* rather than *with* other women) will laugh at. And so we have the idea of the comic actress, who often is the one we are laughing at rather along with. She is the object of the comedy or the goal of the comic. This can be in the form of the dumb blonde or over-reactive wife or the nagging mother. In essence, she is the stage prop. And oftentimes those comic actresses are simply there to react to comedy rather than make it. In the end, they're just the girls that had to be got. The 'things' that the funny guy is going after. Even Chaplin acknowledged this sad reality when he said, 'All you need to make a movie is a park, a policeman, and a pretty girl.'"

That says it all. The girl in the show wasn't necessarily funny; she was an object. A part of whatever else the hero was trying to achieve and often failing hysterically at. Sure, sometimes she was funny (Paulette Goddard, for example, was truly funny), but she wouldn't have *had* to be funny. Making jokes—the essence of "the show"—just wasn't her job. Yet. But until "yet" was realized, she would play the incompetent. And the source of the funny would come from her inherent, female incompetence.

The irony here, of course, is that Lucille Ball herself was amazingly competent. At the same time that she was filming these scenes and supposedly pandering to sexist stereotypes, she was capable of doing her job far better than most other people of any gender. Years later, with TV now an international platform, women are much freer to point out these obviously gendered double standards, and to their credit, they do. To that, I think Lucy would respond, "You're welcome."

Still, Lucy had a lot of power and influence—far more than most people realize to this day. For example, unlike many females in Hollywood at the time, she had the ability to veto comedic situations of which she didn't approve. She often could, and certainly did, control a large part of her character's narrative. According to Dr. Landay, "Everybody involved in *I Love Lucy*—the writers and producer and director—had a very strong sense of what was good for the Lucy character and what Lucille Ball would like and be willing to do. The parameters there were established very early on. Certain ideas about these characters, for example: Lucy could make fun of Ricky's accent, but nobody else could . . . There were certain parameters that would have just gone against the grain . . . she would tell the writers that she didn't like it, and they would have to redo it." Yet another first for a female in comedy. Still, she hardly dictated the show. As the *LA Times* reported in 1952, when interviewers asked Lucy the secret of her show's enduring popularity, she invariably answered, "my writers." More specifically, she was referring to Madelyn Pugh Davis, the sole female writer on that staff and only the second female to have ever been hired at CBS. Madelyn's and Lucille's relationship is, perhaps, the main reason why (as the *New York Times* put it) "the legend of *Lucy* is a tale of two women."

This is most apparent in the expertly crafted friendship between Lucy and her best friend, Ethel—one of Lucy and Madelyn's most memorable co-creations. In every episode, Ethel kept Lucy's secrets . . . and so did Madelyn. Right to the very end. As the *Times* wrote of Madelyn's memoir, *Laughing With Lucy*, "Her unassuming attitude toward her singular career as a television pioneer, and a female one at that, is reflective of her essence; it just wasn't right to brag. And, true to form, at the very beginning of her book, she said she thought that writing unsavory things about people after they died was 'tacky.' Readers were thus not to expect an iota of dirt about the star for whom she wrote."

"Sometimes people called me 'the girl writer'—I didn't mind," Madelyn said in an interview with Tom Gilbert for the Archive of American Television. But when her longtime colleague, Bob Carroll, readily admitted that the men called him by his last name—and that, in fact, they *only* called each other by their last names—it must have felt like they were passing the ball around in a team sport she didn't know how to play . . . but she probably couldn't have cared less so long as nobody on set was calling her "Sugar Tits."

Both Lucy and Maddy started out as girls in the show— one in front of the camera, the other behind—but the "girl writer" didn't just "ride herd on etiquette and outlandishness . . . Because of her sex and then-requisite secretarial training, the typing of the scripts fell to her, too, and so did trying out the plots' more demanding physical stunts—including dipping chocolates at the Farmers Market in Los Angeles and carrying three dozen eggs in her blouse—to determine if they would sit right with a woman or, worse, be too dangerous for the star."

These became what Lucy called "the black stuff"—highly detailed, all-capital-lettered stage instructions in every script. And, again according to the *Times*, "it was upon that she depended to map out such intricate and spontaneous-seeming routines as the 'Vitameatavegamin' commercial, accidentally setting fire to her putty nose while in disguise and many other moments, right down to eye movements, facial expressions and body language."

According to a profile by the Paley Center for Media (formerly the Museum of Television and Radio), which honored her in 2006, "Maddy would type these zany feats in all caps on the script so Lucy would know exactly what she was getting herself into." One of Maddy's scenes called for Lucy to milk a cow. Upon seeing the mangy creature on set for the first time, the appalled Lucy turned to her "girl writer" and said, "You wrote it, you milk it." And Maddy did. Because, at the end of the day, what are friends really for?

Equally notable were Maddy's stamina and commitment to her craft. She cowrote all 179 episodes of *I Love Lucy*, and all 179 are still watched to this day. While Desi Arnaz may have been the "I" of "*I Love Lucy*," Maddy was its eye. She corrected, she judged, she leavened. By her very nature, she helped refine its broad physical comedy with thoughtful details, imbuing it with an unlikely believability that transformed it into a perpetual showcase for the foibles of human nature. Yet her opportunity to do so undoubtedly came as a consequence of much larger political and social changes for women. When World War II upended half of an entire century, according to

Dr. Landay, this altered almost all areas of American life—especially popular culture—from 1941 to 1945.

"We now have women in manufacturing jobs while men are away, which opened doors for new people like Madelyn. She got her first job writing in radio comedy because there was a man who had that job, who then went off to war . . . And so, when we think about women's control over and entrance into mainstream comedy, we have the actresses, some of whom are very powerful in Hollywood (like Katharine Hepburn, who's choosing to do comedy as well as her more dramatic roles, and to wear pants—to *awesomely* wear pants, in fact), but also some women in roles behind the scenes. Those are the women like Madelyn."

Dr. Landay continued, "Even though this environment wasn't one in which anyone could be completely equal, there were a lot of women who were involved. There were a lot of women editors, too, maybe because people thought it was a little bit like sewing in the beginning. And then, as the industry grew more powerful, more money became involved . . . and so, over time, a lot of those jobs became men's professions. We see that over and over again: In the beginning when something is really open and new, there can be possibilities and sometimes women jump in there as pioneers and then they can get pushed aside as it becomes more codified. And, conversely, when something sometimes becomes de-professionalized—like bank tellers, for example—then men leave and those jobs are left to mostly women."

In such an environment, we find the histories of many lesser-known pioneers—women behind as well as in front of the camera. But we don't study those women as closely as we do, say, Chaplin because women's contributions to culture aren't nearly as well publicized and studied and revered as men's.

Women like Mabel Normand—a comic actress of the early twentieth century (who, according to Columbia University's Women Film Pioneers project, starred in at least 167 film shorts and twenty-three full-length features, but whom most people don't even recognize—partly because of the scandals of the 1920s, and partly because almost every source during that time was heavily filtered through either self-interested autobiographies or the Keystone Studios PR machine)—contributed just as much to our culture of comedy as Charlie Chaplin ever did, and the lasting effects of their contributions continues to bind Feminism to comedy and comedy to Feminism.

When Lucy and Maddy hit it off, the term "Feminist" was just emerging—and even when the Second Wave came through in the late 1960s and early 1970s, it was still "women's lib." Still, they'd held these ideals from the very beginning, and Maddy's visual writing style, combined with Lucy's physical comedy, made those ideals shine.

Together, Lucy and Maddy wrote the character of Lucy Ricardo as an actress, like Lucille Ball herself, whose focus (again, like Lucille's) was on her career first and her family a close second. The humor came out of her sincere desire to be in the show, not simply married—which was an almost entirely new way of redefining success for women. And though she was still the screwball, the kooky girl, and she still went through foibles of those temporary jobs, and though she still had the husband that the network and the sponsors insisted she have, both she and everyone watching understood that something was changing: Lucy's character was someone to laugh *with* rather than *at*. Her jokes were more for herself and her female friends than their husbands—or even for the male television executives. Instead, this was entertainment for the ladies (for once), and it wasn't another soap opera where the heroine pines after men. This was a show where the focus lay firmly on what Lucy wanted, and it tapped into an altogether different demographic. Clairol was also very, very interested in tapping into that new market. And this perfect storm of capitalism and confidence changed all forms of television thereafter by shaping the structure *of I Love Lucy*—and all subsequent network series—around first three, then five, and now up to six timed commercial breaks. These required "spots" written into the narrative to showcase sponsors like Clairol forever altered the structure of modern television writing (which is why the earliest dramas were called "soap operas"—their storylines were specifically written for and around the selling of soap). These products demanded storylines that centered around the desires of women, housewives who were in charge of purchasing household products for their families, and *I Love Lucy* was no exception.

In this and many other ways, Lucy not only created what's now known as the TV "sitcom," but she also reformulated "women's comedy" around the central concept of "the somebody": the idea that a woman could *be* the center of the show rather than simply in it. In essence, this also makes her the founder of nearly every form of "pro-woman" comedy on television today—and, indeed, her friendship with Ethel set the stage for almost all of our current positive depictions of female friendship and loyalty.

According to the *Times*, "nowhere in the series is a feminine sensibility more apparent than in the friendship between the Lucy and Ethel characters, a relationship equally as important as—and in many ways more substantial than—the traditional marriage around which the series was centered. The camaraderie, the compassion, the conspiracies and the intimacy the two women shared—not to mention the jealousy, rivalry, squabbling and indignation—are all rendered on the page. The scripts are full of exchanges of knowing glances and the subtle sending of disapproving signals whenever the conversation takes an undesirable direction. There is an undercurrent of communication between the two whenever the men—or anyone else, for that matter—are in the room."

Lucy was the first woman to star on a nationally televised situation comedy that became one of the most popular and highest rated shows of *all time*. Because she had such an amazing platform, what Lucy chose to say—and what her writers, including Madelyn, chose to have her say—was *truly* heard.

Even in 1950, people stopped and listened to Lucy each week, which was remarkable for a woman at that or any other time. Plus, they listened to *her* more than to the men on her show. This was beyond remarkable if you stop to consider that it had never happened before. They'd listened to earlier women on stage and in vaudeville, and of course they'd listened to women's voices on the radio, but these had been smaller, theatergoing audiences or audiences who didn't have to look as they listened through that dial-covered box. Unlike some of its pared-down contemporaries that lacked financial backing from major sponsors (such as Betty White and Del Moore's similarly wacky husband-and-wife comedy, *Life with Elizabeth*, which ran for two seasons from 1953 to 1955), *I Love Lucy* was a big budget broadcast that relied on Lucy's highly physical comedy and astounding talent with props. As a result, audiences couldn't use their imaginations. They couldn't picture anyone else but Lucy. They could never, for even one moment, forget that a *woman* was talking—and that her voice mattered most, since she was "the somebody." Because of all this, and because so many more people were tuning in than ever before, Lucy had more listening power than any other comedienne-ballerina *ever*. This was at a time when women's voices had only counted on any national or political level (outside of a few western states and territories) for about thirty years. Remember: *I Love Lucy* premiered in 1950. Women got the vote in 1920. That's only a little more than *one* generation between nobody caring what any woman had to say (because she couldn't vote and, therefore, had no power to affect change outside of her own home) and everybody who had a TV and a half hour to spare specifically sitting down each week to listen to a woman talk.

Beyond talking, the particular ways that Lucy chose to communicate with her audience radically altered not only the future of "women's comedy" but also the structure of *all* broadcast comedy:

1. She established "women's comedy" as the comedy of everyday life, meaning that her comedy was based around a character whose experiences as a female imitated those of a typical audience member, regardless of gender, and whose comedy in turn permeated her audience's everyday life. The conversation between Lucy and her listeners was, in effect, two-way—and the character of Lucy Ricardo became a part of her audience's day-to-day reality.

2. She further solidified "women's comedy" by becoming the first television character to appear visibly pregnant. Perhaps more importantly, she audibly acknowledged and then openly discussed her pregnancy in front of both men *and* women during the early 1950s, a time when alluding to any aspect of reproduction was considered extremely impolite among mixed company. Audiences had literally never heard a woman—let alone a married couple—discussing "women's issues," and the obvious implication that Lucy and Ricky must have enjoyed some kind of a sex life (gasp!) for her to become pregnant in

the first place was absolutely shocking. Being *heard* and *actually listened to* when she discussed these topics (even when she did so in the subtlest and most comedic ways) forever altered the cultural platform that television was rapidly becoming.

Suddenly, with Lucy pregnant, everyone had to choose: Either confront that reality or stop watching the show. And if they chose the former, they had to acknowledge that respectable women not only engaged in sex (gasp!) but they also enjoyed it (gasp! gasp!). That was an even bigger deal than getting knocked up, I assure you. The fact that, week after week, audiences across the entire country could watch a familiar, lovable, and very *pregnant* woman (who wasn't hiding her belly beneath a giant Victorian-era corset or retreating to her quarters so that fragile minds could escape being accosted by the fact of human reproduction) catalyzed many of the radical social changes of the mid-twentieth century.

I asked Dr. Landay to clarify the impact of this gigantic cultural shift. Did *I Love Lucy* suddenly make it okay for women to have and discuss sex in the public sphere?

"Not yet. That comes a little bit later, but it certainly evolved from the starting point of *I Love Lucy*. That was the 'big bang' that began the conversation about all of these topics, in a way, because Lucy's undeniable pregnancy and her and Ricky's conversations about the baby led to all of the televised depictions of sexuality, sexual preference, alternate sexualities, and even reproductive choice that we're able to watch and listen to on any sort of televised medium today."

Perhaps the most long-lasting effect of Lucy's and Desi's fortitude was that their art helped to close the gap between real experience—people's everyday lives—and what was depicted onscreen. Despite these exaggerated situations, the interactions between the main characters were much closer to a representation of real married life, with its domestic ups and downs, than anything else had ever been. That close approximation, though less impressive when compared to the myriad cable comedies of domestic life today, was at the time very powerful for people to watch.

I Love Lucy's pervasive popularity has yet to be repeated by any other show to date, redefining what it meant for a TV show to be popular at all. The show ran for nearly eight years and entertained sixteen million people a week. People still watch it to this day, which clearly says a lot. Perhaps Lucille Ball and Madelyn Pugh Davis could never have truly imagined the kind of precedent they would set for making real life into real comedy based on real experiences. How their Bothness and Somebody-ness would transform not only our gender expectations but our entire conception of "having it all," and how many future girls in the show—like Tina Fey, Amy Schumer, and even Lena Dunham—would have them to thank.

part three

QUEEN LEAR

"Female: The second sex, who live in the vicinity of Man and are basically susceptible to domestication. The species is the most widely distributed of all beasts of prey. The American variety is especially articulate but can be taught not to talk."
—The Debutante's Dictionary, 1968

the invisible visible

MEANWHILE, IN THE LARGER CONTEXT of American history, the population—and within it, the television-watching audience—was moving into a post-war era. Simultaneously, women who had taken over manufacturing jobs during World War II mostly left the field but stayed in the workforce in general. Poor women and women of color had *always* been working, to be sure— before, during, and after the war—and so this big shift only really took place for middle-class Caucasian women, who'd been primarily working inside the home beforehand. The inroads that women had made into paid work stuck from this point on, making people like Maddy and Lucy permanent fixtures in comedy. All of this progress was highly ironic, however, when America moved into the 1950s, as one of the big themes in American history during that decade was conformity.

This shift made the character of Lucy particularly interesting: here we have this oddball, someone who's not doing the same things as other women—and certainly not a traditional "housewife." As Dr. Landay explains, "You can see why people might be laughing more at someone doing these unusual things and not doing what's expected at all. But there was also a very serious side to this idea of conformity, which was McCarthyism, and the very real way in which people had their careers and livelihoods taken away when they were blacklisted for their political views."

Lucy herself couldn't escape the fervor when she was requested to appear before the House Un-American Activities Committees (HUAC), "where she was being charged as a communist," Dr. Landay told me. "She had registered when she was younger as a communist but so had lots and lots of other people . . . But ultimately she was cleared, in part because of her clout and her power: she was kind of too big to be taken down by that Red Scare. But it was very frightening for everybody involved in *I Love Lucy* at that time." Especially Maddy, who could've been ruined for life, never to write for television again.

There were many other victims who were not cleared. Pert Kelton, the original Alice Kramden in *The Honeymooners*, was labeled a communist (and a "loose woman") and blacklisted. Because she wasn't legally allowed to work, Audrey Meadows replaced Pert as Alice Kramden, effectively ending Pert's career. Other performers were brought down by cowardly informers like renowned director Elia Kazan, who infamously named others in order to save his own career from the government's blacklist.

This contextual fear created censorship that greatly affected what people laughed at and what they felt they were allowed to joke about. In the 1930s, Pert had been playing a bawdy prostitute in vaudeville. Only twenty years later, she wasn't even allowed to play a tame, desexualized housewife on television. As a result, it seemed as if the audience's sense of humor was mirroring politics; humor itself was becoming more conservative.

Even when the Red Scare was over, conformity continued to affect mass culture and entertainment. Reactionary, conservative nationalism took over where the Scare left off. In many ways, even if HUAC wasn't persecuting the people, the people were still persecuting each other. When the majority embraced the concepts of "Americanism" and the straight, white, capitalist values at the center of that, other people who didn't necessarily fit that mold were suddenly afraid to come out of their homes. They began to see the ways in which stepping out of line could have very real penalties and consequences. In reaction, counterculture began to rise in urban areas. Now that so many of the people who "embodied America" were moving to the suburbs, artisans and cultural and political radicals were left inside the cities. The beatniks began to emerge. Coffee shops started to draw in younger audiences and nontraditional thinkers who formed jazz clubs where a new era of outspoken, anti-establishment, oftentimes female and sometimes sexually liberated stand-up comics were born.

Comedians continually commented on Americans' rising nationalism, racism, and reactionary xenophobia. This commentary even played into what Maddy wrote and Lucy performed. The clearest example of this—Lucy's reactions to Ricky's mispronouncing English words—spoke directly to who and what constituted a "real American."

Yet women of the First Wave of comedic Feminism still couldn't—and sometimes wouldn't—associate themselves with the word itself, with sexual liberation, or with gender equality, even while their work was creating these realities and changing what it meant for women everywhere to "have it all," meaning balanced expectations between career and family. While creating this new reality for women that we now refer to as the Second Wave of Feminism (the idea women can work outside the home in the same capacities as men and that they should receive equal pay for equal work), women like Phyllis Diller, Joan Rivers, and Moms Mabley began performing in beatnik clubs and gay bars. There, the substance of their voices began to change as well, creating yet another emergent reality: the content of "women's comedy."

These clubs and bars became forums for airing the public's grievances and promoting debates over racism, sexism, xenophobia, and homophobia—issues that had long been brewing within audiences' and performers' minds—and encouraging new voices from underrepresented communities, including African American, Latin American, and LGBTQ comics. These venues also took up the cause of promoting equal opportunity and freedom of speech for comedienne-ballerinas—a dangerous combination to the Patriarchal status quo.* Here, Lucy and Maddy's forms of physical comedy and the more word-based stand-up comedy grew together in a way that was eventually noticed by executives, who hired these kinds of comics to become staff writers working under writers like Maddy,

---

* Whom I mention, since they so often seek to claim this freedom without a true, constitutionally based understanding of how it actually works: The First Amendment only protects us from the *government* censoring our speech (and certain actions that are considering a manner of "speaking"), and those protections are limited to certain areas/locations/contexts.

That's how the law operates. Private companies, like publishers, for example, can (and will) do as they wish. And therefore: The freedom to speak doesn't exempt anyone from the consequences of speaking.

and who then brought their comedy club experience and their word-based comedy to television. Unfortunately, networks—though they sought out new talent to excite their changing audience demographics—were still stuck in the past. Though newer voices were technically being heard, the vast majority of those voices were men's.

When given an opportunity to be heard, many women of that era—and of today, to an extent—received reactions along the lines of, "Oh, she's just one of the guys." This occurred because of the ways women changed their voices to mimic men's, both in the actual sound and in the content of their comedy, which distinctly mirrored the ways in which racial minorities have mimicked Caucasians' vocal intonations. At that time, there was a certain degree of "maleness" that comedians felt they needed to incorporate into their presentation to be accepted. Their jokes were often tailored toward what they felt men (both those waiting backstage and those sitting in the audience—even those belonging to underrepresented groups) wanted to hear, and what anti-Feminist women in the audience felt comfortable hearing other women say around those men. This constant tailoring proved exhausting; attempting to entertain became nearly impossible.

To ease the burden, comedienne-ballerinas like Lily Tomlin (and Lucy, before her) tweaked their voices for TV audiences and watered down the content they'd honed in live clubs and bars. They also sometimes created characters to hide behind while doing some of their dirtiest, most thrillingly open work. But still, some critics claim, these tactics only brought comedienne-ballerinas out of the frying pan and into the fire. What was the point of going on TV if you couldn't say what you wanted and air your funniest material? Others claimed that necessity became the true mother of invention; that because of network executives' censoring standards and practices, it was now necessary for these women to tailor their work—and so they invented innovative ways of winking at the truth that was, in many cases, considered too "dirty" to deliver to national audiences.

As time passed, comedians like Lily Tomlin began to parody their own "winking" for the camera during the early 1960s. This parody of her own parody was a true meta experiment that demonstrated how far audiences (and standards and practices) have changed from the First to Second Wave of comedic Feminism. In one particular parody of a TV commercial (filmed for a live audience in 1990s), we see Lily edging closer to a true revelation of women's sexual experiences. But she doesn't come right out and say so, speaking as herself, the real Lily Tomlin. Instead, she introduces herself to her audience:

"Hi. I am not a professional actress. I am a real person like yourself. About a month ago, a man came to the door and showed me some products designed to improve the sex lives of suburban housewives. I got so excited I just had to come on TV and tell you about it."

She's clearly recalling those earlier commercial parodies where she played a housewife with laundry issues. Only now, she's selling . . . *not* laundry, I suppose, unless she plans to suggest alternative uses for the spin cycle. With a few well-chosen hand gestures and a pinched, nasally voice, she's here and yet there. Lily and yet *not*.*

It's still riding that line. Not entirely hidden; not entirely open. We can tell that there's some dirty stuff coming, but she's

---

* Most tellingly, a comment below this video reads: "Wait a minute . . . that's not a comedian! That's a girl!"

not *exactly* the one doing the talking. The "not a professional actress but a real person like yourself" is talking for her.

"To look at me, you would never suspect that I was a semi-non-orgasmic woman. This means that it was possible for me to have an orgasm but highly unlikely. To me, the term 'sexual freedom' meant freedom from having to have sex. And then along came Good Vibrations."

The crowd cheers.

"And was I surprised! Now, I am a regular cat on a hot tin roof. This is no threat to the family unit . . . think of it as Hamburger Helper for the boudoir."

This revelation skirts the line even further, revealing the idea that men find vibrators threatening, making them sexually irrelevant to women. This *definitely* goes against the "please cut off any experiences that make men feel uncomfortable" rule, and represents a huge break from the unspoken rules Lily originally followed in her commercial parodies.

"'Can you afford one?' you say. 'Can you afford *not* to have one?' I say. The time it saves alone is worth the price."

Now the crowd is really excited.

"I'd rank it up there with Minute Rice, Reddi-wip, and Pop-Tarts. Ladies, it simply takes the guesswork out of making love. 'But doesn't it kill romance?' you say. And I say, 'What doesn't?' So. What'll it be, the deluxe kit or this handy purse-sized model for the woman on the go? Fits anywhere and comes with a silencer to avoid curious onlookers. Ladies, it can be such a help to the busy married woman who has a thousand chores and simply does not want the extra burden of trying to have an orgasm. 'But what about guilt?' you say. Well, that thought did cross my mind. But at one time I felt guilty using a cake mix instead of baking from scratch. I learned to live with that. I can learn to live with this."

Many other comedienne-ballerinas eschewed characters and music altogether, preferring not to disguise their disguise behind pigtails or soothing music. They stood inside the spotlight, commenting directly to the audience, detailing the reality of women's experiences within a world of masculine and often rigidly traditional values. These women are part of the reason why many comedienne-ballerinas today don't necessarily have to either sing or dance to communicate, nor must they change or hide their appearance to be funny. They can do both, or nothing at all, and use their voices however, whenever, or wherever they want.

Or can they?

Is the price of such freedom, even in the case of one's own voice, eternal vigilance?

talk dirty to the animals

AUTHOR AND CRITIC CAMILLE PAGLIA says that Joan Rivers kept careful watch over her voice. She wanted to make sure it counted, so she "held herself to the highest standard. There was never anything slack or careless about her. On the contrary, she focused the laser beam of her energy and attention on every detail—to give the audience maximum value. On her TV show, I noticed her mic was strapped to her chair leg! She said it was for sound quality, because her voice had such a strident edge. I loved that, and it emboldened me to confront sound technicians at my own public events, where I always request special care and distancing for my 'Joan Rivers voice.'"

But do we *need* to sound strident? Confident? Non-slack and definitely careful? Is there anything especially wrong with a comedienne-ballerina sounding like . . . herself? Apparently so. Enter the modern debate over "vocal fry."

As Ira Glass reported in January of 2015 during a segment of *This American Life* entitled "Freedom Fries," "the women on our staff have been getting emails like this one: 'The voice of Chana Joffe-Walt is just too much to bear. And I turn off any episode she's on. A quick bit of research found an appropriate description, which is vocal fry. How can 'This American Life' have this on the show? It escapes me.'"

Ira then played a clip of Chana saying the phrase, ". . . and Thompson kept hearing that term school-to-prison pipeline . . ." and points out that "her voice kind of creaks on the word 'pipeline.'" This, he says, is vocal fry. Something his listeners, male and female alike, can't seem to stand . . . in *females*, anyway.

Ira went on to say that "a man wrote us in November. Quote, 'Vocal fry is a growing fad among young American women. Miki Meek provides a vivid and grating example of this unfortunate affectation.' Miki, by the way, sounds like this."

And then he played another clip, this time of Miki, speaking in a way that, apparently, this male listener just couldn't tolerate. More letters reached Ira about more of his female co-journalists. Of Alix Spiegel, who cohosted the NPR science program *Invisibilia*, somebody wrote, "Perhaps Alix could cover the vocal fry epidemic. It would be really interesting to hear her take, as she is clearly a victim herself." From Ira's list, it seemed that few if any female radio journalists were spared attack. Elna Baker, Mary Beth Kirchner, Starlee Kine, Yowei Shaw—even investigative reporter Susan Zalkind, who appeared on *This American Life* with the story of the FBI shooting a man connected to the Boston Marathon bombers—received intense criticism for the supposedly grating sound of their voices.

One woman wrote in with the comment, "The growl in the woman's voice was so annoying that I turned it off." A man wrote, "Listen, I know there's pressure to hire females, in particular young females just out of college. And besides, they're likely to work for less money. But do you have to choose the most irritating voices in the English-speaking world? I mean are you *forced* to? Or maybe, as I imagine, NPR runs national contests looking for them."

What seems to be the problem with the sound of women talking?

According to Ira, the term "vocal fry" started to be used widely in 2011 after a study of thirty-four college students at Long Island University found that two-thirds of them had it, usually at the ends of sentences. A reporter wrote a story about that study for *Science* magazine. *Gawker, Huffington Post, Boing Boing,* and other sites linked to it. Within days, it became the most popular article ever published on the *Science* magazine website. Even *The Today Show*'s Matt Lauer was quoted as commenting on "something called 'vocal fry' that is creeping into the speech patterns of young women."

As Ira pointed out, creating such a vaguely medical-sounding term raises the specter of possibility in listeners' minds that talking this way harms young women's voices. Since then, many researchers have said this doesn't seem to be true. But *The Today Show* story said this only affects women. "Is there anything equivalent in men?" Matt Lauer asked his guest, Dr. Nancy Snyderman, a board-certified otolaryngologist and sometime medical journalist for ABC and NBC. She responded that there isn't.

We now know that this is only partially true. There *is* an equivalent in men. While we don't usually *label* it as such— because, apparently, we reserve the polarizing term "epidemic" for those actions we can attribute either solely or primarily to women—men also employ "vocal fry" and just as frequently. According to Ira, "There's now robust evidence that men do this, too. And like a lot of the other coverage, *The Today Show* story pathologizes vocal fry. It says that it's some kind of problem instead of just the way that some people talk. And it teaches viewers to spot it. *Today Show* host Matt Lauer starts the segment saying that he's never heard of this, and ends it saying he'd never noticed it before, and now he's going to be on the alert for it."

It was only when we noticed this in women that "vocal fry" suddenly became a "real problem," and that individuals like Dr. Snyderman began parroting the misogyny surrounding this supposed "epidemic." Like most backlashes to social progress, this issue of vocal fry was directed at the voices we're historically least likely to hear, and now that those voices are being used in ways that don't necessarily reinforce old stereotypes, *we're* being forced to confront our discomfort with change. The truth will indeed piss us off well before it sets us free.* Just because we don't like what some women have to say or how they're saying it doesn't mean those women have some sort of vocal distortion.

The rest of the *Today Show* segment becomes a vocal fry witch-hunt. Dr. Snyderman and Matt Lauer examine celebrities like Kim Kardashian, presenting her voice as "evidence" of the "problem" with women's voices. Like any Salem witch trial witness, Matt doesn't hear anything unusual at first, then promises to "listen more carefully." Eventually . . . ta da! He declares that he can now hear it, too. Whatever "it" is. The rest of us hear only the truth: that there are no witches. If

---

* An ode to Gloria Steinem.

anything, the true pathology belongs to Ira's listeners. Should distortions exist, they are them. "For whatsoever falls from one place is to another brought, and there is nothing lost, that may be found if sought," as Edmund Spenser tells us.

Ira goes to on say that "the *Today Show* story and other stories treat vocal fry as if it's a new phenomenon, on the rise, a fad, an epidemic. But as a linguist at the University of Pennsylvania, Mark Lieberman, has pointed out, there is still no evidence of that, pro or con—no evidence that it is more common now than it's always been. What's striking in the dozens of emails about vocal fry that we've gotten here at our radio show is how vehement people are. These are some of the angriest emails we ever get. They call these women's voices 'unbearable,' 'excruciating,' 'annoyingly adolescent,' 'beyond annoying,' 'difficult to pay attention,' 'so severe as to cause discomfort,' 'can't stand the pain,' 'distractingly disgusting,' 'could not get over how annoyed I was,' 'I am so appalled,' 'detracts from the credibility of the journalist,' 'degrades the value of the reportage,' 'it's a choice,' 'very unprofessional.'"

A younger producer, Stephanie Foo, adds that "lately, in the past year and a half maybe, every time I get together with female radio producers, it's just like comparing war stories. It's just listing off, 'oh, somebody said this about me, my voice this week. Somebody said I sound like a stoner thirteen-year-old. Somebody said that my voice sounds like driving on gravel. Somebody said they wanted to kill themselves hearing my voice.'"

Ira responds, "Listeners have always complained about young women reporting on our show. They used to complain about reporters using the word 'like' and about upspeak, which is when you put a question mark at the end of a sentence. But we don't get many emails like that anymore. People who don't like listening to young women on the radio have moved on to vocal fry."

Producer Chana Joffe-Walt responds, "I'm just trying to speak. Literally, the way that the voice comes out of my mouth bothers you? What am I supposed to do about that? And even now as we're speaking about it, I am noticing every single time I do it, and then hating every single time I do it, and trying not to do it. But trying not to do it is impossible because it's the way that I talk, because it's my actual voice. It's crazy-making."

And then Ira says, "It's funny. Until we started talking about it for this story, I never even noticed it in your voice."

Chana says, "And I didn't notice it when other women do it either until I started to read about the phenomenon of vocal fry. And then I did notice it. And I find it annoying now when other people do it. I mean, I don't notice it all of the time. But if I am thinking about it and hear other people do it—other women do it especially—I become like a woman who hates women."

Ira suddenly hits the bulls-eye. He says out loud what's at the heart of this hunt: "Wow, it's like you've absorbed the messages of your oppressor."

Chillingly, Chana responds, "I hear it in you now."

Beneath the surface-layer sounds of women's voices is, of course, their content. Once we gained a political voice in society, people started listening to not only *how* we talked but also what we talked *about*.

During Gilda's 1983 interview with Howard Stern, he introduced her as "a mystery guest! Are you gonna disguise your voice? You should disguise your voice, or everyone will know your voice in two minutes." When she tries to speak, he shushes her repeatedly and says, "Use a different voice or else you'll ruin the fun. This is radio! Come up with a voice, any voice."

She switches to her impersonation of Barbara Walters, affectionately named "Babwa WaWa."

The first female caller correctly guesses that it's Gilda. Howard teases the caller, claiming it might not be the real Gilda—it might be impersonator Jim Bailey. He changes his voice to impersonate the impersonator. He's suddenly Howard Stern's impersonation of a man impersonating Gilda Radner. It's very meta.

They ask Gilda about her latest book, and kid her about her movie *The Woman in Red* with Gene Wilder (whom Howard insists on calling Gilda's boyfriend, though it's later revealed that they were broken up at the time). After the obligatory PR plugs, they get around to taking questions from callers. Gilda's relieved. She'd rather hear from them than put up with Howard's constant ribbing about "Gene-la" (a play on "bubala," the Yiddish term of endearment). The first guy who calls in wants to know how many she's slept with. Howard answers that, besides Gene, the number must be *at least* ten. When she asks to change the subject, he switches to something even more personal: When did Gilda lose her virginity? This time, she doesn't say anything at all. She barely speaks during the rest of the exchange and then leaves "pretty upset . . . She walked outta here like she never wants to see me again!" Howard says, and then proceeds to freak out because he thinks Gilda hates his guts.

While listening to this interview, I began to wrestle with the age-old virgin/whore complex. Half of my brain is prudishly offended for Gilda (and, like her, completely denying the reality of my sexuality), while the other half is screaming, *Fuck it! We should be able to talk about our sex lives unapologetically!*

In fact, only two years prior to that interview, Gilda herself seemed completely okay with talking about sex—openly, for paying strangers—while in character. After introducing herself and explaining her childhood dreams to her *Gilda Live* (and coed) audience, Gilda announces her first song, entitled "Let's Talk Dirty to the Animals," which details the joys of getting undressed in front of barnyard creatures, yelling "Fuck you!" to a bunny rabbit, and then ordering a bear to "Eat shit!" all because she just doesn't care. "If they don't love it, they can shove it!" she sings merrily.

So did she *start* to care once she got out of character? Did she suddenly lose her sense of humor? Or, more likely, did her character allow her to lose *herself*?

LA-based stand-up Wendy Hammers shed some light on Gilda's duality by discussing her own ability to go on stage, totally uninhibited. Wendy herself started out doing material that was very personal, basic, relationship-driven, and "Jew-y," as she put it. "One bit I did early in my career was based on a character who loved American Express. For a long time, I felt safe hiding behind her but eventually I didn't need to anymore; I could be myself. I could now come out on stage and say, 'I just read this new spiritual book. It is so fantastic! I want to recommend it to all of you. It's called *Do What You Love and the Money Will Follow*. Doesn't that sound great? If it works, by this time next year I'll have a million bucks from masturbating and going to lunch with my friends.' Funny, right? It always killed. There's nothing funnier than talking about that kind of thing on stage. Masturbating, orgasms, you name it. And you know why? Because it's powerful. Those jokes aren't even dirty, really, because they're not *really* about sex. They're about power—and *freedom* from inhibitions."

Much like sexual comedy, creating characters frees performers from their inhibitions through the wide berth that usually accompanies poetic license. To prove the point, Wendy described a character from her second solo show called Cellist Trombone. "She was a very tough Italian girl from a Mafia family, and I based her on a real person I grew up with. She would say things that I would never say, but I felt free to say them when I was playing her. This girl actually told me when we were in school, 'You have a choice: Smoke or pluck your eyebrows.' Those are the only two ways to be cool. I wasn't interested in smoking, so she plucked my eyebrows—only she did it so much that she deadened the root, and now I have to pencil them in. I have no eyebrows. She tortured me. She was a tough, tough broad, who happened to be eleven. Scared the shit out of me. But let me tell you, when I got to do her on stage it was so much fun! 'That fuck! He fucked with my fucking head! *Fuck*!' She was a wild woman. She just *didn't care*."

Cellist Trombone recalls the infamous Depression-era stand-up/singer Sophie Tucker, who hid herself behind the guise of a "Red Hot Mama," and her postmortem protégé, Baby Boom-era comic actress Bette Midler, who hid herself behind Sophie's persona. Early in her career, Bette revealed to *Vulture Magazine* that "when I made up the character we put these sort of terrible jokes in her mouth. She was kind of a throwback, a little bit of an homage to those big-hearted broads who sang and told risqué stories. I like to throw my head back and scream with laughter, but I didn't have a way to put those jokes in my mouth. Some of them were so appalling that if I took credit for them, I felt that I would be diminished in some way. So I made up a character that I felt that I could hide behind. And people recognized her from their own childhood."

Alternately, improv performer Livia Scott used her characters to create a reality of her choosing. "When I was a little kid I did this character called Grandpa Throw Up for my brother. Grandpa Throw Up had a restaurant. He would always greet everybody at the door with, 'Hello. Nice to see you blaaaaaa!'" she said, falling forward, in character, while pretending to barf in my lap. "'Come in! Welcome into the blaaaaa . . .'"—more barfing—"'. . . restaurant!' And then my brother would play along. He'd say, 'Oh, we're so excited to eat here!' And then he would be eating his pretend barf . . . I still do that today instead of accepting somebody else's reality. I get to *not care* what they find realistic."*

Elaine May—arguably the mother of improv—reversed this "chicken and egg" relationship. She also created playful characters, but instead of using them to alter her reality, altering reality inspired her creations. She had as rough a childhood as I've ever heard of in comedy (barring Moms Mabley, whom we'll discuss shortly). Elaine's father died when she was eleven, and she and her mother moved to Los Angeles, where she dropped out of high school at fourteen, got married at sixteen, had a baby at seventeen, and then literally skipped town and moved to the Midwest with seven dollars in her hand.

In Chicago, Elaine finally found a way to channel her imagination. She wore classic beatnik black and audited classes at the University of Chicago, where she met Mike Nichols (her future comedy partner) and lived in a cellar with a single piece of furniture: a ping-pong table. She did comedy every day and every night with the Compass Players, an improv troupe she essentially ran, until she and Mike got so good that the troupe

---

* Personally, I'm never going to accept reality. I intend to grow up to be Angela Chase circa 1994 and marry Brian Krakow.

asked him to leave because his talent was "threatening." Elaine went with him, and they started Nichols and May— one of the first comedy duos to not have a straight man/funny man dynamic where one member was smart (and therefore superior) and the other clearly too dumb to peel an orange (and therefore . . .). Elaine and Mike were equals. She was also so beautiful that Richard Burton once said he hoped he'd never see her again because her beauty was far too dangerous a temptation (and he was already married to Elizabeth Taylor, so you can imagine that his standards were fairly high).

The stuff they came up with knocked the socks off Woody Allen's manager/executive producer, and Nichols and May started performing all over New York. Elaine said they were both such dead-broke theater kids that she arrived in Manhattan practically barefoot and had to get used to wearing heels (this was around 1958, so heels were basically mandatory). Their first album—*An Evening with Mike Nichols and Elaine May*—remains one of the single best satirical sketch comedy collections of all time. Without Elaine's work—she came up with most of their sketches, while Mike handled the scene structures and edits to the final cut—Lily, Gilda, Amy, Tina, and every other improvisational performer you've ever met would have likely become somebody's freaky aunt instead, making up scenes and performing them by herself *to* herself in the garage.

At the heart of all this groundbreaking work was Elaine's outside-the-box thinking. Elaine almost never played a mom or housewife. She played doctors and lawyers and business people. She was in charge. Sometimes she even played men, which was considered crazy, but also paved the way for later ladies to do so. She winked at sex a lot, and she and Mike constantly made fun of how seriously young Americans were taking themselves—lampooning the rise of the "relationship" as romantic melodrama. In 1972, however, Elaine "rejected the notion that being a woman shaped her approach . . . 'It would be hideous to think that either sex took a script and in any way pushed it toward any point of view other than the author's. I don't think it's important whether you're a man, a woman or a chair.'"

She was and still is one of our last living scions of funny, to be revered if not straight up worshipped. As Patton Oswalt, speaking for all of us, exclaimed during her Writers Guild of America award ceremony, "God, I love her! I fucking love her! Avert your gaze as she passes by! That's Elaine May, goddammit!" Her extremely tongue-in-cheek jokes at the expense of heterosexual matrimony and traditional notions of monogamy opened the door for everything from Mary Tyler Moore sleeping over at her boyfriend's apartment to Samantha Jones humping everything that walked on *Sex and the City* to Amy Schumer announcing that she'd contracted genital warts in college while congratulating a girl with Down Syndrome on successfully navigating the perils of "friends with benefits."

As impressive as Elaine's influence on comedy eventually became, it's equally arguable that she inherited the "I don't care" mentality that allowed her to escape both reality and society's gender expectations from Sophie Tucker, a First Wave pioneer and one of the self-proclaimed Red Hot Mamas, whom a Red Hot Mama of the late-twentieth century, Bette Midler, used to indirectly impersonate for her live audience, talking all kinds of dirty to a great number of animals while sporting a spandex Dalmatian-print jumpsuit paired with matching high heels and a fire-engine-red belt. Bette claimed that her character of "Soph" was fictional, but it's clear from her actual performance that Sophie's original comedy made it possible for Bette to feel okay impersonating her as such:

"I was hanging up my laundry the other day, minding my own goddamn business, when my girlfriend, Clementine, leaned over the picket fence and said to me, 'Soph'! How come you always know when to hang out your laundry? You never get stuck in the rain like the rest of us do!' I said, 'Now, Clementine, there's a perfectly simple proposition. This is what I do. When I wake up in the morning, first thing I do is roll over and take a good look at my boyfriend, Ernie. If it's laying on the right, I know it's gonna be a sunny day. If it's laying on the left, I know it's gonna rain.' Clementine said to me, 'Now, Soph', supposing it's standing straight up in the middle?' I said to her, 'Clementine, who the hell wants to do laundry on a day like that, anyway?'"

There's more. Jokes about elephant dicks so large that they leave Soph' feeling loose. About a cop being pulled, feet first, from someone's vagina. When the crowd demands *more*, Bette gets a bit shy. "You're a filthy group. Y'all will laugh at any old thing, won't ya? I have a whole bunch more jokes, but I don't dare . . ." They cry louder this time. She switches back to one about Ernie. He appeared on a show called *The $64,000 Question*. When the host asked, "What were the first words Eve said to Adam?" Ernie didn't have the faintest idea and scratched his head.

"That one's too hard for me . . ."

"You're right!" the host said.

But the crowd wants even more. They scream for her to tell the "taco joke," which she never actually explains*, and

---

* But is rumored to go something like, "If God did not intend man to eat pussy, He would not have shaped it like a taco."

instead replies, "This is a bunch of scumbags! This is a bunch of low lives! You want me to put this on *film*? Eh!" before offering them the Italian hand gesture for something other than "have a nice day!" "I'm dumb, but I ain't that dumb. I know how far I can push the American public," she says.

The crowd has become the Howard to her Gilda, and she'd rather just move on to another bit. (At least she didn't walk out.) The internal battle continues.

Wendy Hammers said, "If you're an actress, performing in a scene with two actors, you have a scene partner, right? But as a comic, your scene partner *is* the audience. Your job is to tell the jokes; its job is to receive the jokes and then return the jokes with laughs. It's like playing a game of ping-pong, with both partners going back and forth."

Today, however, some would argue that Bette should have (or at least could have) given the audience as much dirt as they could take; that the line between civility and vulgarity and between public and private speech has been all but obliterated. Others would argue that, given our current, conservative-led backlash to the entertainment industry and Hollywood as a whole, her audience—depending on their makeup—might have resented Bette's sexualized impersonation. It's always a gamble for a comedienne-ballerina: choosing where to draw the line. Fearing that if she doesn't take enough chances, she'll drop the proverbial ball and her voice will be lost—but if she takes too many, her audience might not return her serve.

Was Bette's joking discussion of sex really all that dirty? In the 1970s (and certainly in the '40s and '50s), we may safely assume so. But what about today? Have we gotten more or less conservative about what constitutes "dirty talk"? Has the line between public and private speech blurred to the point of vanishing?

Take, for example, a mother's publicly posting on the Internet what, for previous generations, would likely have remained extremely private: a text message conversation between herself and her teenage daughter, wherein the teenager journeys to a local store in search of tampons. Tampons so deeply hidden, I might add, that simply navigating the store's aisles becomes a tale of woe to rival that of Odysseus:

Daughter: THEY'RE NOT HERRREEEEE. I SEE NONE.

Mother: I swear on my life they are there. Try near diapers.

Daughter: OH WAIT. They're here tucked away in the a [*sic*] corner, unlabeled. They labeled [*sic*] a tiny shelf of joint braces but not the massive aisle of stuff for your vagina??????

As blogger Maria Guido added, when reposting these texts for *ScaryMommy.com*, "she's learning the secrets of the world at such a young age. Vaginas are never to be mentioned. *Never*. Unless we're telling women what to do with them, of course—but that's a topic for another article."

I asked New York–based author and columnist Mary Elizabeth Williams about the seemingly radical shift from past to present in terms of what women discuss in public (or what they decide to post online, purposefully allowing complete strangers to read, digest, and conceivably tear apart their feelings and experiences). When did the culture begin to crave things that earlier generations, frankly, pretended didn't exist?

"I think a lot really started to change in the 1970s, when you just couldn't escape the fact that everybody was getting divorced," Williams said. "People were leaving their families, and things were changing, and suddenly women were on the pill and could get abortions. It was all extremely different and a much more level playing field. What also happened is, suddenly, you had *Saturday Night Live* and *SCTV*. Ensemble comedy in particular was no longer just an all-boys club. Seeing women every week, on those two shows in particular, interacting with each other and creating characters and doing bits that were more female specific, but were also just about being in the world, not being separate from men but interacting with them, changed our culture a lot. And that change has continued to evolve. Now, when I look at comedy, sometimes I'm really dazzled by how far it's gone to the other extreme. Sometimes I think that card has been overplayed."

"What card?"

"The 'I'm a lady and I'm going to talk about my vagina, isn't that funny?' card. That can be just as much of a trope as 'I'm a guy, and I want to talk about my penis.' There has to be something more underneath."

Inside Amy Schumer's "Boner Doctor" sketch turns this concept on its head. In it, Amy Schumer, wearing a lab coat she claims to have bought on eBay, advises any male members of her audience who might be "suffering" from an erection that lasts more than four hours (a side effect of Viagra) to stop treating this as a medical emergency instead of a true medical *opportunity* . . . that they should remedy at her place, right now, while she's still wearing a short red dress. Nearly twenty years prior, in July 1998, a young Chelsea Handler opened her set with the line, "I am Jewish, and as your MC told you, I will just be talking about cock-sucking my entire act, hopefully." She screams to welcome the clapping crowd, "Look at all the ladies here! This is so exciting! I'm so used to performing in front of men."

Is speaking directly about sexuality inherently "masculine"—while speaking about pregnancy, menstruation, and

the like inherently "feminine"? Beyond these gender classifi-
cations, it's still true that many women lack outlets for sharing their "dirt" (outside of drinking and gossiping with one
another). Telling the truth about their experiences of married
life, including childbirth, raising children, and the joys and
frustrations of simply being with the same partner for a lifetime, is still too often labeled disgusting, impolite, or simply
taboo in mixed company. Many people feel uncomfortable
sharing this level of intimate detail with *anyone*—let alone a
room full of strangers. Yet we share arguably more disgusting
details about our lives every day, multiple times a day, through
our use of social media, with an entire world full of strangers
to judge us.

This psychological paradox boils down to gender expectations. So much of the reality of womanhood is still veiled in
secrecy that we tend to be both disgusted and fascinated by
it. As Mary Elizabeth Williams pointed out, "It's so shocking
because it's not part of the expected narrative. It's not part of
history. We'll read books that are just drenched in the gore of
wartime and battle but you will find very few accounts of the
(often hilarious) gore and mess of childbirth, and the ridicu-
lousness that comes with being a lady. It's an experience no
one dissects in public."

Another mother, Beth Newell of *Reductress.com*, points
out, "I don't think we've really talked about those issues out
in the open, and I don't think the average person knows very
much about pregnancy and birth and what it's like to keep a
small child alive until they go through it. And then they *still*
don't talk about it. I think most women are scared to. They
don't want to scare off the women after them who are going to
become pregnant and have children, so they don't want to dissect that experience out in the open. It's really frowned upon.

And maybe that's why breastfeeding is such a big issue, and why it's a hard thing to talk about: Because people are still so afraid of sex and scared of boobs. Seeing breasts out in the open to feed a baby, all those things. So it's a hard conversation to broach because we have like a knee-jerk discomfort with those things."

Even some women, like Mary Elizabeth and LA-based comic Laura House, are understandably put off by some of the intense focus on those experiences. "A friend of mine put it this way," Laura says. "Her act pretty much takes place between here and here." She gestures to the areas right above and below her vagina. "And, you know, it was true about this particular person. It's not what I respond to, and I wouldn't in guys, either. If guys are just like, you know, 'pussy this and my wiener that . . .' you know those jokes?" She's laughing now. She pulls an invisible pen from the air and pretends to make a note to self. "That's the set list: Pussy this. My wiener that. So stupid, I know. But I guess I'm just . . . afraid of sex. What? No, I'm not. I just feel like . . . I don't know . . . just be funny! Don't try to be the 'funny girl' or the 'funny boy.' *Just be funny.*"

"So what topics do you like to make jokes about?"

"Um . . . vaginas?" she says, with classic upspeak. She starts laughing. I have to admit it's a good twist. "*Just* vaginas. A whole forty-five-minute set. I don't know if you've seen my Netflix special, *Snatch Por Vida?*"

LA-based stand-up and comedy writer Laurie Kilmartin, on the other hand, jokes about anal sex. In all fairness, she only tells one joke, but she still gets nervous *Is it okay if I find this funny?* applause.

"It's funny to be breaking down my anal sex joke," she says, sitting on the couch in her living room in Burbank, California.

"I know. I'm just wondering what makes people uneasy about that kind of sex versus vaginal sex?"

"Well, the same thing that makes me uneasy: your poop comes out of there. It should make all of us uneasy."

"It should make *all* of us uneasy?"

"Yes!"

But I wondered: Could our "talk" become "dirty" simply in the way it's presented, *to* whom, and *by* whom?

As the first transgender comedian welcomed to perform at the All Jane Comedy Festival (formerly the All Jane No Dick festival), Riley Silverman has found that audience members routinely target (and ridicule) certain topics as "female material": Birth control. Dating. Children. Sex. Body dysmorphia. Most of all, periods and pregnancy. What's fascinating is the distance between perception and reality in terms of these topics' frequency. Jokes about periods and pregnancy—though rumored to be both the most common and most offensive sources of humor—are actually so stigmatized that they're rarely heard at all, except for the purposes of protesting this stigma. When someone *does* talk about her period or pregnancy, it's notable, like when LA-based stand-up Cameron Esposito "basically wrote the *ultimate* 'lady parts' joke," as Riley put it.

Cameron's setup describes her status quo: She's a lesbian who's convinced that she'll look like a fifteen-year-old boy forever, and, until recently, she's spent the past thirty-plus years tortured by a monthly bleeding that served no purpose. That status changes, however, when her body suddenly gets a mind of its own. Every night at about eleven p.m., Cameron finds that "I want to make a baby." She then explains in great detail the ensuing "War Against Your Own Womb":

"You might think, well, sure, you've got the equipment . . . No! This is *new shit*!" she says. "They don't even make maternity vests, so what would I wear? I never thought I would grow a baby! I thought I would parent kids but I thought I would buy or steal them, not grow them in my body! When kids are born, they have head hair and teeth and fingernails and gums—so that means before that kid was born that mom had head hair inside of her body! And if you're okay with that, who are you?"

She's yelling this entire exchange directly at her audience. And they're clearly loving every minute of it.

"Whenever I imagine childbirth, I imagine a baby sticks one little arm out of my vagina and then just unzips me. I don't feel great about it, but my body, against my will, keeps me up at night going, *I want to build something!* I keep trying to feed it LEGO sets, and now my apartment is covered in ships."

The ultimate consensus seems to be that women, especially those who also happen to be comedians, should talk however, wherever, and about whatever they want—just as men, especially those who also happen to be comedians, usually do (and have pretty much always been free to do, ever since the end of the notorious Hays Office, which most networks replaced with their own in-house standards and practices). So, if anyone tries to make the point that all "female comedians" talk about is their periods, you should keep in mind—and feel free to point out—that all "male comedians" seem to joke about is their ejaculate.

I've spent over three years extensively researching and watching comedy, and I can honestly say that I have been forced to picture more spunk emerging from more dicks than could possibly exist on this single planet. Do you have any idea how many dick jokes I've heard? I'm so nonplussed at this point that every time it happens, I inwardly shrug. Those who believe that all "female comics" send the same jokes about their vaginas and periods out to their audiences, night after night, tend to conveniently ignore this double standard (much like they ignore the fact that men, too, display vocal fry—or whatever crap we're currently using to make women feel shitty about themselves). Somehow, their rationale holds that while periods are off-limits, dicks and/or their issues with them are apparently totally normal and on point.

Male bookers used to ask Portland-based stand-up comic Susan Rice, "'What tampon joke do you end on?' Even when I never did them. The *guys* did, but I didn't. And it's not that we [the girls] couldn't go there . . . it's that they [the audience] wouldn't come back if we did. There's a difference. And so we were scared to even bring it up. That's why, I'm telling you right now: I don't know one female comic that I worked with from 1983 to 2005 that ever did tampon jokes."

I, too, can feel that cringe in the audience whenever a comedienne-ballerina creeps unsteadily toward "period joke" territory because, much like Lucy and Maddy, I grew up in this petri dish of shamefacedness, and the rules have seeped into my equally saturated core. The rules deem this topic to be one of the many things women who want to be taken seriously should never, *ever* do on stage. I don't blame women for continuing to avoid this taboo for any number of reasons: our own fear, the internal push-pull debate, the war against our own vocal cords, and our subconscious absorption of the age-old shame cloud that surrounds our genitals.

But who's going to change all that? Who's going to rush to the front of the room and let her spilled blood (pun intended) do all the talking? Who is going be the Jesus Christ of Period Jokes? The truth is that a little bit of self-preservation is always involved. And that's exactly how a lot of our subconscious subjugation perpetuates: because not a single one of us wants to die on the cross for a forty-five-minute set on periods.

Right?

Except.

Some brave souls have recently come forward to accept this challenge. Fast-forward to Cameron Esposito's punch line:

"Look, I don't want to make a promise to you. Like that I'm for sure gonna have a baby. I don't know that's gonna happen. But I just want you guys to know that there would be a positive aspect to this; an amazing side effect: That for once in my life my period would not be completely fucking useless to me! Because I have never had a pregnancy scare. And, yeah, I'm a female comic. And I'm standing up here. And I just said the word 'period.' Oh, how hack! Oh, how unnerving! How disgusting! Listen: If you're a guy out there and you think periods are disgusting, I don't think you've ever had an honest conversation with a woman. Because if you think periods are disgusting, you have *no idea* how disgusting periods really are. You shouldn't be able to say the word 'disgusting' without a little vomit rising up into your throat. *That's* how disgusting periods are. I wake up in the night, and I am bleeding out of my body! A crime scene! My body is bleeding *out of* my body! My body is smashing *my body* out of *my body* using *my body*! My body is wringing itself out like a hotel washcloth you might use again! And it doesn't come in an easy, clean, and pourable substance. *Chunks* of my body are coming out of my body! Chunks of my body are being smashed out of my body *by* my body! Sometimes the chunks are so large the only logical thing to do is to pick it up and hold it in your hand just so you can marvel at it. It's the size of a strawberry! A nonorganic, pesticide ridden, grocery store strawberry piece of my body. And this is not just happening to us at home, in our beds—this is happening to us on planes! This is happening to us at work! So if you think periods are disgusting, you can go fuck yourself, because you have *no idea*."

Amen to that. Cameron remains both incredibly brave and incredibly right.

Lyndsay Hailey remarked on how frequently she receives the same note: play the top of your intelligence. "I don't know how many times I've heard, 'Lyndsay, you're going blue again! Lyndsay, you're doing stuff with your vagina again!' It's embarrassing because it makes me feel like I'm not reaching deep enough into myself."

But I'm not so sure that superficiality is truly the issue. If "doing stuff with your vagina" was really preventing "women's comedy" from digging beneath society's surface, then Ilana Glazer's hiding a bag of weed inside "nature's pocket" on *Broad City* wouldn't have revitalized Comedy Central with millennial audiences.

Years earlier, in her screen test for *SNL*, Gilda claimed that she didn't have these kinds of stories. That she didn't have anything to joke about, in fact, except guys and eating. (This may have been true at the time.) But the difference is that this was still a form of progress. Before 1920, we started off not talking about anything at all—"dirty" or otherwise—because we didn't have voices that counted. And then, one constitutional amendment later, we did. Suddenly, everything counted. The real work began. The nation was now listening, so from 1920 to Gilda's time, we had to figure out what to say. And how. And how *much*. And to whom. Though women earning the right to vote didn't form an *immediate* beeline to what, how, and why current comedienne-ballerinas speak on stage—certainly, there were many smaller, progressive steps in between—women's voices would never have mattered without universal suffrage. In today's political landscape, using the former to their best and most truthful effect is a *crucial* way of preserving the latter's existence.

Janeane Garofalo and other comedienne-ballerinas of the late 1980s' and 1990s' "alt comedy" scene were both aloof on stage and nakedly honest, breaking the wall between performer and audience, playfully chiding them for laughing, and generally re-creating comedy as DIY: personal, vulnerable performances without the studied mannerisms that the women before them had learned from men. Their comedy is technically "blue"—which we'll discuss in just a bit—but not purposefully so. It's not purposefully *anything*, really, since their performances are rarely polished or perfect, thus creating a sense of danger that, especially when it comes to Janeane, results in electrifying comedy as we listen to her go on random tangents that don't seem to lead anywhere, but then hit on a moment that's cathartic for the audience. In 2013, Justin Gray wrote for Splitsider that "there are those within the comedy community who, to this day, take issue with Garofalo's reliance on notes on stage, not to mention the many people who abandoned her idiosyncratic style of comedy during her foray into the realm of political activism during the George W. Bush administration. Sprinkle in a healthy dose of lazy sexism and you have a comedian who, despite being instrumental in practically re-inventing the form of stand-up comedy, receives little of the accolades that she deserves."

These women moved the ball forward to today, however, where there's arguably no winking *at all*. Most commentary on anything relating to women or sexuality or reproduction is blatantly stated and clearly understood. How did that happen? How did we go from *not* talking to winking to, some would say, yelling?

According to Rosie Shuster, "Women sat in comedy clubs all those years, listening to millions of dick jokes, and eventually said, 'It's my turn.' And of course you want women to be able to share their experiences with each other on the airwaves, just as men have been doing for *so* much longer."

To this, co-creator of *The Daily Show* Lizz Winstead added, "It was pretty sexist back in the '80s, too—not that it's all cleared up now, but it was a time where women comedians were told 'don't talk about *women* things!' Which basically meant, 'please cut off any experiences that make men feel uncomfortable and only tap into part of yourself.' Which people just passively accepted and went along with back then. We all just sort of subconsciously followed the same directions that were handed down to us. We started saying, 'Oh yeah, I would never talk about my period or having crappy sex or whatever,' you know? It was bizarre. But that's all changed, and now we've started asking, 'Why is a woman's experience not interesting if she can make it funny? Why would you ever put those parameters on a human being?'"

During our conversation at Second City Hollywood, comic actress Angelina Spicer said, "The more noise and the more offended or shocked and amazed people are by my work, it's better for me because it has a lasting or more poignant reception. I don't set out to change the world. I don't approach it that way. Some might say, 'Oh you should do better. Or you should use your platform as a way to influence minds and things.' But I feel like it's my perspective and it's going to be unique from anybody else's anyway. So people are going to react whichever way from it. In stand-up, I find that I do go against the grain of what most other women are speaking about."

"How are your jokes different than other women's?" I asked.

"Sex. It's pretty pervasive. Sex, dirty jokes, poop jokes, fart jokes. It's self-deprecating, but it's also gross. It's not self-deprecating to the point where . . . It just isn't clean. I make it a point to not do any of that when I'm doing stand-up because I feel like—It's what everybody else is doing, number one. Number two, as a black woman, sometimes I am not given the same opportunities as other women are and I really need to cherish those opportunities and not blow them talking about how great I suck dick. That's not a representation of me. It's a waste of time. It's a waste of opportunity. And, ain't nobody got time for that. I'm not sitting up there placating an audience, talking about how my vagina smells. I'm not doing it. *No.* I feel like talking about those things would placate the bookers. It would also placate the other comics in the room, because guy comedians can be filthy, so they'd get a kick out of it. They'd think, 'Oh, you're just one of the guys!' or 'Let *me* scratch and sniff!' No. We're not doing that. There are other ways that I can separate myself and differentiate myself other than talking about pervasively sweating. *Not doing it.*"

"Is it progress that women can tell dirty jokes?"

"I think it's progress that we have a *choice* as to whether we *choose* to tell dirty jokes. I think it is progress that we're able to talk about whatever we want to talk about, and that we're given opportunities to speak."

Maybe exercising this choice is why, according to actress Leslie Bennetts, legendary comic Moms Mabley "talked about sex incessantly. Her humor leaned toward the sly double entendre rather than the straightforward use of obscenity that would become popular with such later black comedians as Richard Pryor. Although Moms herself was a lesbian . . . her favorite persona was that of 'dirty old lady' with a penchant for younger men. She made fun of older men, subtly ridiculing the ways they wielded authority over women as well as the declining of their sexual powers. Her signature line became: 'Ain't nothin' an old man can do for me but bring me a message from a young man.'"

But today, the pendulum seems to have swung back the other way. Today, that choice is possible, but in order to appear smarter or funnier or simply more adept at their craft, many comedienne-ballerinas seem to be moving away from choosing to "talk dirty." Whereas Moms and Sophie and so many others chose and continue to choose to address their audiences frankly, and reveal, even through pinpricks, all the assumptions about women and women's conversations, and to lay bare all the "dirtiness" that so many find impossible to pair with femininity, some millennial comedienne-ballerinas are using their freedom of choice—gotten, perhaps, through this very "dirtiness"—to specifically become "cleaner." In so doing, they are straddling both past and present. Exercising their choice in order to choose an earlier sensibility, one that was present far before choice was an option, especially for them. But the true underlying issue seems to be less about what these comedians are choosing to talk about, dirty or otherwise, and more about our reactions to that choice. Comedians may have changed, but have audiences changed with them?

During our conversation from the red movie theater chairs in the audience section of the Magnet Theater, NY-based stand-up comic Ayanna Dookie revealed, "I feel like we're still at the bottom of the totem pole, as far as who gets opportunity and who gets to speak. Even when I structure my audition set to specifically avoid dirty stuff, audiences still expect me to talk about certain things based on stereotypes about black women.

I'm biracial, but I'm seen as black, and so I'm expected to talk about sex, and to be loud and brash. Maybe that's why I go so far out of my way to make sure I *don't* talk about sex, and to make sure that I'm *none* of these things, because I don't want people to write me off before I even open my mouth."

She sighed and sat back, tapping her perfect manicure on the armrest. "I don't even want to talk about having a boyfriend on stage because some audiences will respond with, 'Here we go with boyfriend and period problems again . . . She has nothing else to talk about,' but then I'll go to an open mic and hear six guys in a row do either porn or dick jokes and nobody says, 'He has nothing else to talk about.' They always assume those guys have more to say and more to offer in terms of perspective and that not all of them will present that perspective in the same way. And God forbid I say anything about a yeast infection. Not that I'm going to try to convince everybody yeast infections are funny but, you know, people just shut down. They visibly roll their eyes and whisper things like, 'We don't want to hear about that.'"

Shelby Fero is a fair-skinned, strawberry-blonde Caucasian. She experiences the exact same pushback from audiences—this time, full of stereotypes about what young white women are supposed to talk (and not talk) about on stage and how they're supposed to act while speaking. "I try very hard not to bring up sex in my acts . . . even though, when you google me, one of the first things you'll find is my talking about how bad I am at sex," she said, sitting on her bright-orange sofa, which lit up her strawberry-blonde hair like a beautiful frame around her face. "It's hard because there's still a minefield. If you talk too much about sex in certain ways that are exploitative, you can get a reaction, but that reaction gets conflated with positive feedback. Some people think any feedback is positive, but that's not always true. So, it's hard. Talking about sex doesn't get the most positive reactions that I've seen, personally. For girls, it always comes off as weirdly braggy. At an open mic, if a girl starts telling a story about getting hit on when she wasn't interested or being pressured to have sex, boys will freeze up, like, 'Why aren't you happy about that?' or 'I don't get the joke. Why would you be uncomfortable in that situation?'"

Putting our experiences out there, however we choose to do so, is really the ultimate goal. Speaking our truth, whether that entails telling "dirty" jokes about sex, or sexuality, or menstruation, or reproduction, or "clean" jokes about getting turned down for a loan—it doesn't matter. All that matters is that people listen, truly hear, and then spread it around. Pray that somebody listens. That those new messages begin to mingle. That with time (and luck) they overtake the old ones. That we start to change the default settings. That we stop telling ourselves to shut up because "no one wants to hear that."

Like so much of this conversation about what topics and words truly constitute "dirty talk," who's listening to women speak, how much, why, and possibly most importantly, which of us are the *real* animals—the audience members or the comedians—my conclusions swing back and forth.

The truth is that we're all exhibiting a little (if not *a lot*) of the traits traditionally associated with both genders. And we'd all make so much more—and better—art if we could get over this idea of masculinity versus femininity, of "men talk this way" and "women talk this way," and just start talking however and saying whatever we want. Out loud. On stage. To *everyone*. To deny this and ignore our similarities ends up hurting everybody. Everyone's voice should be respected, "vocal fry" be damned. Everyone's words should count, dirty or otherwise. We're *all* the animals. Let's *all* act like it.

Maybe when we remove the rest of the boundaries, when nothing's taboo, and we can all freely laugh at whatever's funny—abortion jokes, anal sex jokes, period jokes, *any* kind of jokes that ring true and "punch up" at powerful figures— then comedy *will* finally flow for women. Maybe then we'll fulfill our destiny. Maybe then we'll grasp Gilda.

Beyond sex and abortion and all the other "dirty" words a woman can (should? must?) use, there are others that have morphed over the past three generations from rarely heard to constantly mined to conscientiously avoided, and which are now included in what some comedians define as "going blue."*

This now pervasive tactic for endearing oneself to an audience roared on stage via Phyllis Diller's and Joan Rivers's routines, and men like Louis C.K. and Marc Maron now base their entire brands on spewing a certain level of self-deprecation. But how did a comedian essentially shitting all over herself for the benefit of strangers so successfully dodge the bullet that has traditionally killed the careers of other "blue" comics?** Is it possible that sex is viewed entirely differently from self-hatred because it's embraced instead of forbidden? Is

---

* Frank discussions of anatomy and sexuality, which often include self-deprecation.

** For example, once again: the hilarious Pert Kelton, who—both before and during World War II—successfully portrayed a bawdy prostitute in vaudeville and yet was fired from the role of Alice Kramden during the first season of *The Honeymooners* and replaced by Audrey Meadows— mostly because the new wave of conservatism rolling through Congress under McCarthy's Red Scare of the 1950s labeled former prostitutes (and

it even more possible that self-loathing is actually an accept-able form of *self-love?*

Though she considers most "blue" comedy lazy and some-what hack, comedienne-ballerina Angelina Spicer noted that using her distaste for her own body to elicit laughs at her own expense is arguably better "because that's your truth. If you hate your hips or you hate your cellulite or you don't like what you see in the mirror, that's liberating to other women in the audience. They might say, 'Oh God, I've got the same hip issue. Or I have the same muffin top thing.' It's liberating, in a sense, to get up on stage, in front of a whole lot of people, and reveal those things about yourself. It's difficult to do. I think it's more difficult than telling the 'scratch and sniff vagina' jokes. That same girl who's talking about how many blow jobs she gives in a weekend is probably not the same girl who's talking about the body issues, and the latter demands a deeper sense of vul-nerability in my experience."

Today, in this current wave, "not caring" is another way of "going blue," since it means telling the jokes that *you* want to tell, in the tone of voice (fried or otherwise) that *you* want to use, regardless of whether women are the only ones laughing. It means being okay with that, and being okay with the fact that some men (and some women) are *never* going to laugh because they (1) don't relate, (2) don't understand your point of view, or (3) don't like the sound of your (or any other wom-an's) voice. Because #Patriarchy.

---

those who played them on stage) as no longer harmless sources of humor for "real" Americans but, instead, "unchaste" forces that might destroy the sanctity and harmony of nuclear families. "Going blue," when it butted against the hypocritical politics of Patriarchy, first made and then destroyed Pert's (and many others') career(s).

Gilda did this in 1979 when she took to the stage with *Gilda Live* to freely express herself, to say more and go further than a late-night sketch show could have ever allowed, even in its earliest, most ambitious days, when pushing the latest social and political boundary was far more important than promoting a celebrity host's latest movie (though they did a lot of that, too). Gilda wanted to talk dirty to a whole new audience of animals. And her obscene barnyard anthem, while totally fine for current cable comedies like *Inside Amy Schumer*, was way too dirty for late-night NBC (and probably still is). Going "blue"—at least, on network television—was a pathway to oblivion for "girl comics." Even today, as some women turn their dirtiness into comedy gold, once they go "blue" they can sometimes never go back. Even Amy Schumer has recounted that, once men began describing her first performances as "mostly about sex stuff," she felt the label became permanent. Now she would be expected to focus on "sex stuff" every time she took the stage or risk disappointing her audience. She eventually joined those whom she could not beat, so to speak, by turning the label into the title for her 2012 special, in which she used her "ditzy comic persona" to "allow her to satirise a world in which women think they can control men easily if they wear little and think less."

Would Gilda have gone further on stage today? Would she have stayed to answer Howard's questions, free from embarrassment? Does the makeup of the audience determine the tone of the comedy?

For example, improv performer Cody Lindquist said that whether her husband is listening determines her answer to the question, "Do you share child-rearing duties equally?" Which sort of implies that, if he weren't listening, she might change her answer. Which further implies that some women who also happen to be comedians might tend to censor their speech depending on who's listening to their comedy. With this in mind, I asked Cody whether her hesitation applied to all men, other than her husband. Does she tailor her jokes, either in terms of substance or delivery, according to whether or not the audience is coed?

"Well, if you're scared, and you don't know comedy well, and you're trying to figure out what you're doing, you think, 'that'll work—everyone's going to laugh if I make a joke about sex!' I don't necessarily think that this happens because there's only men in the audience, because women laugh at it, too. Maybe it happens because sex is the most basic, normal thing that everybody experiences, and because women and men are both sexual creatures. So that seemed like the easiest thing to do."

"Were dirty jokes easier for you, too?" I asked.

"Yes. But I also started performing in New York in 2006, so maybe I was just different then. I was twenty-six at the time, and I made a lot of sex jokes. I'm a tomboy, and I grew up with three brothers, so . . . my jokes never pulled punches. I swore a lot. I don't know how much of that is because I grew up around men, and that's just what I'm used to, or how much of it came from the fact that everyone in my class was a guy, or because making jokes about sex or your body *felt* easier. Ironically, that was *less* embarrassing.

"But then I took more classes," Cody continued, "and I worked with more people, and I learned at the UCB to avoid *always* going for the easy joke. To avoid going blue *all* the time. Sometimes, blue comedy is fun and hilarious, and there's a time and a place in everything, but as you learn more, you realize, 'I can use things from my life. I can do a character about somebody that I saw on CBS who was singing to herself, and she was hilarious to me and hilarious to the audience around me, and it's not dirty, it's not sexual, it's not easy—it's a complex weird character who made me laugh.' And so, as I started to get more confident in myself and my comedy, and as I got a bit older, I realized that my voice had changed, but I don't know why."

It's understandable that Cody, like many of us, isn't sure how change happened. It's hard to separate decades of social programming from what we really feel and think. As time progresses and we get to know ourselves better, we gain confidence, we begin sorting these issues out, but there's always that person inside—some of us call her "*that* girl"—who continues whispering in our ear, telling us all of the things that society wants us to hear, to believe, and to perpetuate.

Comics who are really good at what they do are great teachers in this way: they help us to sort through all our deepest programming. They help to decode all the messages that so often make it hard to tell our own wants and needs and desires apart from society's. Have you ever had a great teacher who could make you really understand? Whom you loved, despite their retaining authority?

That's why comedy is so hard, and why being funny is so accomplished. It requires both accessibility *and* authority, which is not a terrifically funny concept when you explain it. Riding that line between seeing and hearing, light and dark, rightness and wrongness, us and them, is the painstakingly difficult job not only of comedians but also of entertainment as a whole. Those are its most ancient roots and purest purpose.

At its onset, we can see from even the earliest Greek plays that comedy was a way for society to work out a moral dilemma. It was always the theater of debate, intended to simultaneously reflect society while also teaching it something about itself. Today, this debate has evolved into every aspect of entertainment and manifests wherever a comedienne-ballerina takes something verboten and magnifies it. Speaking up may make her "edgy," but could we move society forward without this edge? In a broader sense, comedy opens the door to analyzing the essential questions of "What are we all doing here? How can we have fun with what's happening?" and then invites its audience to find an answer. In this way, Wendy Hammers is right: comedy is a relationship between two partners who teach and learn from each other, passing sound waves back and forth through the dark. And maybe this (rather than detecting which gender rules to follow) is the toughest part.

"What does this joke mean?"

"What did that laugh mean?"

"What answers does it give me?"

"What's the *truth*?"

This is perhaps its straightest, most direct point: *There are tragic things happening, but let's figure it out together.* Communicating this to her audience is what a comedienne-ballerina does best. But while she's sharpening society's latest edge, she herself is left bleeding. Her honesty may reach and therefore relieve her audience's pain, and in so doing push us all toward collective social progress. But are we worth it? Is her effort to push us forward actually creating a more truthfully cohesive society? Or are we all just "dirtier" now?

LA-based author and comedienne-ballerina Sara Benincasa thinks the pain is worth it; that the gains made by earlier rule-breakers, edge-skaters, and social scapegoats were necessary to form today's comedy landscape, and we therefore owe it to them to keep up the "dirty talk." For her, both Gilda and Carol Burnett first shone a light on all that was possible.

"I'm sure I must be the hundredth person to say how much I love them," she commented. "I used to watch Carol with my mom, and she would make my mom laugh, and I remember feeling like I wanted that, too. She's a sketch actress, I guess. She never really translated as a stand-up to me until I remembered that she used to always take questions from the audience ahead of time, before the show started, and that's riffing. That's a kind of stand-up. I think I picked up on that as a young girl watching her talk and hearing the audience talk back to her."

"Did you ever see Gilda do the same thing as Carol?" I asked.

"Oh, yeah. They were both always, in their own subtle way, breaking all the rules."

"What rules were they breaking?"

"Rules about what 'the girl in the show' could do—about being a woman who was a performer, a comedian, a beloved object of affection, and who also made herself look ridiculous sometimes. She wasn't afraid to take a pratfall. She wasn't afraid to wear the goofy ensemble. She wasn't afraid to get a pie to the face if that's what the scene called for. And she wasn't just the secretary. She wasn't just the wife. She wasn't just the mother. There's nothing wrong with being a secretary, wife, or a mother but when those are the *only* roles you're permitted . . . there's something wrong with *that*. She could do so much.

"And Gilda, specifically, did so much for both the baby boomers of her time and for millennials today—so she meant a lot to my parents *and* she meant a lot to me. Her comedy bonded us, in a way, across generations."

Even identifying as something other than maid/mother/wife/secretary/nurse was skating the edge of acceptability within the gender code. Before Gilda and Carol could even *find* this edge, women like Moms Mabley, Phyllis Diller, and Joan

Rivers, and much earlier comedienne-ballerinas like Sophie Tucker, Belle Barth, Pert Kelton, and hundreds of others had to create it. It's actually a relatively recent notion that "going blue" is the "easiest" (read: "laziest") thing to do on stage. For earlier generations of women, this was, in fact, the hardest, most fraught comedic choice.

enter through the wound

IN THE 1960S, WOMEN LIKE Joan Rivers began appearing on TV. Joan's look fit very much into a feminine type—a type that was not in any way going against the grain—yet her humor ripped holes in the fabric of gender. On April 23, 1967, she appeared on *The Ed Sullivan Show* in her little black dress and her perfect string of pearls and her perfectly coiffed hair and her perfectly done makeup—then promptly began ripping apart this one-sided, gender-based expectation using familiar territory—husband-shopping.

Later, on *The Carol Burnett Show*, she exclaimed that "the whole society is not for single girls! Single *men*? Yes! A man, he's single, he's so lucky! A boy on a date, all he has to be is clean and able to pick up the check, he's a winner. You know that. A man could call up anybody in the whole world—'Hello, I saw your name in the locker room, I thought I'd give you a quick call'—but a girl can't call. She has to wait around for the phone to ring, right? And when you go out, you have to be well-dressed, your face has to look nice, and the hair has to be in shape. The girl has to be the one who's bright and pretty and intelligent and a good sport. Howard Johnson's again? Hooray, hooray! A girl, you're thirty years old, you're not married, you're an old maid. A man, he's ninety years old, he's not married—he's a catch! Isn't that true? It kills me!"

Through all of these seeming hysterics, Joan remained very feminine, and she kept her topics completely within the boundaries of a feminine role, but she also moved away from the punch line–based comedy favored by male performers and popular until the late 1950s in which you stood in front of a crowd and told joke after joke, each with a setup and punch line. By the 1960s, Joan was telling longer stories, which became the basis of stand-up comedy and solo performance as we know it today.

The ways in which Joan differed from her predecessors seem like steps of evolution: women like Phyllis Diller had created comedy by mirroring men; Joan moved into ignoring men altogether. Phyllis delivered her comedy through a series of set-ups and punch lines; Joan engaged in conversational comedy, giving and taking with the women in her audience and "reading the room" for these women's reactions. Her material was based on social commentary, personal reflections, and cultural critiques—much like Lenny Bruce, who was known as a "shock comic," focused on exposing society's deepest flaws and confronting them directly with his audience. But while Joan also exposed and confronted the gender-based double standards, her act focused solely on what she considered "women's concerns," telling her version of the truth about women's lives.

Beyond this, Joan distinguished herself by drawing her material directly from her own private life, which was considered incredibly TMI (and certainly "dirty") for the time.

She wasn't joking about some imagined person, like Phyllis's make-believe husband, Fang. And she wasn't dressing up like a different person to play a character *based* in truth, like Lucy and Moms Mabley. Instead, Joan's character was Joan. She played only herself. Her jokes were funny because they were *true*. She described something that rang true within the typical marital situation for women at that time, and she described that situation as she honestly saw and understood it. Joan wrote toward vulnerability. In this way, she was expressing a huge duality: dressing very much as was expected of a woman, yet speaking and acting in ways that were expected of men.

Through this combination in Joan's comedy, the subconscious narrative began to emerge that maybe, just maybe, women could be *both* feminine and masculine—and that society should view this Both-ness as acceptable behavior. I asked LA-based writer and stand-up comic Shelby Fero, who was only twenty-one at the time of our conversation, how much she knew about Joan Rivers.

"I've seen some of her old late-night appearances. Her jokes are always funny . . . but when I'm listening to her, part of me says, 'Now make a joke about *something else*. Make a joke about *anything* else. You're so funny! Come on! *Just do it!*' And then reading some of the lines from that movie she directed with Billy Crystal, which were just satirical in the broadest sense, I thought, 'Why didn't you tell *those* jokes out loud? Were we stopping you?'"

I turned this over to Mo Collins, a veteran of sketch and improv comedy and a favorite of mine since *Mad TV*. "Why did Joan channel her best jokes through Billy Crystal's voice? Why didn't she go back on *Ed Sullivan* and tell them herself?"

"That's always a question of society's edge, and its the definition of 'acceptable.' That's the networks and everyone saying, 'Here's the line. Don't cross it.' *That's* what stopped her: the line. The rules. That's what stops all of us unless we're on a stage where our words aren't being televised, and we can say whatever the fuck we want."

At the other end of the generational spectrum sat Rosie Shuster, who agreed. Though these three generations were separated by at least forty-five years of experience, a common thread ran through.

"I also think that sometimes guys viewed 'women's comedy' as unrelatable to *anyone* simply because it wasn't channeled through *their* point of view. The guys just didn't believe there would be any appeal simply because it didn't necessarily appeal to them. But now, there are far fewer rules, and so it seems that everything appeals to everyone—and maybe that's because comedians can say *anything*. Like now, I was just watching an old *Inside Amy Schumer* episode, and she was talking to the audience while wearing not much more than her panties for a good solid chunk. It was hilarious stuff, and it was brand-new ground, but you *never* could have gone there long ago. Maybe all that's changed because there's so much destruction going on around us. There's as much need to laugh as ever in this crazy world, and so we've relaxed the rules on what's 'too dirty' to talk about."

That's comedy's job. It's also the job of entertainment as a whole: to get us there, meaning a place of common understanding where we, as a society, can work out a moral dilemma. Comedy was always intended as a way to educate an audience. Showing us our reflection, taking apart some piece and magnifying it beneath a comedian's spotlight, teaches us all something about ourselves. While it's long been said that truths are told in jest, the word "jest" implies that you're trying to be funny, whereas, to be funny, you have to be committed to the truth—and to loving your audience enough to bother teaching them anything. So to do its job properly, comedy must be a combination of both truth and love.

Near the end of her career, Joan was able to go much further across "the line" by embracing both truth and love. When she appeared on *The Tonight Show Starring Jimmy Fallon* in 2014, she playfully called him "ethnic" for being Irish, though she herself, like all Jewish comedians, was ostracized as a non-white "ethnic" comic until the 1970s. Then she proceeded to tell him how dry her vagina was by joking, "I took a bath tonight, and all the water went WOOSH!" up her crotch, and claiming that she wants to do porn but because of her age "nobody wants to hear an old lady talk about coming unless she's going for the door." The expletives fly out of her mouth in such rapid fashion that her 1967 performance seems, in comparison, fit for church. She even insists that she was late because of a misdirected flight followed by a broken-down limo, ending with, "The Nazis killed six million Jews and you can't fix a carburetor?"

In Joan's mind, she was telling the truth (as she knew it) and loving the subjects of her jabs, all at once. She was also joking in a way that earlier audiences had only ever given certain men (like Don Rickles, Mort Sahl, and Jerry Lewis) permission to do, and which Phyllis Diller had once described as "mock hostility."

Phyllis Diller wrote that she never intended to be dirty, "but a lot of people would read innuendo into what I said. For instance, when I'd impersonate supper-club entertainer Hildegarde singing, 'The Little Things You Used to Do,' I'd sexily go all the way up the octave just repeating that line and comment, 'He was a very small man.'" Phyllis claims that she wasn't referring to the man's genitals, but was instead suggesting that he was a "small thinker, a shallow person." This is hard to believe, considering that she was in her late thirties to early forties at the time and already had six children, but Phyllis maintained that she "was so innocent that it took me years to learn that I was dirty." More likely, however, is the idea that Phyllis wanted to have her cake and eat it, too—meaning she wanted the laughs that "talking dirty" to her audience could bring without the backlash that so-called "blue" comics often experienced (especially if they were women).

Phyllis's comedy was inspired by the "blue" comics of the First Wave's generation: so-called "brassy chicks" like Belle Barth and Rusty Warren, who "turned the air blue with their crude jokes in after-hours hangouts." She claimed that they were far too X-rated for television, but their inappropriate commentary only fueled Phyllis's own career. So while she was apparently just the right amount of dirty for TV, when she was live, on stage, she wasn't dirty enough. The audience wanted more, just as they did years later from Bette Midler's Sophie Tucker impersonation. Maybe that's why people kept reading more into Phyllis's songs than she supposedly intended.

As for those "brassy chicks," Phyllis Diller still owed them a lot.

Joellyn Wallen wrote for the Jewish Women's Archive that Belle Barth often impersonated singers like Sophie Tucker, Al Jolson, Harry Richman, and even Gypsy Rose Lee. Born Annabelle Salzman in East Harlem, New York, on April 27, 1911, Belle grew up with a virtual audience of siblings—three brothers, Moe, Abe, and Saul, and one sister, Paula. Not much is known about her childhood, but according to Joellyn, "Upon graduation from high school, she billed herself as a singer-pianist who also did impersonations." Singing her way through popular standards and performing imitations kept

Barth employed on the vaudeville circuit through the 1930s and 1940s, but "the character of her act changed in the 1950s, when she began to mix her two talents—music and comedy—and added a splash of 'red hot mama' for good measure. In other words, Barth capitalized on the emerging field of adult comedy that emphasized overtly sexual material. This sort of comedy teetered perilously on the brink of obscenity, and the police were often part of Barth's audience. However, as long as her acts were confined to small clubs, avoided religious gags, and maintained a one-liner approach, delivering her most vulgar punch lines in Yiddish, she avoided clashes with the law."

This method of delivery came off as less crude (they couldn't understand what she'd just said, anyway), and those who could understand her enjoyed the "sweet and salty" shtick. Critic Ron Smith points to this interplay as the element that made her comedy particularly effective: "She was especially good at contrasting a coquette's conversational sweetness with the sudden brawling howls of a Brooklyn bordello madam," a particular skill that, far from leaving her unable to communicate with her audience, became her primary method for hammering home her point. No one in his right mind ever accused her of having vocal fry. In fact, Barth herself described her own act in a classically cool third person: "She says dirty words in a cute way and everybody digs her the most."

Belle was better known in the press as one of the "Red Hot Mamas," along with Sophie Tucker and a singer named Pearl Williams. In her excellent 2008 thesis, *America's Madwomen: Jewish Female Comedians in the 20th Century*, author Grace Overbeke details the contributions of these Mamas—and of Jewish comedienne-ballerinas in general—as one of history's best-kept secrets. Before the 1970s, according to Overbeke, Jewish female comedians like Fanny Brice, Molly Picon, Jean

Carroll, and others eschewed political humor and instead channeled their subversive energy into jokes about domestic life. While women were certainly not allowed to joke about their periods, their sex lives, or anything men might find "unpleasant," these women were granted membership into the Club of All Things Domestic (a.k.a. *not* political due to the "perception of women as lacking important social and political insight," according to Overbeke). She goes on to write that "in the late 1930s and 1940s, this domestic humor took a decidedly sexual bent in the routines" of Pearl Williams and Belle Barth, who "took up [Sophie] Tucker's mantle of sexually subversive humor in the 1960s but did so in ways that reflected the anger of the Feminist movement at that time."

Sophie Tucker began by performing in her family's diner in Hartford, Connecticut, at the turn of the twentieth century. She got a big break in 1907 when she booked a role in Joe Woods's New England vaudeville circuit playing a blackface-wearing "coon-singer." By 1910, however, she'd gotten rid of that crazy and gross idea and started touring around and gaining attention with her singing numbers. One of her hits included the perfectly titled, "No Man is Ever Gonna Marry Me," which just screams, *This! This is why we needed Feminism in the first place!*

Irrespective of their minor differences, these Hot Mamas—Sophie especially—were some of the very first to assert that women, regardless of their age or size, were highly sexual beings with libidos to rival any man's. Even worse (or better, depending on your perspective at the time), Sophie specifically insisted that Jewish "Mamalas," as she called them, should come out from behind their ovens and start sexing it up.

June Sochen wrote in her essay "Talking Back" that Lenny Bruce referred to all comics as either predators or prey. Once they took the stage, they had to choose which label to assume. But Overbeke claims that this distinction reveals more about the onstage/offstage personas of many comedienne-ballerinas of that time, who were almost forced (by both external societal pressures and their own internal absorption of those pressures) to meekly acknowledge their "subordinate roles" as women and accept that their success precluded the possibility of their having any kind of love (or even sex) life off stage.

According to Overbeke, Sophie's personal life as a Jewish woman in the early twentieth century was filled with emotional trauma and repeated victimization by her philandering partners (to whom she apparently remained devoted, often blaming herself for their cruel infidelities, possibly because Feminism was another fifty to sixty years away, and who has the energy to fight the Patriarchy while wearing a whalebone corset, anyway?). Meanwhile, her professional life was markedly different. At home, she might have been prey, but on stage, Sophie behaved like a real predator. Necessity became the mother of Sophie's invention, and the suppression she felt by both the Jewish and American patriarchies drove her into show business where she could change the world by truly being *herself*.

Women's voices were hardly celebrated within Sophie's household. Robert Mock writes, and the Jewish Women's Archive confirms, that the Talmud forbids a woman to read the Torah because "a woman's voice is a sexual enticement, as is her hair and her leg." Sophie was to abstain from doing anything that might attract men's attention—like, for example, stand-up comedy. Instead, she was supposed to conform to the Jewish idea of feminine modesty, known as "tznuit" or "halacha," and—even more importantly—to keep clean, in word and deed, through the ritual of "kashrut," or keeping kosher.

Sophie's parents kept their household strictly in line with these commandments about female subordination and modesty.

Sophie wrote, years later, that she grew up unable to criticize her father for anything he did simply because he was the head of an orthodox home. Even after she became famous, she was still expected to keep up the charade of subservience whenever she visited her parents. "I had to stop being a headliner and the boss, and remember that I was just a daughter, who had to sit back and let the men of our family take the lead. Even Son, the eldest grandson, ranked ahead of me when it came to our religious ceremonies."

On one hand, she had to keep quiet and repress all of her thoughts, feelings, criticisms, and experiences . . . and on the other, she'd found the liberty to voice them all. Prey vs. Predator. Woman vs. Comic. On stage, she was the independent, sexy Red Hot Mama who demanded that men conform their minds to hers rather than the other way around. Off stage, Sophie was expected to "throw her arms around" a man's neck and turn herself into "a clinging vine all the rest of her life," meaning that she was to be, at all times, financially dependent— since a woman's independence in this area was considered a deep affront to a man's masculinity. This relationship extended beyond her religious household and into society's messages for all women—both open and subliminal—encouraging them to remain weak and easily preyed upon, regardless of their talents and abilities. The implication has always been that this pretense of weakness will make them happy.

The title of an article in a 1944 issue of *Ladies Home Journal* says it all: "You Can't Have a Career and Be a Good Wife." This article vehemently counseled women against speaking their minds and having ideas of their own, stating that "it's good to have one partner vigorously emitting ideas and challenging the imagination . . . and that person needs an audience who is wholeheartedly interested, and who will put everything aside to give *him* encouragement."

This mindset fills women with self-sabotaging anxiety and stems from unfair gender expectations. Using it only serves to reinforce the automatic settings with which we've been programmed. Through it, we don't live as our true, honest selves, but as default reflections through the car's rearview window. As academic sources have noted, "the author of this article, who identified herself only as 'a successful career wife'—meaning, of course, that being a wife *was* her career—stated that marriages were rarely successful when both spouses worked. 'Successful career couples,' so-called, try to keep up a glossy surface, hoping it will not crack and expose the disappointing makeshifts underneath, she explained. She listed the common reasons that women might want to continue working after marriage—the desire for extra money, the yearning for stimulation and socialization outside the home, and the urge to express themselves through their work—and then dismissed them as selfish."

On stage, Sophie bucked all of that "you're so selfish" brainwashing. According to Overbeke, "Tucker's subversive tendencies exploded through her stage persona" and she was "the pioneer flaunter of taboos, who made illicit laughter more comfortable." But at home, it seems that her strength waned. She gave in to gas-lighting by her husbands. She even blamed her inability to conform to gender norms for the failure of her relationships: "Both marriages were failures, due, I can honestly say, to my earning capacity . . . no red-blooded man can stand that situation."

Tucker's partners were blatantly unfaithful, yet she still couldn't blame the status quo. This *How can I lower myself enough to be loved?* way of life has filled normally happy women with rancid inferiority complexes since before we invented actual doormats. It's like watching Stella Kowalski in Tennessee Williams's masterpiece, *A Streetcar Named Desire*, when she refuses to believe that her husband Stanley raped her sister Blanche. There's no doubt, objectively, but she just can't bring herself to believe anything negative about him. She refuses to believe him capable or to see that she's irrationally enslaved, choosing to remain loyal to a ruinous mindset rather than seeking out actual happiness on her own terms. She gaslights herself willingly. The result is disastrous: Blanche is sent to a mental institution while Stella remains "happily" married to both Stanley and her own delusion.

The Stella Syndrome illustrates the effect of Patriarchy on women's psychology, as demonstrated by Stella's willingness to not only participate in but also promote her own subjugation. Male Supremacy, Stella shows us, offers protection at the price of silence. Women like Blanche, who are not silent, must either stop talking or face Male Supremacy's darkest element: Rape Culture.

Written for her master's thesis at the University of Florida, Natasha Patterson's "A Womanist Discourse Analysis of the Comedic Discourse of Jackie 'Moms' Mabley"—another comedienne-ballerina of Sophie's generation—explains that Male Supremacy's continued success is rooted in and renewed by Patriarchal ideology.

Patriarchy works to ensure the continuation of both White and Male Supremacy by reproducing systems of domination and subordination. These systems use images, concepts, and premises to provide us with a framework through which we represent, interpret, understand, and "make sense" of some aspect of social existence—an existence framed both by and then around White and Male Supremacy. In short, Supremacists create our idols, and our idols reinforce Supremacy, forming a social ouroboros.

Today, this same gas-lighting is seen in everyday phrases directed at both men and women—for example, rebranding basic sensitivity toward other's feelings as "political correctness." But in our culture, we have certain phrases that are specifically designed for men to use in gas-lighting women: "Locker-room talk" is one. "Boys will be boys" is another. Both imply that certain misogynistic behaviors are forgivable and even inevitable, and if we take issue with them, we're just being "bitchy." We're essentially told that we're asking for too much when we acknowledge Rape Culture. Or when we insist that bragging about sexual assault be stricken from the definition of "acceptable" conversation. Our cultural backlash to Feminism has made this behavior not just acceptable but electable. We're accustomed to the Stella Syndrome. We know it works but we never talk about it. Instead, we use it—and we allow it to use us.

On stage, Hot Mama Sophie fought the Syndrome and remained a predatory force. It saw her through the rest of her career and many failed marriages and personal tragedies, continuing to personify a character for her to hide behind. The Mama spoke for her, allowing Sophie to transform into a sexually aggressive woman who initiated encounters with strange men whenever she chose. Her song "He Hadn't Up 'Til Yesterday" was so dirty for the time that theaters banned her. The *Chicago Examiner* claimed that some of Sophie's songs were "red, white, and blue, and some of them omit the red and white," but the way she spoke—and what she spoke of—was less an attempt to shock and awe her audience than to free them. To encourage them to rebel against all the age, size, and gender stereotypes about women's sexuality that insisted women were weaker, less interested in intercourse, and unable to achieve happiness without pretending to be less-than. Sophie's songs declared that women have sexual feelings, that they have a right to them, and that they could (and should) state them—openly and loudly.

Today, women like Portland's longtime stand-up hero, Susan Rice, who came of age in comedy during the early 1980s, have kept the spirit of the Red Hot Mamas alive, though they tend to smile more and use far fewer "fuck yous." In her stand-up routine on aging not so gracefully, she asks a trick-or-treater, "How old are you? Seventeen? Well, come on in . . . betcha that ninja costume's hot, huh?" But when she flashes her sheepish grin, she insists, "No! They've gotta be eighteen! I'm not going to jail for a turtle."

But in the 1930s, the devastating nature of a comedi-enne-ballerina's duality—her public freedom versus her private subjugation (often reinforced from within and by societal expectations)—was never more poignant than in the lyrics from Sophie's ballad, "I Just Couldn't Make Ma Feelings Behave." She tells us that she's prepared to reveal the truth about her sexual experiences: that she can "warm up" cold men, give old men back their "flaming youth," and leave both feeling like they've had their tonsils removed from her kisses alone . . . but in the end, she knows that she'll have to "turn her damper down," meaning, sadly, that even a Red Hot Mama felt she had to make sacrifices to survive within the Patriarchy.

A decade later, in the 1940s, twenty-something Phyllis Diller encountered yet another sadly confusing set of expectations urging women to treat men one way before marriage (hold them at arm's length to create the illusion that they were hard-to-get sexual prizes) and then a radically different way after marriage (cling like vines around their necks to create the illusion that, as the "weaker sex," wives needed their husbands' support—financially, emotionally, and even physically). This enforced passivity bled over into Phyllis's professional life. "I didn't chase things," she wrote. "Once I delineated my dreams, I knew they would come to me, and these included love. Nothing will help more to make a man turn and run the other way than sensing you want him. That's why my advice to girls is, be a prize, not a trap. After all, men are supposedly the aggressors. They want to chase, so you've got to run . . . or at least crawl. Run but hesitate."

Which is it? Are we to be dependent or independent? And is this any different from today's impossible catch-22, where women are expected to be perfect mothers, sexy wives, and successful career women—all at once and, most importantly, on our own, without expecting our partners to share any of the burdens? Will we ever be ourselves beyond the characters—or partners—we hide behind?

Part of the answer lies within the history of "women's comedy." In using this outdated term, we're often referring to a lineage of performers who have, traditionally speaking, also happened to be female, who worked in a male-controlled field, and who *had* to care whether men (both off stage and on) laughed at their jokes. So in the process of progressing into the era of "I don't care," how much of that past should we choose to take with us—especially since we're trying to drop the segregationist adjective from our vocabulary?

When we consider all sides, an answer seems to emerge. We don't choose. We can't. All we can do is add to it. Much like truth, it can't be changed, so we must turn history into history *plus*. A woman who goes into comedy does so to hear her own voice speaking her own history. As a result, her humor (and with it, those echoes of fearlessness) comes from everywhere—most especially from past comedians. She grew up watching previous generations of performers who influenced how she performs today, adding herself to history. That's the thing about the past. You don't simply repeat it; it repeats in you. For this reason, every generation must ask itself anew: Shall I create a past that the future celebrates or seeks to avoid? Shall *mine* be the example those next in line uphold or risk repeating?

Almost everything about our current comedienne-ballerinas boils down to a mixture of past and present: half their own contributions and half the contributions of those who came before. It's all part of the same double helix. In this way, women like Gilda created a space for Tina and Amy, who then created space for you. To be remembered, one must remember.

With this in mind, I asked Dr. Landay, "I wonder if there would be a place for women in comedy without Feminism?"

"Not the same place," she answered immediately. "There's a great example from something Amy Poehler said, that Tina Fey wrote about in her book. A situation where Amy Poehler was joking around, and one of the men said to her, 'Wait, that's not cute.' And she says, 'I don't care.' And to get to that point *is* a Feminist idea, where the woman doesn't care whether the man likes what she's just said or done, that that is not the most important thing."

Rosie Shuster once said of the First Wave generation, "If you're a woman in comedy, especially if you were a woman in the early days of stand-up or in the early days of working the circuit, to be able to be out there, even if your jokes were very self-deprecatory, or if your routine was very much a self-loathing, 'look at me I'm so ugly!' kind of bit, simply by getting up and doing it and having that courage, you'd already succeeded. You'd already started taking back that power, and setting the stage for other people to take a little bit more, and a little bit more, and a little bit more. So I absolutely have the greatest admiration for the women who were doing it under the roughest, most difficult circumstances."

One of these women included First Wave Comedic Feminist Frances Marion, best remembered for pushing society's edge forward as not only one of the most renowned screenwriters of the twentieth century but also as one of the most respected dramatists ever. Frances was born in San Francisco, where she modeled and acted and had some success as a commercial artist before going into journalism—like Nora Ephron and so many other talented comedians who also happened to be women would later do. Frances served in Europe as a combat correspondent during World War I and then moved to Los Angeles, where director Lois Weber hired her as her assistant. Under Weber, she learned everything she could about writing for film. Her talent eventually attracted the attention of silent film star Mary Pickford. The two women began a long relationship as both friends and artists, with Marion writing Pickford's most memorable, Oscar-award-winning films, including *The Big House* (1930) and *The Champ* (1931). When she died in 1973, Frances remained one of Hollywood's most enduring talents. What's less well-known about Frances is that she discovered one of Lucille Ball's biggest influences: comic actress ZaSu Pitts.

ZaSu's trademarks included an extremely "woe is me" voice, doe-like blue eyes that gave her a distinctively forlorn look, and a timid stance that she accented with fidgety hands. She was born in 1894, thirty years after her father, Rulandus, lost his leg in the Civil War. The family was originally from New York, but traveled around much like Lucy's, settling first in Kansas and then in Santa Cruz, California, when the job market in the Midwest collapsed (and the winters turned out to be worse than in New York). ZaSu joined the drama department in high school, where she learned to use her less-than-glamorous looks and inherent shyness in screwball comedies featuring wallflower characters. She first appeared on stage in 1915, when Frances spotted her. They became fast friends, and Frances helped ZaSu to score a number of bit parts in Douglas Fairbanks's and Mary Pickford's movies at Paramount. Pickford did ZaSu the same favor until ZaSu was finally cast as the lead in 1919's *Better Times*. She did at least four more big box-office comedies, focusing on her strengths: character roles like the twitchy, timid beautician or the best-friend/partner-in-crime to the Great Depression's many Jennifer Lawrence prototypes. She worked steadily through the 1940s and '50s until, like Gilda, she was diagnosed with cancer and passed away at age sixty-nine.

Of course, while these and many other white comedienne-ballerinas were pushing boundaries, comedienne-ballerinas of color were working far harder under far more difficult circumstances, doubly burdened with both race and gender. There's a wide swath of history here, but since Jackie "Moms" Mabley was one of the first stand-up comedians who also happened to be female, we'll start with her before moving on to a few of her peers. As always, their stories are a mix of wonderful and truly terrible. The earliest pioneers can always be recognized by the arrows in their backs.

Natasha Patterson's thesis again provides insight into these circumstances, breaking down the historical, cultural, social, and political context surrounding Moms's journey to the stage and her hard-won status as a seminal rule-breaker whose efforts helped both Civil Rights and Feminist activists achieve their common goals.

Leslie Bennetts reported in 1987 for the *New York Times* that Moms was born Loretta Mary Aiken in 1894, the great-granddaughter of a slave, and one of sixteen children whose parents died tragically. "She was raped at the age of eleven by an older black man and raped again two years later by the white town sheriff. Both rapes resulted in pregnancies; both babies were given away. Loretta's father, a volunteer fireman, was blown to pieces when a fire engine exploded, and her mother was run over and killed by a truck while coming home from church on Christmas Day. At the age of fourteen, Loretta ran away to join a minstrel show."

She steadily honed her act by eventually joining the African American vaudeville circuit under the Theatre Owners Booking Association. There she met fellow performer Jack Mabley, who became her boyfriend for a short time. At some point, she took on his name, becoming Jackie Mabley, but eventually everyone called her "Moms" out of respect for her reputation as a mentoring, mothering spirit. According to Bennetts, "the career she launched as a runaway child ultimately earned her not only such material perquisites as a chauffeur-driven Rolls-Royce and a sable coat, but also a place in history as a show-business pioneer." But underneath her success were the bumps and bruises of breaking the mold. Although it is unclear whether she was ever legally married, Moms bore another daughter (possibly fathered by Jack Mabley), who later became a drug addict.

Clarice Taylor (who played Bill Cosby's mother on *The Cosby Show*) portrayed Moms in a play by the same name that opened at the Astor Place Theatre in 1987. According to Taylor and Bennetts, Moms' comedy skated many different edges all at once: racial, gender-based, and sexual. Taylor claimed, correctly, that Moms "was finally discovered by whites in the 1960s, and did a crossover. But most of her jokes at the beginning were 'in' jokes. She talked about things black people understood. She talked about white people, and she told us things we wanted to hear about them."

This switching between "in" and "out" jokes, each chosen for a specific audience, demonstrates the idea that we switch our speech based not only on the gender but also the race of our listener(s). But Patterson also notes that, as the civil rights movement wrought the changes necessary to enable Moms to gain national exposure, her humor (or her ability to switch effectively) proved universal. Still a favorite at Club Harlem in Atlantic City, where she performed with such legendary figures as Count Basie, Duke Ellington, and Cab Calloway, in her later years Moms also appealed to national television audiences via Merv Griffin, Johnny Carson, Flip Wilson, Mike Douglas, and the Smothers Brothers. In the end, the most poignant impact of Moms's story is its clear illustration of invisibility. Despite her groundbreaking work, amazing fame, and ultimate influence on "women's comedy," few people know her name, demonstrating how underappreciated the contributions of comedienne-ballerinas of color remain, even today.

While the works of women like Naomi Ekperigin, Whoopi Goldberg, Sherri Shepherd, Maya Rudolph, Kim Wayans, Jessica Williams, Lady Roz G, Leslie Jones, Mo'Nique, Thea Vidale, Tiffany Haddish, Wanda Sykes, and Phoebe Robinson are easy to enjoy online or in person, unfortunately, as Patterson details, "the majority of scholarship on stand-up comedians has largely ignored or limited the contributions of women, particularly women of color." In fact, only one scholar, Elsie Williams, places the various generations of comedians within their proper social and historical contexts, or describes how they used their comedic performances as "satirical protests against the traditional roles relegated to women."

Patterson claims that, throughout the years, the creative responses of African American humor have adapted to their environments, manifesting in four distinct types of characters: the Plantation Survivalist, the Accommodationist, the In-Group Satirist (which refers to Moms's early in-jokes), and the Integrationist. "In Elsie Williams's *The Humor of Jackie Moms Mabley: An African American Comedic Tradition*," she goes on to explain that, whereas survivalist humor was "developed by the slaves as a survival tool, accomodationist humor was first initiated, directed by the slave masters themselves, and later appropriated and claimed by the slaves. However, in-group satirist humor"—like Moms's—"had two functions: conflict and control. It meant poking fun at the white oppressor, by shedding the victim's mask and appropriating the stereotypes," which partly explains Moms's apparel (a baggy housedress, oversized hat, and worn slip-on sandals) and vocal inflections (a rasping lilt she created by imitating an older woman attempting to speak without her much-needed dentures) while performing. On the other hand, "integrationist humor was similar to in-group satirist humor, except that it including [*sic*] Blacks laughing at themselves, poking fun of others, addressing controversial subjects—all in front of an integrated audience."

During the 1970s, integrationist humor was largely used by TV shows like *The Jeffersons*, which confronted racism head-on through the clashes between two African American families—one wealthy, the other middle-class. Language alone shows the two families' socioeconomic divergence, and when one of the richer men points out that the Jeffersons are clearly poor, Mr. Jefferson levels the playing field by jumping up and confronting the man with, "Nigger, what the hell did you say?" cutting him "back down to size." The show's live (and integrated) audience goes wild.

Patterson also writes that "the first type, plantation survivalist, can be traced back to the days of slavery when it was developed as a mechanism to deal emotionally and psychologically with the effects of slavery and used as satire against the injustices and dehumanization of the 'peculiar institution.'" In order to survive repeated degradations, Patterson explains, "the plantation survivalist was essentially the slave trickster who used his wit as barter for some advantage or gain. In folktales, a rabbit, often symbolizing the plantation survivalist, would feign weakness, practice deceit, or simply outwit his opponents."

If this sounds familiar to advice from women's magazines of the past, which encouraged women to feign inferiority to either gain some advantage (e.g., happiness) or to simply survive legal, emotional, and financial captivity, it should. Is the history of "women's comedy"—having long ago been segregated from "comedy" as a whole—that much different from the history of "black comedy" as it was segregated from "white comedy"?

The similarities seem striking, especially when comparing the use of humor to survive repeated degradations to the humor employed by generations of comedienne-ballerinas to psychologically survive subjugation. Forty thousand years of gender-based oppression and violence—largely due to husbands' legal ownership of their wives and children for much of this time—created "women's comedy," just as four hundred–plus years of slavery and racist oppression created "black comedy." These movements' histories are obviously different, yet their shared purpose of equality—and with it, freedom—binds them together.

For women of color who also happen to be comedians, these dual oppressions apply equally in shaping their voices. This is why it remains so important for women of color to seek support from both civil rights and Feminist activists, since neither racial equality nor gender equality *alone* can ever fully address their needs. Seeking both, together, all women can be agents for positive change for our gender, and in addressing under-discussed facts about women's daily realities, comedienne-ballerinas have always been and continue to be agents for this kind of change. But has that change actually occurred? And if so, how much? Does life imitate art or does art imitate life?

fighting for laughs

THE FUNNIEST COMEDIANS — AND THE BEST writers—are, without exception, some of the angriest people. Their art tends to imitate their lives and vice versa. Part of this stems from the self-loathing that invariably accompanies talent (mediocrity, after all, pats itself on the back while genius is preoccupied with punching itself in the face). The other part is driven by a deep-seated disappointment that turns inward for some, resulting in depression. For those driven rather than depressed by their anger, the result is an almost enviable tirelessness—especially in artists. I don't know about you, but I personally can go from zero to Cyrano de Bergerac in about thirty seconds. Great talent, and the anger that so often drives it, can hurt an artist's personal life, and especially her family.

Phyllis Diller experienced this in trying to support her six children while jump-starting her stand-up. They were often neglected and split apart to live with relatives. Her youngest son was once found hitching a ride home after he'd been inadvertently forgotten at the beach. He was seven years old. One of her daughters had to be institutionalized for schizo-phrenia, which Phyllis suspected she inherited from her father. Later on, she became estranged from yet another son, who'd been forced to give his parents the money he'd earned sweep-ing floors. They needed it to pay the bill at a seedy Manhattan hotel where they were staying.

Heralded author John Banville once said of artists and per-formers, "We are ruthless. We're not nice people. We might be interesting; we might be diverting . . . but mostly it's just slog. You see, because you have to concentrate so deeply and sink down into yourself as far as you can go, you lose sight of the people around you. The people you are writing about can be more real than the people you live with, which is very cruel on the people you live with."

While many who read this might attribute Banville's being a bad companion to his being self-absorbed, much like any stand-up comedian who uses her family in her act, the point here is that those two traits—talent and self-absorption, tal-ent and anger, talent and ruthlessness—are often one and the same. Those who say otherwise are selling something, or else, as budding artists themselves, they don't *want* it to be true—but this hardly means it isn't.

For anyone who is any good at excavating the human con-dition, an extraordinary amount of self-searching is required. That ability to singularly focus on oneself for long periods of time is usually labeled as the mark of a self-centered asshole. But talent demands brutal honesty with oneself *about* one-self, and especially about one's own personal moral failings. It inflicts hero worship. It is parasite to a host. Those who resist losing themselves don't usually perform at the same level. Have you ever read a masterpiece that wasn't written by some variation of a tortured asshole, who was likely a terrible mother or selfish partner? I haven't. Maybe I'm simply not that well-read. Or maybe that says something about Both-ness. Maybe art is an area in which the possibility for true fulfillment falls apart. Since lasting art reflects pieces of the human condition, and because art is driven solely by sustained suffering, it only makes sense that immense, parasitic talent would drive out the thing that, if embraced, would bring so many hosts so much happiness.

In the face of all this, some comedienne-ballerinas still strive to move in a less selfish, more supportive direction. Like Gilda hugging Judy Carter on a toilet in 1970s New York, they try to encourage those pedaling fast behind them to catch up. Stand-up comic Wendy Hammers claimed that this reaction came from "a lack of generosity from other people in the past. I never wanted to repeat that. I try to be encouraging of other women, especially young comics, and check in. Ask them if they feel they're getting enough stage time. I remember, years ago, meeting Letterman in an airport. I was coming from a gig. He was just sitting there, by himself. And he was so kind. He asked me things that you would ask any other colleague, you know, 'How's it going? How many nights a week you doing stand-up? What are you working on?' Just being part of a community as a comic."

Given that he is a white, male, heterosexual, cisgender comic, it's hard—though not impossible, of course—to view David Letterman as having experienced any of the same intense battles or the amount of scapegoating as comedienne-ballerinas of any generation, including his own. And so when we consider why women are often so much angrier, so less likely to offer assistance, we must remember where they've come from. We must examine their scars, not to excuse, but to better understand that anger.

Sitting on stage at iO West, LA-based stand-up and comedy writer Laura House said that it's often hard for trailblazers to overcome the past and avoid bringing that reactive anger into the present. Sometimes its effects spill out unintentionally, either in front of an audience or when interacting with other comedians. "You would see Joan Rivers in interviews when she said that she doesn't give people breaks. Phyllis Diller, on the other hand, seems very nice. But I think it was just so fucking hard for them that once they got big, they clung to it *hard*. That was the mindset you had to have—of climbing to the top. They were the only women they knew, really, and comedy was and still is *so hard*, and when you don't get a break, you've got to toughen up. And sometimes these women, both then and now . . . once they get to the top, the climbing has turned them into terrible people.

"But the good news is that this is all changing now. The business is opening up more. I find women in power now, who are going out of their way to find new comedians—like Wanda Sykes on *Last Comic Standing*. Women are connecting in ways they never were able to before. Whereas, I think even only twenty years ago, there was a sense of like: 'Look, there's only room for one woman here, and it's me.' Now, we can work more as one big team and there's less competition."

When we discussed all of this underlying competition, Eliza Skinner commented, "If I were going to give advice to women, anytime you find yourself judging another woman on anything, just cut it out. Just stop. Whether it's if their voices are annoying. Whether it's that they seem sexy. Whether it's that they aren't funny. 'She isn't even fucking funny! Fuck her!' You're just making it worse. There should be every type of woman in the public eye and everywhere. There should be every type of female character. And we get charged now with being a certain type of woman: 'You should be like a certain type of strong, confident woman, that's it.' Like I read articles about women saying that other women shouldn't appear so weak on stage. Or women shouldn't talk about such explicit sexual things. And it's just limiting what women are allowed to be . . . Think about how many male comics have built their career on talking about how fat they are. How ugly they are. How awful they are. And to say, 'Okay that's another area that you're not allowed to talk about, women. Can't talk about these things or these things. Or these things or these things. You can only talk about *these* things. So find a way to make a career in that.'"

"And yet don't sound similar to everyone else," I added.

"Yeah! Exactly. And how many male comics sound similar to other male comics? 'Cause there's been so many of them. But if a woman does it, 'Oh you're just ripping off her, or her, or her.' And it's tough. You're going to have the whole world doing that. When women do it to other women, it just feels like they're punching themselves. You know? Like this is what I hate about me. And it really kills me."

Longtime comedy writer and stand-up Laurie Kilmartin claimed that a sense of competition keeps her going. After many years of performing her own material and then writing for other well-known comedians, her desire to win the silent battle to be heard and acknowledged for her talent (which, even after only a few moments in her company, is obvious) sharpens her edge. "I feel like that all the time on stage. Every time something works, I'm like, 'Um-hum, I'm still in first place. I'm ahead of you guys!' I know it's a very competitive thing. Sometimes people, after a show, they'll say to you as a comic like, 'Wow, it must feel so good to make people laugh.' And they're right, in a way; it does feel good . . . but probably not in the way you think. It's not in a generous way. It's a very sort of selfish declaration of, 'I'm here, and I'm a person, and I demand attention!' So it's not, you know, loving and positive. Even though you pretend it is on stage because you're trying to impart the persona that you're nice—I'm not a mean person, don't get me wrong—I'm just saying that my core reason for why I still like to perform is that I'm angry. And I'm not done being angry."

So do the means justify the ends, or do the ends make us meaner?

Today's performers continue to bleed for our societal benefit, pushing us all forward by pairing truth with jest, and yet many comedienne-ballerinas—like Laurie—feel that their efforts remain underappreciated. While "male comics get up on stage to get laid," she said, "female comics get up on stage to get heard. And I think we're never heard. Even now. Like, take my abortion joke for example . . . it gets a lot of mixed reactions. Some people boo or get real quiet until I make it very clear that I had the baby, you know? That I didn't go through with it. That I'm a mom now. Until they know that, they can't feel safe. They're, like, '*ugh*—where is she going with this?'"

Even today, there are mixed reactions to women exercising the same level of reproduction freedom that men have enjoyed for centuries. Only the bravest comedienne-ballerinas are willing (or able) to expose the underlying connections between these mixed reactions and our capitalist politics, or to confront the Right to Life movement's true purpose within any capitalist society: to prevent women from exercising choice so that those women can provide bodies for war.

In Adam Smith's economic theory of the Invisible Hand, wealthy countries engage in war (usually to gain power through additional lands and resources taken from the vanquished). We don't throw our wealthy or our intelligentsia to the cannons, however. We never have. And so we need bodies. Poor bodies. Expendable bodies from non-academics and non-"job creators." This is why, during the Civil War, wealthy Southerners could get out of conscription by either paying $300 or sending a paid replacement in their stead. Only very rich people had $300 in 1861, I assure you. Guess who fought for the Confederacy? Not rich people. And guess who had enough money to actually own any slaves? Not poor people. The people who actually fought had literally no real skin in the game. They died to help rich landowners keep their property, and they later deserted their posts when that poverty continued, resulting in the common rallying cry denouncing this nationwide conflict as a "rich man's war, but a poor man's fight."

Today, the same holds true. We usually don't send doctors and lawyers and scientists and rich kids to war. Instead, we fill most of our ranks with members of the middle and lower classes: kids whose parents can't afford to pay for a bachelor's degree on their own, or who are terrified of taking on massive student loans, or who went to such lousy high schools that they find themselves underprepared for any level of postsecondary education. We offer many of these kids the opportunity to sign up for military service, as a way to either pay for college or learn a specific trade useful to the nation's defense. In essence, the military has taken over for trade schools and scholarship funds. In the midst of technological revolution, what other choice do these kids, the military, or our nation's taxpayers truly have? It's not as if millions of low-skilled manufacturing jobs are still waiting around for those who cease their education after earning a high school diploma or GED. So there they are: going to war while wealthier people go to school. Without the poor, the rich would have to fight their own wars. So what do we do? We make sure the poor don't have equal access to birth control and abortion by allowing companies to avoid providing either to their female employees, by defunding organizations like Planned Parenthood, and by making abortion so incredibly shameful that few if any of the millions of women who have one each year will come forward and ever admit it (for fear that they will be humiliated, ostracized, threatened with rape, and even killed.) We make abortions so hard to access and afford in many Right to Life states that poor women can't get one at all. So they give birth. And our capitalistic war machine gets bodies. And the cycle continues.

Is this part of the reason we feel uncomfortable joking about abortion—because our the-poor-give-birth-so-the-rich-can-go-to-war assembly line is so currently and dangerously real? Do we need to feel comfortable joking about it? In other words, is the past necessary to make the present enjoyable?

Abortion is hardly new. It's been legal in the United States since 1973, and has existed for millennia before then. Many male comedians discuss abortion, birth control, and a wide range of sex acts in graphic detail on stage all the time, without audible sounds of discomfort emanating from the audience at the blatant use of domestic violence and obvious misogyny to get a laugh. So why do we cheer openly for [INSERT ANY MALE COMIC HERE] but nervously clap for Laurie? Why does the sound of a woman poking fun at a legal, common, safe, and arguably routine procedure make us so terribly uncomfortable?

Laurie attempted to answer this question by comparing it to social evolution, in that "people are still in the process of grasping how women talk, on some level. Some of them assume 'Oh, women don't talk like that' when, really, we just don't talk like that to *you*. Plus, in my joke, I say the A-word, and then I claim that I had one, which is not only very hard for women to admit but even harder for people to hear and then confront as true. Sexism, violence, and abuse . . . all that, they're used to. But honesty about how many millions of women have abortions every year? How *one out of every three women they've ever met* has had one? Maybe not so much. The funny thing is, though, that it's a joke. It's not even true. I didn't *actually* have an abortion."

"So how do you frame the punch line around an experience that's *not* based in truth?"

"I push them out as far away from me as I can, and then I pull them back. I *know* I'm going to lose people at first. I *like* doing that: pushing them out and then pulling them back. And then revealing that I lied. That I didn't have one at all. I like going, 'Yeah, don't worry about it. I'm a mother—and it's even worse!' If anyone should be able to joke about abortion it's somebody who *didn't* have one, you know? I mean, someone who *did* have one obviously gets to joke about that real experience, but second place goes to somebody like me, who's stuck raising the child. If I can't talk about it, fuck you. You know? I'm in the trenches with an eight-year-old every day, so I'm going to talk about how much I fantasize about having had an abortion."

"So basically, all women have the right to poke fun at abortion: Both those who've had abortions and those who haven't?"

"Yep! Basically."

"Do you ever think we'll get to the point where an abortion joke is no longer 'blue'?"

"Oh no. I don't think so. I think America is crazy. It's not like the Netherlands where people don't give a shit. America's super religious, so I don't think it will ever stop. I used to do a different abortion joke in the early '90s, when I was working the road in the South. And, I don't remember it now, but it was kind of a light one. Just a little pinprick. Just a little 'ding-ding,' and then I'd go right on to the next joke. I would just do it very quickly, go in and out, so that people wouldn't dwell on it. I wouldn't point out that I'd just done an abortion joke, like comics do today. There's a thing today, where people doing an edgy joke feel the need to spend ten minutes confronting the audience about it, like 'You can't handle the truth!' That's not the way to reel an audience back in. When I see that, I always want to tell them, 'Just do that joke, and then do your next joke, and by the end of your set you will have had, say, 75 percent of an audience in the middle of Tennessee laugh at an abortion joke.' They might not remember it afterwards, of course, but you did sort of . . . you did it. You pushed them an eighth of an inch forward."

Phyllis Diller echoed this sentiment, writing that everything has to be impeccably timed when you're going for laughs because every audience is different. Every performer is, too. She had to go with the flow and rely on her instincts, because "it always takes people a moment to digest a joke before they'll laugh." It strikes me that this kind of talent—this innate patience in changing the world hairsbreadth by hairsbreadth, room by room, laugh by laugh—isn't something that can be taught. Invisible bars are all around us, and there are some who are truly born to break through.

In the 1970s came the brilliant, message-shattering, boundary-pushing, obviously Feminist sitcom starring Bea Arthur as the title character in *Maude*, a spin-off from the role she'd played as Archie Bunker's neighbor. *Maude* was to *All in the Family* as *Frasier* was to *Cheers*.

Bea Arthur's groundbreaking work picked up where Marlo Thomas's *That Girl* left off in the late 1960s. *Maude* was created and written largely by television legend Norman Lear, who, according to writer and activist Amanda Marcotte, "prided himself on creating sitcoms that grappled with the big political issues of the day." But Norman pushed the envelope to an entirely new level when he created a sitcom about a middle-aged Feminist on her fourth marriage—a loud-mouthed, grouchy, opinionated Feminist who, shockingly, was treated like a full human being who gets by just fine, thank you very much.

In 1972, *Maude* had what turned out to be a singular event in television history: a major character dealing with an unintended pregnancy by terminating—and it ends up being okay. (Her character lived in New York State, where abortion was legal in 1972.) You'd think something that happens to over a million women a year would merit more than one portrayal on prime time television in the thirty-seven years since Maude terminated her pregnancy, but in TV Land, abortion is rarer than coffee shop employees who can afford enormous Manhattan apartments.

Whereas Marlo brought American television viewers their first single girl protagonist, Bea revitalized the spirit of Sophie Tucker with her bold portrayal of a middle-aged woman who, at forty-seven, still—*gasp!*—dares to have a "red hot" libido and not apologize for it. When Maude gets pregnant—*gasp! gasp!*—things get even more shocking when she—*gasp! gasp! gasp!*—actually discusses her options for engaging in a 100 percent legal medical procedure and there's not even any sad music to remind us all that she's a tragic figure.

Equally impressive are Maude's family members, who, rather than throwing tantrums or shame-circling her with their pity, fear, or silence, intelligently consider the situation and then voice their support for Maude making up her own mind based on the freedom of reproductive choice.

Norman Lear aired that entire discussion in 1972. In 2004, network censors made Shonda Rhimes change "vagina" into "va-jay-jay."

If that episode aired on network TV today, Maude would've had to clasp her friends' hands as they offered their heartfelt support and then hang her head in all her slut-shamed agony before "bravely" deciding to keep the baby to either raise herself or hand over to an adoption agency, promoting the still so very popular moralist fantasy that every kid born out of wedlock automatically gets adopted into a loving, white, heterosexual, financially stable, cisgender, two-parent home. In creating such a forward-thinking (and, perhaps even more importantly, *speaking* and *acting*) character, Norman proved that not everyone who is pro-woman is a woman.

It's unlikely "Maude's Dilemma" would ever see the light of day today—at least not on prime time, though Lena Dunham and Co. have tackled the subject a bit more bravely on HBO, and the character of Paula (played by Donna Lynne Champlin) from *My Crazy Ex-Girlfriend* readily and unapologetically got an abortion.

But as of 2017, much of the Western world has begun to relapse into the "darkness of the 1930s," as Prince Charles of England described it, and it is unlikely that Paula—or any character like her—will survive to mimic "Maude's Dilemma" on prime time. In fact, a complete backtrack from these kinds of equality-driven episodes is ripe to occur, which will likely end this promising start before it's really taken hold. Indeed, we are likely to lose much of the ground we've gained since *Maude*. As Amanda Marcotte detailed in 2009, a character from the 1970's "with a new and unwanted pregnancy might tell her husband, as he makes a drink, 'Make mine a double. I'm drinking for two now,'" but no matter how edgy sitcoms are supposed to be in our current century, it's doubtful that anyone would dare put that joke onscreen these days.

It's not that abortion is entirely unknown on TV. It's just that these characters tend to exist for only one episode and may not have any lines. They later turn out to be "the dreaded and foreign Woman Who Aborts. They usually get to be pathetic, such as the teenage girl who is victimized by holy-roller parents and needs a secret abortion on *Battlestar Galactica*. Sometimes they get to be injured or silenced dramatically, such as the woman in a coma whose husband tries to abort her pregnancy when he learns that the baby might be gay. They get to be undeveloped characters that exist mainly so that male doctors can wring their hands about the morality of abortion. When it comes to main characters, if the possibility of abortion comes up, it's dismissed as a real option. And we learn that decent women would sooner die than share a waiting room with the sort of sluts who get abortions."

Further, "when it comes to imagining how women relate to pregnancy, it's incredibly obvious that most TV writers are men who dearly wish to believe that nothing is more precious to a woman than accepting a man's seed like it was the touch of God himself. The only exception I've ever seen in the years since *Maude* was an episode of *Sex and the City* in which a character contemplates having an abortion. The show had a unique opportunity to set a new standard, between having a spot on HBO (where envelope-pushing is mandatory) and having four characters that often laughed in the face of prudish, misogynist sexual norms that don't really make sense for actual women's lives. I give a grade C in courage to the episode 'Coulda Woulda Shoulda,' an episode where Miranda gets pregnant accidentally, decides to terminate without much fuss, and then, in classic TV fashion, decides to have the baby at the last possible minute. So why not an F, since the show relied on the usual cop-out? Well, they did put abortions in the past of two of the other major characters, Carrie and Samantha. And in both cases, we learn it was absolutely the right decision for them, and it's also implied that it's unfair that men aren't expected to handle the fact of abortion realistically. But they still didn't have the courage to show a character making the decision in the here and now."

Rosie Shuster says that this willingness to suffer the consequences of pushing society into new territory reflects back not only to her time at *SNL* but to the comedy of the 1970s in general. "When Richard Pryor did some of his first concerts and he was like in n-word territory and he was able to not only flirt with taboos, which is how I like to put it sometimes, he was able to shine light in an arena that nobody could even touch. And I think there's a parallel thing with females. Sometimes, if you're breaking new ground, it's on the cusp between really uncomfortable and/or hilarious."

Humor is so fluid in terms of where people find those boundaries. I tend to think of it anthropologically. During our conversations, I asked about the boundary between public and private, masculine and feminine, inside and outside. Where's the boundary between what works and what's fun? This boundary is where comedy happens. It's also where the Trickster goes back and forth over the line between predator and prey. Comedians' placement of the character of the Trickster in their stories determines their connection with the audience and how much truth they'll tell. Women of earlier generations—from Sophie to Lucy to Joan to Bea—were skating dangerously to make comedy and, through it, reveal a greater truth. While performers like Lenny Bruce spent their stage time unapologetically (and violently) indicting the public's rampant racism and hypocritical imperialist ambitions with punch lines like, "Everybody hates Americans because we fucked all their mothers for chocolate bars," comedienne-ballerinas had to worry about getting too "dirty," lest it stain their careers forever.

Natasha Patterson uses similar language to describe the ways the construction of the black female identity by comedienne-ballerinas like Moms challenged and resisted the process of hegemony by white Americans by "providing a voice . . . critical of the economic, political, social, and cultural status quo."

In these ways, the Trickster jumps over boundaries to simultaneously entertain, shock, and reveal our common flaws for the common good. The same can be said of "female comedians" resisting Male Supremacy by criticizing its financial, political, social, cultural, and linguistic enslavement of women's minds. These common flaws were never more perfectly lampooned than on televised sitcoms. During the 1970s, shows like *Maude* clearly celebrated the gains made by Feminists who had been fighting for women's reproductive freedom since Margaret Sanger opened the first birth control clinic in 1916 (it was immediately shut down by police, who locked her up for thirty days). Unfortunately, watching *Maude* makes today's backlash against gender equality—as evidenced by Congress's strident efforts to defund Planned Parenthood and many Supreme Court nominees' pledges to overturn *Roe v. Wade*—all the more starkly evident.

According to Marcotte, "it's not that Maude doesn't struggle with her decision to abort, but the reasons given in the show are refreshingly realistic . . . Abortion is presented as a sensible option for women dealing with unwanted pregnancy, which is exactly how many women experience it. Too bad TV writers since have been afraid to tell this basic truth."

In her 2016 NPR interview with Terry Gross, Sarah Silverman echoed the sentiment—perhaps shared by Norman Lear—that talking about taboos helps to take away their power to shame us all and scare us away from stepping over society's latest edge. "I do enjoy and feel compelled to talk about things that are taboo. One, because I think I'm a troublemaker inside. If someone says, 'Don't say that,' it's all I want to say, you know?"

"Who made it that way?" I asked Mo Collins. "Who creates the edge?"

She thought before she answered. After a moment, her eyes grew wet, and through sudden tears, she finally smiled. "Anybody who steps over it."

But have we stepped so far over the edge that we've lost the point? Is the new version of edginess embracing "clean comedy"? Is it true (as a twenty-one-year-old Trump supporter once told me) that "the only way to be progressive any more is by being conservative"? Is the future *really* to be discovered by embracing the past? As distasteful as I personally find this idea, history tends to suggest as much. It's long been said that everything becomes new again if you wait long enough. (I'm reminded of this every time I see someone my age wearing the same white, low-top Converses that my father wore to track practice in 1968.) But sometimes we tend to forget it. Sometimes we think we exist only in the now. We mistake re-creations for inventions. We fall victim to the Columbus effect: the false belief that we have made what has long existed. In terms of comedy, this translates into a stubborn insistence on mistaking "Yes, and" for "Let It Be." When we persist in our ignorance, believing our present wholly disconnected from our past, history shows that we end up re-fighting the same battles we've already supposedly won. If we're going to regress, we can't do so in slices. We can't replay only the good times; rest assured the bad times will tag along.

Phyllis Diller would agree. Phyllis, who'd never intended to be a comedian at all until her jealous, backbiting first husband, Sherwood, convinced her to get into comedy as a way to make more money.

While she was busy paving the way for future comedienne-ballerinas, Phyllis realized that if she listened to every criticism from every jealous mediocrity she ever encountered, or took every "no" she ever heard for an answer, she'd never accomplish anything. She'd have given up on her dreams and divorced Sherwood (as her mother constantly urged her to do) before he ever began pushing her into comedy.

"I knew I was in trouble," Phyllis later wrote in her memoir *Like a Lampshade in a Whorehouse*, "but I told her, 'I can't make that decision all by myself.' Instead, I sought the opinion of my dear friend Reverend Glass, the minister at the Presbyterian church where I was music director. I called him, he came over to the house, and we had a very civil conversation:

'Does he beat you?'

'No.'

'Is he a good father?'

'Yes.'

'Does he fool around?'

'No.'

'Then you have no problems and no grounds for divorce.'

"Thanks in part to these incredible words of wisdom, insight, empathy, and understanding," Phyllis wrote, careful to dip each word in heavy sarcasm, "I stood by my apparently model husband," who also routinely raped her, faked heart attacks to ruin her performances, refused to visit the hospital each time she gave birth, and jealously told everyone that *he* was the real person behind her imaginary husband, Fang. He even went so far as to open a checking account under the name "Fang Diller"* to try and ride Phyllis's coattails as far as possible. "However, I also think that, subconsciously, a better voice told me to hold on," she wrote. And so she stayed with Sherwood. She also credited him for pushing her to become a stand-up comic in the first place. "I never would've thought of that. Timing is everything, and it always is."

Even into the 2000s, established comics like Paula Poundstone experienced similar backbiting antics. "After Bob Costas and then Greg Kinnear had left the position, *Later* invited me to host their one-on-one interview show for a week. It was sort of an unofficial audition for a permanent position. With coaching and practice, I have done a good job as an interviewer in the past. I actually got a CableACE Award for my work as an interviewer on my extensive four-episode HBO talk show. I beat out Larry King and Charlie Rose, and Larry King became bitter and had me on his show and didn't show up to do the interview."

This envy comes from Male Supremacy's ouroboros. In order to maintain this dominance over the fine and performance arts, women have been led to believe in the supremacy

---

* Fun fact: Until 1974, credit card companies flatly refused to issue women credit cards in their own names. This meant that you would have to get a male co-signer (like your dad or your husband or your little brother) to attest to your "credit-worthiness." It wasn't until the Equal Credit Opportunity Act that card companies were no longer allowed to discriminate against potential card holders on the basis of sex.

of a mythological, lone wolf artist—a cross between the Marlboro Man and Jackson Pollock. This, we are told, is the true *artist*. This alone is what true *art* is supposed to look like. In reality, it's just a way of devaluing the collaborative methods at which not only women but also a large number of men excel. We have this in common, and it could connect us, but instead we're told—either directly or through billions of subliminal messages—that we should go it alone. That we shouldn't be so needy. That we should suppress those parts of ourselves that crave collaboration, or else we will never become "real artists."

On November 22, 1975, Lily Tomlin—by then a well-known "real artist" and consistently enthusiastic collaborator—hosted *SNL*. This was its first season. Rosie Shuster and Anne Beatts wrote a sketch they thought Lily would enjoy called "Male Sexual Harassment." It was an attempt to dissect some of the ridiculous and ridiculously common events that occur when living as a female.

The scene opens inside a classroom, where Lily, as a construction forewoman, is demonstrating a lesson with a hydraulic drill. Her all-female students are dressed in hard hats and jumpers. "Well . . . that's how the hydraulic drill works. Now that you've got the technical stuff under your belt, I think it's time ya got some moxie—what I call 'streetside savvy.' Now, here are a few choice facial expressions—you know, for when you're not on the construction site—and the noises that go with 'em. For instance: 'Hey, ay, ay, ay! Chicky, chicky, chicky, chicky, chicky! Hey, ay, ay, ay!'" Here, she purses her lips and signals with her fingers. "And, this is a killer . . ." Now, she's imitating some kind of cross between cunnilingus and a motorboat. "Yeah, it drives men crazy! Okay, now Exchange Student Danny, over here—hey, you!" At this, Dan Aykroyd (referred to as "Danny" in the transcript from the episode) walks over in a brief coat concealing skintight short-shorts and a red tank top.

During our conversation, Rosie revealed some uncomfortable truth behind this sketch: None of the male cast members "wanted to play the guy that the Hardhats were heckling. But the women were only saying real things they'd heard before, dozens of times, walking down the street. Stuff like, 'Hey, you wanna come do squat jumps on my girder?' But no guy wanted to hear that. None of them wanted to switch places and walk in, wearing a pair of shorts, totally vulnerable, like a woman would normally be. It was a pretty simple switch, where we just turned the tables, but seeing their instant, knee-jerk discomfort with that role-reversal was fascinating. Belushi turned it over to Danny, and Danny was a good sport and finally did it, but I don't think he was too happy."

Lorne Michaels backs up Rosie's claims that Belushi passed the ball to Dan, and Jane Curtin's appearance on Oprah, years later, revealed that Belushi was rampantly against the "girl writers" at *SNL* in those days. "There were two things John didn't do," Lorne said. "He wouldn't do drag, because it didn't fit his description of what he should be doing." (Belushi later made an exception and appeared as a gluttonous Elizabeth Taylor on "Weekend Update.") "And he didn't do pieces that Anne (Beatts) or Rosie (Shuster) wrote. So somebody would have to say that a guy had written it or something."

According to LA-based improv performer Betty Cahill, who appeared on *SNL* during its 1991–1992 season, Belushi wasn't alone in his bias, which had been passed down from seminal comedy instructor Del Close. "When I studied with Del, I was only one of two or three women in the class, along with Susan Messing. We were three out of twenty-five total.

The rest were all these funny guys—David Koechner, Kevin Dorff, Andy Richter . . . and we were all pals. But Del Close would look at me and the other women in the room with incredible disdain. He didn't hide his utter dislike for women. And so one thing I became determined to do was to make that guy laugh . . . He used to say, 'Women aren't funny. Women are there as a function in the scene—as the wife or the mom or the whatever.' As a result, we would be put into these roles, so it would be a challenge as a girl on stage with all of these funny guys to not simply be the wife or the mom who doesn't serve any other purpose, to instead be the wife or mom who was also a fun character on her own, somebody whom you were watching and listening to, wondering what she was going to say or do next. We had to work so much harder to make our roles interesting and cool and original. We had to step up our game to such an extent . . . Which is ironic, because when you're working hard on stage, people can tell and it makes them uncomfortable. It sucks the funny out, normally. When you get laughs is when you're just having fun and not working at all. When you're being yourself, letting words flow, and not caring what anyone thinks of you.

"I no longer care what anyone thinks about what I do," Betty continued. "When I go on stage, I go for me and to try to crack myself up. So, while learning from Del made me work harder in one way, it also made me realize that the hard work is a lie. In comedy, it should come easily. It shouldn't be work at all."

"Male Sexual Harassment"—or "The Hardhats sketch," as Rosie Shuster called it—worked so effectively precisely because of its comedic flow, because the women writing it, like Rosie, and the women performing in it, like Gilda and Lily, went onto the set trying to crack each other up rather than whoever happened to be listening. The experience of gen-der-reversal in a sexual harassment situation made sense to them, whether or not men understood what that kind of experience felt like. The women in the audience understood exactly what the girls in this show were trying to say, and exactly the male-dominated power they were intending to punch.

According to Rosie, the Hardhats sketch made the male cast members feel a vulnerability that women feel constantly but that these men wouldn't have recognized as a part of their normal, everyday existence. There was a new kind of exposure. There was an unfamiliar disempowerment. They were ganged up on. In showing how women felt then and continue to feel in male-dominated spaces, which is almost every public space, it was comedy based in truth, whether "dirty" or "blue" or otherwise. The girls were surprised by how much release the sketch provided, and how much better they felt after sharing that truth.

"It was a powerful thing to watch the women of the show really get into it," Rosie said when we spoke. "I mean, Gilda, Jane, Laraine, and Lily all had that team mentality going . . . They were the ones doing the wolf-whistle for a change, even though it wasn't even in the script! They just drew from their own lives. There was a whole other level of something primal going on."

Nearly twenty years later, when Betty Cahill was on the show, the writers' room had changed. Rosie, Anne, and Marilyn had long moved on. In the early 1990s, it was again a room of men, with a male head writer, Jim Downey, who felt that sketches about little girls playing with Barbies, for example, were "too girly" to make sense to *SNL*'s audience. These kinds of scenes were exactly what made Gilda beloved nationwide but now they were "too much of a girl thing," Betty said. The head writer's response was that the scene would be far too expensive to make. I asked Betty, "So does capitalism drive content or does the audience?"

"Both. One is exactly the other. Whoever's watching or buying tickets to see the show is whom most comedians will try to please. But the thing about this sketch is that men could've related to it, too. Boys played with GI Joes at that time, just like we played with Barbies. Everyone understands that joke. But back then the gatekeepers were different. And they just didn't get it."

The same was true for the gatekeepers of stand-up. Of this time, writer and TV critic Emily Nussbaum wrote that "from the sixties to the eighties, Johnny Carson was, for aspiring comics, the model of a scarce resource: to get to the big time, you had to make it with Johnny. But Carson, notoriously, didn't like female comics. In Yael Kohen's *We Killed: The Rise of Women in American Comedy*, from 2012, the show's talent coordinator Patricia Bradford recalls the atmosphere: 'They hired women over their dead bodies. They just didn't want them there.' Even popular comedienne-ballerinas—Totie Fields in the '60s, Elayne Boosler in the '80s—couldn't get traction. 'I don't ever want to see that waitress on my show again,' Carson told his booker about Boosler, when she was considered a top stand-up, the peer of Jerry Seinfeld."

During the mid-1970s, however, *SNL* began to shake the gate, hiring an unprecedented number of women for its writers' room. As a result, funnily enough, sketches like "Male Sexual Harassment," "The Sleepover," and all of Gilda's beloved characters like Judy Miller, Roseanne Roseannadanna, and Baba Wawa suddenly started to "make more sense."

But then, when the 1980s brought about a return to traditionally heteronormative, Caucasian, Patriarchal values under Ronald Reagan, backlash occurred. The gate was once again fortified by boundaries reminiscent of the 1950s: these so-called "girly" sketches about "women's issues" largely disappeared, and by 1990, after a decade of this conservatism, there were few women left in the room.

Another wave rolled in with the election of Bill Clinton in 1993, and progressive values once again permeated American culture both on stage and off. By the late 1990s and early 2000s, the economy was once again booming, calls for greater diversity were being answered, and Tina Fey took her place in 1999 as the first female head writer in the show's history. The period from 1999 to 2006, under Fey's leadership, is often referred to as *SNL*'s Second Golden Age. Millennials today revere the cast and writers of this time as much as their baby boomer parents did the original 1975–1980 cast. Betty regretted leaving the show and missing this seismic shift: "I always wished that I could have worked there when Tina was the head writer, because I think she would have gotten my humor more. I would have felt so much freer to really express my own voice around somebody like her than an older guy who may or may not care what a twenty-six-year-old girl from the south side of Chicago thinks about anything or what she has to say about the world. Maybe I'm wrong, but I don't think I would've automatically assumed, as I did at that age, that what I had to say didn't make any sense and shouldn't be heard."

Perhaps the real problem lies in our notion that today is so much better than yesterday; that the past is always bad and the present always good. We use this notion to justify our continued efforts to divorce the two. But both "good" and "bad" are sometimes relative, highly dependent upon shifting mores, and they always come in interchangeable waves. In fact, during the 1980s, many comedians who also happened to be women and/or people of color might have preferred the past, at least in terms of what they were "allowed" to talk about on stage and what made mostly white, mostly male audiences, bookers, and network executive gatekeepers squeamish. A wave of progress that gives voice to the marginalized and unheard is inevitably followed by backlash, quieting those same voices. Some things change while others remain the same. Some kinds of sketches, regardless of which wave of history we're all currently surfing, draw consistently touchy responses.

Even years after the Hardhats sketch, Rosie recalled the reaction to her commercial parody "Mommy Beer" (featuring a beer bottle with a nipple on it that the male cast members, dressed as cavemen coming back from a hunt and dragging their clubs, drank from as greedily as hungry babies). "The guys' reactions were a little primal, too—just as the girls' had been when playing construction workers in the Hardhats. It hit some nerve in the guys, where suddenly sucking on the beer bottle was . . . let's just say they got very squeamish."

"Where do you think their squeamishness came from?"

"From repressed memories of sucking on Mommy's tit!"

I asked Beth Newell of *Reductress.com* for her thoughts on this early commercial parody. "Do you think that has anything to do with gender roles? Or what's considered 'dirty' or uncomfortable for one gender or the other to discuss openly, in mixed company?"

"Oh yeah, for sure . . . Chelsea Peretti has a joke about how if men were getting their periods they would talk about it all the time, about how blood was coming out of them. And I think if men could breastfeed, they'd be showing off their boobs to everyone constantly. Like, you know, boobs would be out everywhere. Everyone would be like, 'Isn't it so great that boobs do this?'"

Before she became a stand-up comic, author, mother, and director of the documentary *Women Aren't Funny*, Bonnie McFarlane grew up on a Canadian farm without television, and so she never knew that American comedienne-ballerinas faced such intense gender politics. "It was only when I started actually *doing* stand-up that everyone kept telling me that women aren't really good at it. That's when people would say to me after my shows, 'I don't really think *women* are funny, but I thought *you* were funny,' which, by the way, every female comedian hears every second show. I feel like saying to them, 'I don't usually enjoy this kind of compliment, but from *you* it's actually not bad.' Also, for a long time, when you got on stage as a woman . . . there was a little bit of a shrug. The men in the audience were kind of like, 'Well, okay. Let's see.' There was zero enthusiasm, simply because of your gender, so you had to make them comfortable and let them know that you weren't going to be a prude, or worse—a Feminist, God forbid!"

I asked New York–based comic Aparna Nancherla if she hears these same sorts of comments.

"I definitely do."

"What does that mean to you?"

"It's funny because the word 'Feminist' gets tossed around a lot. So many women say things now, like, 'Oh no, I'm not a Feminist, I'm a humanist!' or whatever. And I think, because the term has the root 'fem' in it, these women, like most people, assume that these issues of equality and what you can and can't say on stage *only* affect women. But the real meaning of this word is pretty simple: Feminism means women should be considered the same as men and that's it."

I wondered why that idea is so revolutionary, why it inspired so many different, and often negative, reactions in both men and women. I told Aparna, "I'm really interested in why women respond in such mixed ways."

"I know," she said. "I think it threatens a lot of our pre-existing ideas, and some of them aren't necessarily ones that we explicitly talk about. They're internal traditions in society, and when those are challenged, people push back. 'Wait, no! Why are we making such a big deal about everything?' When, really, we should be saying whatever we want—*especially* about these things that are traditionally not discussed. These are the things we need to be talking about, both on stage and off, because talking about them would make all of our lives so much better."

Others, like longtime Upright Citizens Brigade performer Amey Goerlich, believe that women should change their entire mindsets when it comes to talking to audiences or being part of any show. They don't think that demanding equality—or being equally aggressive about sex on stage—is the way to true parity with audiences. "I don't think *anything* is effective that has an air of like aggression to it," Amey says. "I think you just have to present yourself in a way that has nothing to do with 'I deserve this,' or 'You should give this to me.' You should just be present. You should just act like, 'I'm a part of this.' Not, 'I'm a *girl* who's part of this,' or 'I'm a *guy* who's part of this.' No. Just *be* a part of it."

"Just *be* in the show?"

"Yeah. Exactly. If you don't act like you want to be treated like a girl, you won't be."

Back in LA, Mo Collins seemed to agree. "It feels a little bit loaded in the 'I'm trying to be in the boys' club' department. Meaning, girls—women—going so far in the other direction, implying things like, 'Yeah, I'll have sex and not think about it. I'll suck your dick. I ain't got no problem with it,' and that kind of thing because they think that will make others—other comics, audience members, etc.—respect them and listen to what they have to say up there. They're trying to empower themselves, I think, but at the same time it actually feels like a step backward. You know? Because those aren't the *real* ways that we empower ourselves as women. Those ways just aren't enough. It's just not enough. You don't have to do that to get into 'the club.' The club is not owned by one specific gender, but it is perceived that way."

As Eliza Skinner noted, those perceptions waste our time—and wasted time is wasted opportunity for growth. "Every time that I get on stage and have to deal with someone heckling me or the comic before me, being sexist or an asshole or anything, any time I have to get on stage and deal with that, rather than tell the jokes that I've prepared and that I want to talk about, that takes time away from me," she said. "That takes time away from my development. And that happens a lot to female comics: They get a lot of opportunities early on, but they don't get to get good as fast as men because they're scrutinized in a different way and because they have to spend so much time saying, 'No. I'm not here to suck a dick. Also, what you just did was dumb.' And then they find a way to make their responses funny, and not just angry, because it's a comedy show and not a complain show. So . . . it just sucks."

This brings us back to Feminist writer and columnist Lindy West, who later wrote of her own heckler, "I asked him why he chose me."

He told her that her pride—being proud of who she is and where she is and where she's going—stoked his anger. "You almost have no fear when you write," he said. "It's like you stand on the desk and you say, 'I'm Lindy West, and this is what I believe in,'" he said. "'Fuck you if you don't agree with me.' And even though you don't say those words exactly, I'm like, 'Who is this bitch who thinks she knows everything?'

Lindy asked him if he felt that way because she's a woman.

"Oh, definitely. Definitely. Women are being more forthright in their writing. There isn't a sense of timidity to when they speak or when they write. They're saying it loud. And I think that—and I think, for me, as well—it's threatening at first."

And, of course, she explained, that's exactly why she does it: because people don't expect to hear women at all. Because history has so rarely listened, and it has taught us to absorb this silence. "I want other women to see me do that, and I want women's voices to get louder."

"I understand," her troll responded. "Here's the thing. I work with women all day, and I don't have an issue with anyone. I could've told you back then if someone had said to me, 'Oh, you're a misogynist. You hate women.' And I could say, 'Nuh-uh, I love my mom. I love my sisters. I've loved the girlfriends that I've had in my life.'" In a stunning move, he demonstrated his own growth in this respect, admitting, "But you can't claim to be OK with women and then go online and insult them—seek them out to harm them emotionally."

Lindy wrote of this, "In my experience, if you call a troll a misogynist, he'll almost invariably say, 'Oh, I don't hate women. I just hate what you're saying and what that other woman is saying and that woman and that one for totally unrelated reasons.' So it was satisfying at least to hear him admit that, yeah, he hated women."

With this in mind, I asked Eliza Skinner, "Do *women* hate other women?"

"I think it's more about doing whatever it takes to join 'the club.' So women who want to be cool with those kinds of guys will be, like, 'Hey, don't worry! I'm not going to give you guys a hard time about being sexiest. You know how I'm going to prove it? I'm going to say something shitty about that girl, too. Yeah, her tits are weird! Ha! Can I be in "the club" now?' And then they get rewarded for it. And because there were always traditionally more men than women in comedy, they've never needed to join a female club. They've never needed to be 'just one of the girls.' Only now that's changing, and there's more of a need for that. It's more attractive now, which means we have fewer women who are coming at each other with knives. There was no way you could make friends with other female comics for a long time. It was really tough because everybody was ready to throw the first punch to prove to the peanut gallery of dudes that you were a guy's girl; you were a cool girl."

In essence, more opportunities for women have led to less competition, which has led to fewer women trying to hurt their own gender in order to gain entrance to the "boys' club," which has led to more opportunities for women to be kind to one another, to "Yes, and" each other's work, which has, today, formed a sort of "girls' club," which we'll discuss in more detail later. Another kind of ouroboros has begun to form, but it's still very new—only rising to the surface in the early 2000s.

Unfortunately, before the "Tina and Amy" era of the early 2000s, the history of women "Yes, and-ing" each other on the set of *SNL* was a mixed bag. Some helped the cause while others hurt it. Victoria Jackson has said of her time at *SNL* (1986–1992), "We had this meeting, and one of the producers asked us what was wrong with the show. And everyone was supposed to say something, but no one was saying anything. And it was all of us sitting on the floor like high school or kindergarten or whatever. And finally I go, 'OK, I'll say it in one sentence. You really want to know?' So then I was shaking, and I stood up and told everyone that what was wrong with the show was those two women—I pointed to Nora [Dunn] and Jan [Hooks]—and all the things they did bad: they didn't cooperate in sketches, and they slammed doors in people's faces and backbite and backstab and all that, you know. And then there was, like, silence, and no one said anything. And so they both got up really slowly and walked out of the room. And then I said to the others, 'Thanks a lot for standing up for me.' And Dana [Carvey] goes, 'You didn't hear anyone disagreeing, did you?' And everyone burst out laughing."

After Victoria's comment, fellow *SNL* star Jan Hooks said that Victoria "had a pretty good gig. I just have a particular repulsion to grown women who talk like little girls. It's like, 'You're a grown woman! Use your lower register!' *And* she's a born-again Christian. I don't know. She was like from Mars to me. I never really got her."

The guys, on the other hand, seemed to "get" each other on many levels, and many shared a bond within the safety of "the club." In a wave of backlash, the 1980s and very early 1990s under first Reagan (1981–1989) and then George H. W. Bush (1989–1993) were a time when those who resented women's empowerment rebranded Feminism as an ugly word. They sought to push back the gains made by the civil rights and women's liberation movements of the 1960s and 1970s, and they either delayed or altogether ignored new calls for equality by the emerging gay rights movement, which was experiencing rising stigma over the AIDS epidemic and even violent discrimination by a misinformed public.

Meanwhile, women—both gay and straight—were attempting to fight their own battles against the same silencing stigma attached to being labeled as Feminist. For Betty Cahill, the

1991–1992 *SNL* season was a period where being labeled a Feminist, much like being labeled gay, drew an immediate and often negative response. "It meant that you were ready to take on any man and fight him on anything he might say or think, and that you wanted to change him . . . but really what it means is that you're not going to take abuse. You're not out to change men so much as to change *yourself*. You're going to alter your reactions. You're going to stick up for yourself when others try to change *you*. You're going to be loyal to yourself and to your female friends and not betray them or leave them behind just to get guys to like you."

Still, on the surface at least, Betty was having fun. She went to the same McDonald's where Gilda used to order fries, late at night, only to puke them back up either on the side of the road or when she got home. Only Betty wasn't there alone, as Gilda had often been, but hanging out with David Spade and Chris Rock. She never had anything against any of them. They were always great to her. But that's just the thing: the problem is rarely ever against *individuals*, but the policies set in place to give advantage to those individuals over women. The default settings we're all taught to embrace. The subconscious behaviors and deep assumptions we all make. The fact that one minute Betty was hanging out in the basement of 30 Rock with David and Chris, who treated her as their equal, and then the next minute she was supposed to learn how to be funny from Del Close, a man who seemed to believe that women, quite literally, were not and could not be funny. "I was just trying to get the same position that they [Chris and David] had," she said. "I was just trying to be in the show."

Chris Rock claims that his time at *SNL* was the best of his life. "I honestly tell you, I made friendships that will last for the rest of my life. Most people had to share—they had a part-ner in their office. I had a four-person office: Sandler, Farley, Spade, and me shared an office. And those are my boys for life. For life. I love those guys."

Not that it was always this easy for the guys in the show, or that men aren't competitive with one another in different, perhaps even more brutal ways—certainly much more overtly competitive than they might be with women, whom men often subversively undercut rather than openly challenge. The differ-ence, of course, is that this competition was acknowledged. It was out in the open and, in some cases, expected. The rumors of Chevy Chase fist-fighting Bill Murray backstage are legend-ary. The stories of John Belushi egging both of them on to retaliate against Chevy for leaving the main cast are equally shocking.

Meanwhile, women like Betty had to pretend like nothing was happening. She couldn't just have it out with someone and throw things to air her grievances. Nothing could be discussed at all, because no one acknowledged her inequality. She had to smile while fighting against the immutable characteristic of being a female in a male-dominated space, and her fight was far harder because it had to be won in secret. She, like all the other women on the show, wasn't claiming to be *more* talented than the guys; she was claiming to be *equally* talented. They were simply trying get others to recognize what lay beneath the obvious surface: a subconscious bias rooted in the belief that these guys were more talented *because* they were guys.

In reality, they were all talented. But the fact remains that these particular "guys in the show" were receiving far more focus from a room of predominantly guy writers, who wrote far more sketches featuring other guys, and then, when the audience primarily saw guys performing, this reinforced the belief that visibility equals talent. Which, in keeping with this bizarre snake-eating-its-tail analogy, leads back to our starting point: a subconscious bias. Since bias so often becomes belief, this bias leads many to believe that "women aren't funny" and that guys are "naturally" better at comedy simply because they're more visible.

On top of everything else, these women had to wrangle with the Rule of Two, an unspoken practice that continues today, determining the makeup of almost every comedy lineup. Most commonly enforced by comedy club bookers and venue owners, the rule dictates that no more than two "female comics" should appear in any show not specifically designated as some variation of "ladies' night" (implying that the comedy will undoubtedly poke fun at "ladies' issues").

As a result, comedienne-ballerinas (much like cool girls seeking to join "the club") find themselves competing against one another to be chosen. One slot, I've heard from several comedienne-ballerinas of color, is always reserved for a white woman—unless, of course, "the show" is specifically designated for women of color. Otherwise, the default settings take over: according to several of my interviewees, out of a typical lineup of five to seven performers, 72 percent will be male, 28 percent will be female, and a *maximum* of 14 percent will *possibly* be females of color.

This rule is yet another example of the Patriarchy's divide-and-conquer strategy. Separate and destroy: get them to fight each other in order to distract them from the fact that they shouldn't have to fight anyone at all.

"Especially in the beginning," Betty Cahill said, "there were times when I wished I were a guy, because I knew that I would be in the guys' club instead of being over here, by myself, as a girl . . . but then I started meeting all these other women. They were so much fun, and so intelligent, and so cool, and they made me *laugh*. So we formed a girls' club. While the guys still had theirs, we had ours, too."

rewiring the ficus tree

OVER TIME, AS PORTLAND-BASED STAND-UP comic Bri Pruett pointed out, "I think that some men are getting really tired of 'the club,' because they're tired of having the reputation of being sexist that comes along with being a member of that club. It's become important to them to be, like, 'Hey, that's not who we are. Male comic does not equal shitting on women. It does not equal being hateful toward people.' So they have a real reason to speak out about it and to be Feminist and not racist and all that stuff. There was a quote from the guy who made *BoJack Horseman*. He had a great quote about how as a writer, you want to write the cleanest, most pared down version of the joke that you can before you sort of evaluate the comedy of it. And one thing that he noticed was, if he's telling a joke where gender is important, and the two characters that you're telling the joke about are female, a person's like, 'Why are those characters female?' Because they think of male as being a default—a default setting."

"Because of language," I said.

"Yeah."

"Remember when we were learning how to write essays and the standard fallback for all pronouns was 'he'?"

"Oh, right! 'He.' Sure, I remember learning to use that for everything I wrote. It was the default."

"Right. And writers had to sort of stop and think about whether using the alternative made sense. Some went out of their way to start using 'she.' It was their reaction to an automatic setting."

"Right! And, in the case of *BoJack*, we're talking about *animation* for fuck's sake. You know what I mean? Like, the *least* real-life, rooted-in-truth type of entertainment—and even then, he was uncomfortable at first using female characters. But when he began pushing those boundaries in his own work, he figured out that it actually worked fine."

"I think, in a way, he actively rewired himself."

"Yes! Rewiring is *hard*—especially for women. I mean, I'm a thirty-year-old person. I really am pretty young. You'd think my brain would be really malleable . . . but I have so much to learn."

"And *unlearn*."

"And unlearn. Yes. *Mostly* unlearn, I think. I've had experiences where people ask me to change the pronoun that I address them with and it is really, *really* hard for me. Everything we do is so gendered. It's all about presentation, almost like we're performing as ourselves *for* ourselves . . . and for others. We're all doing it all the time. I can't even imagine, I mean you think about a computer using CPUs, how much of my brain all day is thinking about what I'm doing—if this is feminine enough; if I'm making a choice to be masculine. 'What do I look like? What do I sound like? How are the women going to receive me? How are the men going to receive me?'"

"'Am I taking up space?'"

"Yes! 'Am I taking up space?' And how much of that energy could be put toward actually being funny? Or remembering math equations . . ."

Or unlearning a language. Releasing ourselves from, as Natasha Patterson writes, the role of communication "in constructing, disseminating, and maintaining the values and norm systems that serve the dominant Patriarchal class interests."

Put more simply: fighting against the divide and conquer. Examining the words themselves at their most basic level. Undoing the default setting for our brains, which have learned to see the standard everything as male and anything else as a deviation from "normal." A special subset, a niche, an exception to the rule that should be spoken of and viewed separately:

Women's Issues
Girls' Soccer
Chick Lit
Lady Doctor
Female Senator
Women in Business
Female-driven
Girl Writer*
Comedienne
Actress
Women's Comedy
Female Comic
Feminist Comedian

----

* In 1965, Joan Rivers was selected to appear on the "death slot" (the last ten minutes) of *The Tonight Show Starring Johnny Carson*. Emily Nussbaum wrote that "the gig was a mercy booking . . . In her black dress and pearls, Rivers was introduced not as a stand-up but as that rarity a 'girl writer.'" Sound familiar, Maddy?

As Luisa Omielan put it: "I shouldn't be a 'feminist come-dian.' It shouldn't even be 'feminist comedy,' because that's suggesting that other comedy *isn't* feminist. Maybe that other kind of comedy that's been around forever should be labeled as 'clichéd,' or 'tired,' or 'sexist comedy,' but it isn't. Instead, it's simply 'comedy,' while my kind of comedy is labeled 'feminist comedy.' Maybe we should come up with two entirely new cat-egories! Maybe the two categories should be 'outdated, misogy-nistic comedy,' and 'comedy.' Did anyone ever think about that? I mean, why am I always the one with the special adjective?"

The problems now arise less in the pronouns or adjectives (which, in the last decade or so, have become less black and white) and more in the verbs. Since circa 2000, the issue has become less about "male" versus "female," and more about our society's con-fusion between "yes" and "no"—a systemic problem that has, slowly but surely, translated into a feeling of, "Well, I didn't tech-nically say 'no,' but I'm not feeling great about what happened next . . ." And this is how history's slopes become slippery—what might appear on the surface a simple matter of biased pronouns and adjectives morphs, over time, into a language of biased con-sent. It starts with the seemingly innocuous words we use in our daily vernacular—then eventually trickles into those we codify by and within our legal system: words like "legitimate" versus "statutory" rape. Phrases like "consensual sex." *

This last one gets me the most. As one especially astute online meme put it, adding the descriptor "consensual"

---

* Even words, like "wizard" and "witch," are segregated into male and female viewpoints, where the male term is considered either positive or neu-tral while the female term has become a derogatory slur. To call someone a "witch" isn't very nice, but try calling someone a "wizard" and he'll just get confused as to how that's an insult. (Because it isn't. It means "wise.")

"implies that there is such a thing as 'nonconsensual sex,' which there isn't. That's rape. That is what it needs to be called. There is only sex or rape. Do not teach people that rape is just another type of sex. They are two very separate events. You wouldn't say 'breathing swimming' and 'nonbreathing swimming,' you would say 'swimming' and 'drowning.'" All of this revisionism—changing words from what they literally mean into what we'd prefer to simply imply—is a part of our society's sickness. If nothing else, women have finally, after thousands and thousands of years of Male Supremacy's programming, begun to consciously rewire their language, to pick up on their own self-loathing, and in so doing reject the idea that any of this ever was or could have been their fault. They're unlearning all the things they've been taught to apologize for. Most importantly, they've begun calling rape by its true name. Crime doesn't need an adjective. Rape Culture, on the other hand, absolutely depends on our assigning one.

The process of unlearning these adjectives is (either fortunately or unfortunately, depending on your perspective) lifelong. Our words are small components of a Patriarchal, oppressive language that needs to be recognized, and the process of unlearning all the damage we've internalized needs to start as early as possible, maybe even before the learning begins. Thankfully, we can work together to overcome the harmful effects of binary language and the many subconscious ways we brainwash ourselves, and our children, into not only seeing anything that's described in masculine terms as normal and anything else as separate and thus inherently unequal but also into passively accepting their own oppression and victimization.

At the end of Joan Rivers's Vegas act, she tried to do something similar for the women in her audience. She would offer one of them a reward in the form of a ficus tree, dragging it across the stage, struggling, as the orchestra watched but refused to help. She describes the moment in *Still Talking*: "I say, 'Fucking liberation. We did it to ourselves.' Women love that line. I am raging out like King Lear—Queen Lear—screaming into the wind, screaming for all us women."

I often think about Joan's screaming out all her rage-filled, dirty laundry—talking to us animals to try and set us free. She was fearless, as she had to be. After Joan's husband, Edgar Rosenberg, committed suicide, Joan's performances changed viscerally. She seemed then like a bundle of nerves—a very high-strung woman, clutching pearls, exploding her immense pain and obvious fear onto her audience. *That's* powerful. But then, making anyone laugh is powerful because making anyone laugh is a form of love. Loving your enemy is manifested by putting your arms not around the person but around the situation that you're mocking—the joke that you're making—in order to siphon power away from those who misuse it, at which point they can become human, too.

Today's comedienne-ballerinas are still doing exactly this. Putting their arms around their audiences—enemies or friends—is their gift. It is their offering of a reward. Sometimes their arms are jokes. Other times their arms are pointed topics and powerful questions; attempts to first connect with and then wrap their arms around any woman who'll listen. Today's comedienne-ballerinas prepare their embrace by asking themselves questions, too: *Am I talking about what's true, what's funny, and what my audience wants to hear? Am I talking about what my audience* needs *to hear?*

I think, as Joan likely did, that the answers to these questions are akin to a ficus tree. They're the opposite of defeatist. They're a branch to cling to while screaming into the wind or shouting in a forest. Because at the end of the day, we're all ghosts, driving meat-coated skeletons, made from dust, riding a rock, hurtling through space. We should fear *nothing*. A woman who fears nothing and follows her gut makes a sound—a voice that that cries out long after she's gone, riding herself away, straight through the stars. She lifts herself up by her Self, and doesn't let herself droop down, for her Self is herself's only friend, and herself is her Self's only foe.*

---

* An ode to Bhagavad Gita 6:5.

part four

LOOKISM

"What do Americans think is beautiful? Guns? Barbecue? Perhaps the most beautiful woman in America is one made entirely out of brisket and holding a revolver?"
—Poppy Carlton from BBC's *Almost Royal*

punching up

BACK IN 1952, AFTER LUCY gave up on becoming a ballerina in Episode 19, she asked a comedian dressed as a Marx brother to teach her a burlesque act instead. While many people use the term "burlesque" to refer to a form of striptease typically performed by women, its original definition refers to a comedic performance involving comedians, who were usually men (with a few exceptions, such as Moms Mabley and Jorie Remus). Thus, the comedian responds to Lucy's request with, "I don't know about doing this bit with a dame. These bits are done by two men."

"Couldn't you just pretend I'm a man?" Lucy begged. When the comedian finally agrees, he gives her a set of new clothes to wear and clown makeup to apply all over her face. When she puts them both on, she is transformed into a boxy, unfeminine figure, her gender suddenly switched from traditionally female into male by a shapeless suit, a bolero hat, and thick circles of makeup covering her eyes, nose, and mouth. With her femininity covered, the scene can once again be played by "two men." Lucy is now someone the comedian believes he can teach. But as he explains his routine, he routinely forgets who Lucy is, mistaking her for the man she's dressed up to be, and slowly becomes convinced that she is, in fact, the man who stole his ex-wife. He tries to beat Lucy up, pummels her with a pie to the face, and finally sprays her with water. The lesson abruptly ends, and the audience goes wild.

In reality, the comedian's reluctance to teach Lucy based on the unspoken rule that a burlesque act is "usually played by two men" was completely typical and normative for 1952. In fact, until 1661, this tradition was not just "usual," it was a legal requirement—and it serves as the basis for what we now know as "ladyface."

The history of men dressing as women to get other men (and women) to laugh at the expense of women stretches back across many centuries and countries. The most predominant legend for the origin of boy players—as these early ladyfacers were supposedly called—dates back to a time when the Church of England forbade women from performing as actors on stage—because only men went to the theater and women who performed for men were considered prostitutes. During the sixteenth century, thanks largely to the infamous* reign of Henry VIII, there was very little substantive separation between church and state, and the king was technically the head of the

---

* Wherein he broke England away from Roman Catholicism and proclaimed himself the Supreme Head of the Church, all so he could divorce his first wife, Catherine of Aragon, and live guilt-free with his mistress, Anne Boleyn, who played hard-to-get long enough to become the second of his six wives and first of (at least) two murder victims.

church. The practical result of all this was simple, yet absolutely terrifying: Whatever the church/king wanted suddenly became not only secular law but also religious commandment. Still, breaking the law/pissing off the church became almost unavoidable, since there were only so many stories male playwrights could invent featuring only male parts (not everyone can aspire to become a young David Mamet, and nobody wanted to spend the next five hundred years watching various remakes of *Glengarry Glen Ross*), and so some male actors trained from the age of eight or nine to eventually perform adult female roles for their audiences.

This legally required cross-dressing came to a grinding halt during the seventeenth century reign of Charles II, whose mother, it's rumored, dearly wanted to be an actress—until conservative clerics abused her for her ambitions and added fuel to the smoldering, revolutionary fire of public opinion, which already held the royal family under Charles I as utterly corrupt, licentious, and debauched. This fire ultimately exploded into the English Civil War, ending only in 1649 when Charles I was beheaded and Charles II, then still a teenager, was exiled with his mother and siblings to Holland. He spent the next twenty years grinding his teeth, allegedly marrying his first of many mistresses, siring bastards, and planning his revenge on Oliver Cromwell's Evangelicals.

When English peasants finally got tired of Puritans banning all the fun stuff, everything from dancing to drinking to even celebrating Christmas, the monarchy was restored and Charles II came back to power. One of his first orders of business was supposedly doing away with legalized ladyface. If the legends are indeed true, however, it's more likely that Charles II changed the laws in order to appease the most famous of his mistresses, Nell Gwyn, who was an "orange girl."* Nell was so great at "selling oranges" that she sold one (or several) to Charles II. She also, supposedly, wanted to perform on stage rather than solely behind it. Once Charles (again, allegedly) made this legal, Nell did in fact become something of an actress. In a way, today's American comedienne-ballerinas only exist because of Henry VIII's and Charles II's overactive boners.

While the legal necessity of ladyface allegedly died out with the Stuart monarchy, the tradition of auspiciously straight men donning drag remains, especially in the world of comedy. But is this a tradition that embodies women's lack of options? Does the image of a man in drag continue to anchor comedy to a repressive time when women were legally forbidden to go on stage, and therefore had few options to create their own comedy? Or are we poking fun at this form of discrimination because we've moved past it?

"When a guy's *entire act* is his dressing up like a girl, it's *such* a *scream*!" Eliza Skinner answered. "Even removing all the trans issues from that, of which there are *tons* (and to which I can't really speak that well) . . . as a woman that's a huge bummer because, c'mon! Was there *no* woman that would have been hilarious in that part? Was there *no* woman who would have been hilarious doing that voice? Is it really that funny if it takes a man putting on a dress to make it funny? Monty Python was much more of a 'dressing as women because there weren't any women in the group' kind of thing, and also they thought it was funnier for them to dress as women and play

---

* A female of the Stuart Era, who carried baskets of fruit around to places like the Globe Theatre, soliciting dudes who were there to watch "plays," a.k.a. the seventeenth-century version of TV, and buy "oranges," a.k.a. the seventeenth-century version of "strange."

silly characters than it would be to hire *real* women to come in and play those characters. They thought that real women would look too good. For them, the joke about putting big blokes into dresses was funnier than having female comics be on the show . . . So, doing that sort of thing today just takes parts away from women in the same way that white actors putting on blackface took parts away from African American actors, and in the same way that Mickey Rooney dressing up like an Asian man for *Breakfast at Tiffany's* took a part away from an Asian man, who should have been able to play that role far better and certainly less offensively."

Sadly, although she inspired Eliza to go into comedy more than anyone else, even the beloved Miss Piggy was portrayed by the voice of a man. "What are you going to do?" Eliza asked, throwing up her hands in exasperation. "Guess you can't have everything."

Some performers, like Mo Collins, believe that ladyface can be complimentary. "We can't be women *without* men," she said. "Men are very necessary for us to shine. Not mandatory . . . but I find necessary. We need them to help us compare and contrast, to heighten what's so funny about being female sometimes."

But Eliza Skinner maintains that we shouldn't so easily dismiss ladyface because we haven't yet fully dealt with sexism's harmful effects on society, and thus we haven't actually moved past the mindset behind such discriminatory laws; even if the laws themselves are gone, the motivations for them remain. In her opinion, the act of dressing up as *a* woman in order to mimic *all* women shouldn't get such an easy pass. "It's still very clearly poking fun *at* women when men dress up and act out scenes using unfair gender stereotypes about how women walk, talk, and act. When I see a man play a woman, the man is never playing the straight woman. He's never playing some-one about whom he would honestly say, 'Wow, what a great example of a woman!' It's always an exaggerated negative or an outright lie about women. It's also a snide comment that implies, 'Women are *so* like this, aren't they? Aren't they *just* like this?' to his audience."

"You think it's more of a caricature of all young women in the world versus commentary on *a* young woman in *a* funny situation?" I asked her.

"Exactly. I think that, at its core, it's a punch-down per-formance . . . focused on poking fun at groups of people who are already, usually, hanging from the lower rungs of society."

Riley Silverman agrees. "It's straight, cisgender, male come-dians taking advantage of their audience's fear without bother-ing to do anything to fix it."

A man dressing as a woman is laughable but, like Lucy's burlesque performance, a woman dressing as a man is under-standable. It subconsciously reminds us of all the reasons why a woman might sincerely wish to "pass," both on stage and off. Both are a way of tricking an audience. The former might be a way of getting them to laugh, whereas the latter might be a way of getting them to leave you alone.

Many women over millennia have dressed in men's cloth-ing for any number of reasons: to protect, elevate, and upgrade their social positions, and to escape our collective fear and dis-trust of the female gender. As we've discussed, we don't cele-brate females. We hide away their "issues" as disgusting and impolite topics of discussion. We segregate their very real strug-gles into the subcategory of "women's" rather than human concerns. In fact, association with anything of or relating to femininity is actually the source of some of our worst insults and greatest fears. Naturally, many women seek to escape it through dressing as men. This is the sort of escapism that's been happening since women dressed up as men to join the Civil War and get out of their oppressive Victorian-era realities. (That's how crappy it was being a woman in a whalebone corset.) This past and present reality is hard to fix and even harder to comfortably mock.

"I used to have a hard time whenever Lorne would put Garrett in a dress," Rosie Shuster said of Garrett Morris, the first (and only) person of color in *SNL*'s inaugural cast, who—even after taking most of the blame in the press for its growing reputation for rampant drug abuse—stayed loyal to the show from 1975 to 1980. Apparently, Garrett wasn't happy "going home to the 'hood' each night, having appeared *yet again* on live television as a woman. We were all well aware of that, but it was especially squirmy for me, personally—watching his discomfort when I had no power to help." Sometimes the problem with ladyface isn't the inherent biological difference between the genders but the negative social, physical, financial, emotional, and legal ramifications of being raised (and then treated) as a female. Maybe the reason we have such a problem seeing ourselves as both of any two things is that one gender (male) is still treated as vastly superior to others. As a result of this unequal treatment and presumed male superiority, females (and especially those who outwardly identify themselves as female, vocal Feminists, and fearless comedienne-ballerinas) experience everything from the subtly gas-lighting "I don't usually like female comics, but *you* were funny" to flat-out, in-your-face online harassment (as in the cases of Lindy West and Jessica Valenti). Belonging to the female gender has, since the beginning of the Patriarchy, carried negative consequences, which have made some comedienne-ballerinas disassociate with this disadvantaged gender. They want to be comedians, not necessarily female comedians.

In some types of comedy, and especially with ladyface, the female gender's disadvantages are openly exploited, laughed at, and then blamed on the disadvantaged (more Stella Kowalski, anyone?). This is partly why, as Eliza Skinner argues, big differences continue to exist between men's and women's approaches to ladyfacing. Men dressing up as women isn't often intended to achieve the same comedic effect as women dressing up as men. The former is usually done for an entirely different, and much broader, purpose than simply sending up, for example, Justin Bieber as an especially douchey but ultimately singular individual—not his entire gender. The latter is a giant "See?" to the audience. It's the male performer's sly wink as he reveals his version of "the truth" about "how all women *really* are."

The target of a joke often reveals a comedian's intentions. Whether the bull's-eye is set on a person of power or a victim of power determines the course of the comedian's entire performance.

In the end, as Eliza points out, the performer is the one who should be parodied—if nothing else, for the intense cowardice such performance reveals. "You couldn't find enough funny things about white men? *Really?* Why don't you go make fun of *yourself?* Go make fun of yourself, and then when you run out of material, you can come for me."

Targeting a person of power is what comedians across the spectrum refer to as "punching up." It's the preferred type of comedy for any performer of integrity, since it's usually a choice between mocking a victim or a victimizer. Conversely, when the punch line lands on the victim, this is referred to as "punching down." Intention, purpose, and effect act together to determine whether someone's comedy is viewed as conciliatory, emancipatory, or demeaning. Sometimes attempts to reach out and understand comedians who engage in this third option only encourage continued "punch downs." Sometimes unity for the sake of comedy isn't the most important priority.

These differences in purpose, intention, and effect explain why comedienne-ballerinas like Eliza Skinner often have a problem with ladyface in *any* context, since it's a kind of gender revisionism.

Lorne Michaels once told *Vanity Fair* that "so much of what *Saturday Night Live* wanted to be, or I wanted it to be when it began, was cool. Which was something television wasn't, except in a retro way. We wanted to redefine comedy the way the Beatles redefined what being a pop star was. That required not pandering, and it also required removing neediness, the need to please. It was like, 'We're only going to please those people who are like us.' The presumption was there were a lot of people like us. And that turned out to be so."

But did pleasing those people really require ladyface? Was that really the cool, new thing to do, imitate a form of comedy that had died out in the 1660s only to be revived in the 1960s? That seems about as "retro" as it gets. Or perhaps everything old does indeed become new again eventually. And what about the reverse? Could female-to-male drag have proven equally pleasing? While male-to-female drag gags are a British comedy mainstay (see Monty Python), the reverse is far less common. Is that why Lorne so rarely tried it? Is that why so many men (in fact, every single male cast member at *SNL* except John Belushi, who only relented once) wound up in dresses, but so few women wound up in suits? The better argument, based on all of this, is that Lorne, who grew up watching the traditional British and Canadian comedy mainstays of his youth, simply re-created what he knew. We are all far less unique than we would like to believe, and we all pander quite a bit more than we'll admit.

Maybe Lorne truly believed he was redefining comedy—and in many other sketches that didn't touch on gender-based stereotypes, *SNL* did exactly that. But, like many revisionists, in terms of reinforcing Male Supremacy through ladyface, *SNL*'s idea of how to "redefine" comedy was to repeat the past but change its name. These weren't boy players anymore; they were now the Not Ready for Prime Time Players.

Had the show truly intended to reach for something entirely new, it would have featured the women—in drag. It would have upended ladyface instead of reinforcing it. It would have taken more cues from the forward-thinking comedienne-ballerinas performing in bars and clubs across America during this time.

By the 1960s, women like Phyllis Diller had already begun hiding their gender in a similar way, parroting what they saw—as Lorne and Lucy did—but winking at it instead of repeating it. This became the new wave of actual gender-based rebellion. Perhaps that's why Phyllis was considered, by some, to be an acquired taste. Most new delicacies are. But female audiences had absorbed ladyfacing, too. And so they laughed, though sadly at their own expense. They stood straddling a line between male and female, with one foot in a new world and the other in the old.

As Portland-based stand-up Susan Rice described her, Phyllis was "clownish when she first started, with the wig and everything. Women of that generation were used to seeing Milton Berle in drag, but all of a sudden here's Phyllis Diller, and she's saying things that Milton Berle couldn't get away with. Red Skelton was that way, too. He dressed in drag, too, you know. But once Phyllis hit on *Ed Sullivan*, she exploded. And then she got more garish and more garish and more garish and it was . . . that was the sign of the times. It was totally emblematic of the '60s. It was crazy."

Phyllis wrote that newspaper columnists used to label her "the female Bob Hope." She was famous, at her peak, for hiding her femininity behind fright wigs and loose-fitting dresses that made her appear flat chested (though she was a 38D), and for her noticeable stance—much like a ballerina's plié, she would stand with both heels relatively close together and her toes pointing outward in opposite directions. But she didn't start out that way.

In February of 1955, she attended an open audition (there were no open mic nights back then) on the last Saturday of the month at the Purple Onion, where the person in charge of choosing talent was "Barrymore Drew, an older gay guy who had been a radio star in Chicago" as well as a member of a famous theatrical family. Phyllis described him as "tall and elegant, although he always wore sandals," and a "wonderful housemother as well as a gentle person with a great sense of humor," who once told her that he'd always been torn between wanting to be either Mary Pickford or Douglas Fairbanks. He just couldn't choose whether he was a lady or not, and it's a shame that, in those days, he felt the need to be strictly one or another rather than a bit of both. Phyllis, too, started out choosing to be Mary, dressing up for her audition in a tight black cotton evening dress and rhinestone-strapped high heels that she referred to as her "whore shoes"—a play on the word "horseshoes." *

---

* What's so funny about this is high heels were literally created by French prostitutes, whose English customers so admired the sexiness of the courtesans' footwear that they brought pairs home for their poor cuckolded wives to wear, too (when they were done fighting off the brain-melting syphilis). Consider this historical tidbit every time your corporate dress code mandates heels as a part of "professional attire." Which profession

Phyllis wrote extensively about her extremely feminine fashion in those days, making her debut on Monday, March 7, 1955, in another form-fitting cotton dress borrowed from a friend. So she wasn't always trying to hide. Or perhaps she hadn't started hiding *yet*. Perhaps it took her many years to learn. Perhaps she first needed to take the temperature of the room. Maybe she spent years observing her audience's comfort level, absorbing preconceived notions for what comedy "should" look like based on what it almost invariably had: a man. Sometimes a man in drag. Sometimes a man in drag who got laughs. And sometimes a man in drag who got laughs less because he was funny and more because he was willing to appear in drag.

As she became more famous in the Benny Hill, Monty Python, and Dame Edna era, Phyllis's style mimicked theirs, much like the "female comedians" of today's era who often internalize and then either consciously or subconsciously mimic the jeans/hoodie/thick glasses style they observe in their

---

are they encouraging, exactly? Similar confusion led to an explosion of "bottle blonde" hair in Roman times. In Rome, natural blondes were usually Gallic slaves, and thus considered barbarians. Thus, since married Roman women had traditionally black hair, and prostitutes were supposed to be socially inferior to these ladies, many "working women" were forced to dye their hair blonde—both as a system of castigation and as a type of ancient advertising. It didn't work that well, however, when Roman husbands purchased sexual services, leading their wives to believe that these men preferred prostitutes *because* of their hair. The wives tried to compete by dyeing theirs blonde, too, or forcibly chopping the hair off their slaves to make into wigs, once again making supposedly high-class ladies indistinguishable from prostitutes. This vicious cycle continues today in the form of Bravo TV's *Housewives* reality show franchise. Just kidding!**
** I'm not kidding.

fellow "male comedians." Chicken? Meet egg. The past is never dead. It's not even past.*

Phyllis's style ended up making her look as "dragged-out" as they did. For her, as with so many current comedienne-ballerinas, art imitated life, and her life ended up imitating her art.

But nearly forty years after Phyllis began, by the early 1990s, some improv performers were turning the tables on ladyfacing, too. Most memorably, Julia Sweeney's character "Pat" (a sexually indeterminate office worker and an obvious comment on gender roles) appeared on *SNL* from 1990 to approximately 1994.

To transform herself, Julia used beige lipstick and colored her eyebrows, then padded her body into near shapelessness, wore a tightly curled wig, and donned more traditionally masculine clothing that could now suit any gender. "I did the character Pat at the Groundlings, and it was part of my audition for *Saturday Night Live*," she says. "I'd been an accountant for five years, and there was one person I worked with who sort of drooled and had the kind of body language of Pat. I started trying to do him. I was testing it out on my friends, and they were just like, 'Yeah, it's good, but it doesn't seem like a guy that much.' So then I thought, 'Maybe that's the joke. I'll just have one joke in here about we don't know if that's a man or a woman, just to sort of cover up for my lack of ability to really play a guy convincingly.'

"I think it was the Christmas show or something—a John Goodman show. I put it up with Kevin Nealon in it. Just showing how humble I was about that sketch, I didn't even cast the host opposite me. They put it on as the very last sketch of the

---

* An ode to William Faulkner.

show, and I didn't think it got a great response. I felt happy with it, but it wasn't like, 'Oh, new recurring character.' And the audience responded, but I think they were also really confused by it, or creeped out by it.

"A couple weeks later, though, Roseanne Barr hosted, and she had seen that show, and she said, 'We've got to do that character.' And I said, 'Oh, OK.' So Christine [Zander] and I wrote a Pat sketch for Roseanne and I to do, and when I came on during the sketch, I got this fabulous entrance applause, as if the audience knew the character. That was actually one of the most beautiful moments in my life. And it was completely unexpected.

"People would always ask about Pat's sex, and I didn't have an answer. To me, Pat, by that point, had sort of taken on its own personality. This sounds really 'actor-y,' but I felt like I was just playing Pat. Pat was this other person. And I didn't know Pat's gender, either."

Splitsider once reported that "*SNL*'s recurring character mold, as well as male/female cast member divide, would have gone largely untested without Pat's existence. And for a featured player whose first year was spent in an overcrowded cast with thirteen men and a mere three women, perhaps Sweeney sensed that a joke on the gender issue was the best way to get around it. Whatever the case, Pat's smarmy, pleading face will, for better or worse, remain the thing on *SNL* for which Sweeney is most remembered . . . Pat was a creepy yet instant recurring character hit," perhaps because the show's celebrity hosts played everyday people who would encounter Pat (short for either "Patricia" or "Patrick") and try to discern Pat's gender without coming right out and asking the question, leaving both them and the audience deeply frustrated whenever Pat never came right out and answered this question, either. In fact, Pat's comments and reactions seemed oblivious to any gender confusion. "A typical example might be, 'Sorry if I'm a little grumpy, I have really bad cramps . . . I rode my bike over here, and my calf muscles are *killing* me!'"

The entire sequence demonstrates the idea that neither Julia herself nor the character she plays fits strictly within either gender paradigm. Much like the dynamic between Lucille Ball and Lucy Ricardo in "The Ballet," neither the comedian nor her character truly fits the binary mold. This inability to fit into the either/or system can be both positive and negative for the performer's future. Beyond comedy, "The Ballet"—which, as we've discussed, constituted something of a beginning for comedienne-ballerinas like Amy Schumer and Maria Bamford, whose comedy embodies both the traditionally masculine and feminine—speaks directly to our current, ongoing debate over "identity politics," which have been blamed for everything from "political correctness" to Hillary Clinton's loss to Donald Trump. But Lindy West has pointed out, "identity politics" are essential to the survival of all kinds of groups, including women, racial and religious minorities, and other victimized populations including rape survivors, the handicapped, and even veterans of the Vietnam War. Their identities help them to withstand near-constant financial, legal, social, and certainly legislative attacks during times of conservative backlash against Both-ness.

Today, many scholars have proposed that gender characteristics are not fixed. They can and do vary across time and between or even within cultures. Contemporary scholars have even proposed that gender and its extension, sexual identity, are best understood as occurring along a continuum rather than a binary.

Still, our country, much like our comedy, hasn't yet fully figured out how to stop punching down at trans people. We use the same bully's defense that sexists and bigots have historically leveled at Feminists and other activists: "So what if I hit you first? How dare you hit back! Now, *I'm* the real victim in this situation I created." We ridicule "others" for calling out microaggressions and seeking trigger-free safe spaces. We claim they're overreacting and that they need to be less sensitive. Yet we never curb our own behavior in causing their offense. Instead, we come to our own defense. We strike first, and when they point this out, we conveniently switch cause with effect, claiming that reaction is somehow more offensive than action. If we'd rather not hear a wince, we should, perhaps, stop punching.

I covered this exact issue for *Forbes* in March of 2016, only thirty-six hours after North Carolina Governor Pat McCrory (who has since been voted out of office) signed House Bill 2, the Public Facilities Privacy and Security Act. This Act put in place a statewide policy that banned many transgender individuals from using public bathrooms. The bill was largely a response to—and also undid—the city of Charlotte, North Carolina's attempt to protect these same individuals from exactly this kind of discrimination by the state. Immediately after signing, McCrory tweeted, "Ordinance defied common sense, allowing men to use women's bathroom/locker room for instance. That's why I signed bipartisan bill to stop it."

As this flawed reasoning demonstrates, our society tends to react strangely and often irrationally to anyone falling into a sexual orientation and/or gender identity gray area. This also includes so-called "metrosexual" men, who aren't gay but display certain behaviors that we've stereotyped as "gayish." Chris Kattan, an *SNL* cast member from the 1990s, once told *Vanity Fair* that "there is a little generalization of casting people just in the sense of, like, 'Well, this character's tall and skinny—get Jimmy.' Or 'He's the dad or somebody—get Will.' And, you know, 'He's gay—get Chris.' I would be the guy who would dress up in drag or dance or something. I know some people do think I'm gay. I've had people ask me if I'm bi more than gay. And I'm OK with it, and I like it, because I'm not gay, so actually for women it means I'm not threatening. It doesn't bother me too much. I think there's femininity, something feminine, in my characters that's easy for me. The way I move my body and my rhythm—it comes out a little gayish."

We also owe these "gayish" comedians of the 1990s a huge debt of gratitude for our current bevy of LGBTQ marvels, including Alison Grillo, Jeffrey Jay, Bethany Black (supposedly Britain's *only* self-proclaimed lesbian transsexual comic), Janet Mock, Laverne Cox, Laura Jane Grace, Lana Wachowski, Erika Ervin, Adam Torres, Alexandra Billings, Tom Phelan, Ian Harvie, Ni Ching, Rocco Kayiatos, Zackary Drucker, Hailie Sahar, Harmony Santana, and Mariana Marroquin, Alexandra Grey, Sophia Grace Gianna, Julia Scotti, Hari Nef, Trace Lysette, and my personal favorite, LA-based stand-up and online columnist Riley Silverman, whose insightful commentary helped to reinforce my suspicions that comedienne-ballerinas are essential to guiding all little children (of every or no gender) toward the realization that *nobody* fits some myopic mold of "man" or "woman."

"I'm a comedian, and I think of comedians as my peers," she said, "so they're the first voices that I listen to . . . and I think Ellen's coming out as a lesbian in the '90s, when I was in high school, was a turning point for me, consciousness-wise, because our country had never *really* talked about gay issues like marriage equality before."

It's true. Stepping back a few years, to 1993, older millennials were around eleven or twelve years old when Pedro Zamora married his husband on season three of *The Real World,* and then passed away after living for many years with AIDS. He, too, used his platform to help others and to encourage teenagers to not only practice safe sex but to talk about their alternate sexualities and identities. He'd contracted HIV by having unprotected sex with women, breaking the idea (held over from Reagan-era stigma and pointed silence) that only homosexuality led to infection. He was the first gay man I'd ever seen in my small southern town in North Carolina, and my television became the medium that opened my eyes to a largely silenced reality (much like audiences watching a pregnant Lucy were suddenly faced with the reality of female sexuality).

In 1996, the year before she came out publicly, Ellen appeared on *The Rosie O'Donnell Show.* Rosie asked about all the rumors flying around regarding her upcoming season, and Ellen responded, "I don't know how this happened, because we were really trying to build this up slowly, in a way that would be, you know . . . that would change people's opinions, basically. We do find out that the character is Lebanese."

"Just out of the blue?" Rosie asked.

"Well, no, there have been clues. You've seen her eating baba ghanoush, if you watch the show at all, and hummus . . . and she's a big, big fan of Casey Kasem and Kathy and Jimmy's . . ."

"Hey, I'm a big fan of Casey Kasem! Maybe *I'm* Lebanese?" Rosie asked.

"You know, that's funny, because I pick up sometimes that you *might* be Lebanese . . ." Ellen said.

"I think that's great, because a lot of other networks wouldn't take the risk, going different ethnically with a character like that."

"Well, half of Hollywood is Lebanese."

"Really? I didn't know!"

"Yeah, people don't know. So we have to change people's perspectives about being Lebanese."

Even before this ode to perfectly timed satire, Ellen became the first stand-up comedian to make five-year-old Riley laugh. Riley retains the visceral memory of sitting on the tile in her parents' living room while they were watching Ellen do her now iconic bit about airplane food. Years later, Ellen's coming out in the middle of *prime* prime time (remember: network TV had almost no competition in the 1990s, and nobody used the Internet very much, so we're talking about roughly as many viewers watching *Ellen* as watched *I Love Lucy*) sparked another kind of realization for little kids like Riley, who identified as female but who had male bodies. Something changed inside of her. The world suddenly tilted her way. That kind of courage connects Ellen to Gilda to Lucy to Maddy to Moms to Sophie to Carol to Marga Gomez to Laverne Cox and to all the other unwitting blocks on which our humor has sharpened its knife. All of them deserve the Medal of Freedom that President Barack Obama awarded Ellen in November of 2016.

"See, I didn't know that 'transgender' was even a thing until I was eight or nine," Riley explained. "I kind of stumbled upon it in a *MAD* magazine of all places, reading a comic book parody. I can't remember if it was *MAD* or *Cracked* magazine, but it was parodying the first *Batman*, when Vicki Vale entered the bat cave and Bruce Wayne steps out of a side closet wearing his Batman suit and says, 'There's something I need to tell you,' and, as a psychiatrist, she answers, 'Oh, I get it. You're a transvestite.' I remember asking my babysitter at the time, 'What does that mean?' And she goes, 'Oh, that's a word for men who like to dress up as women.' My mind exploded. It was like, *BPOOF!* 'There's a word for that? I'm not alone?'"

Today, in terms of embracing our greater cultural (and perhaps global) shift toward a gender continuum, author Sara Benincasa admits to having been "a bit of a shit in this department." At one time, she says, she was highly transphobic, and this feeling was rooted in her conflicted emotions about her own emergent bisexuality. "I didn't understand transgender issues. I didn't understand why someone would want to admit and embrace who he or she really was. All of that was really about me, honestly; I didn't like some things about myself, and I was scared of being different from the folks around me. I didn't feel that I was a different gender than I presented on the outside, but I certainly felt very conflicted about being sexually attracted to both women and men. I thought that this part of myself was disgusting, and so it bothered me that there were people out there who were willing to admit how they truly felt. I resented that. It wasn't an active hate, but it was definitely fear of 'otherness.' It's so interesting now to speak to different Feminists, as I do, and to hear that there are still some Feminists who carry that same fear. To me, it's ridiculous to imagine that Feminism could possibly exclude *any* woman—regardless of how she identifies, or where she was born, or how she was born, or the gender of the body into which she was born. Now, all that fear or whatever, it seems ridiculous to me. For a lot of Feminists who are younger than me, that kind of fear never came into play. They don't even care. Whereas I had to learn to stop caring about stupid differences and start embracing them as both transgender *and* women, or transgender women *and* my fellow Feminists. I went through that personal evolution of learning to be less of an asshole and more of a loving and inclusive person."

Years later, Sara is open about many of the issues that once plagued her: bisexuality, "assholishness," and even agoraphobia (which she refers to as "agorafabulous!"). But as a cisgender woman, who presents as extremely feminine on stage, Sara is on one side of the spectrum. On the opposite side is Riley, a transgender woman who also presents with a definite femininity. Somewhere in the middle are women like Marga Gomez, Jane Lynch, Rhea Butcher, Cameron Esposito, Tig Notaro, Rosie O'Donnell, Lily Tomlin, Janine Brito, and Paula Poundstone, who identify with the female gender they were born with, but don't necessarily present as feminine performers.

Comic Janine Brito has said that she believes Paula Poundstone to be the most underrated comedian ever, and that she credits Paula with inspiring some of her own work. "I remember watching her as a kid. Then, when I did the Great American Comedy Festival in Norfolk, Nebraska, she was the MC and the headliner, so I got to watch her live. She really does improvise everything. A lot of comics who 'riff' just sort of ask open-ended questions and have enough material that fits most people's standard answers. They put the square in the square hole," like a fortune-teller, or, as Paula has described herself, a baseball player in a batting cage. "They're, like, 'That's weird that you have that job. I used to have this job,' so that it *seems* like they're thinking on the fly, but in reality, if you know them and watch their act a few times, you're like, 'No, that's a bit that you're just delivering *as if* it's off the top of your head.' But Paula really *does* think and interact in the moment with her audience—and yet it's still tight and on point and hilarious. She a master at riff delivery . . . Me and the other comedians backstage were, like, 'How is this woman just not the most famous comedian on the planet?'"

"How *is* she not the most famous woman on the planet?" I asked.

"Because she presents *real* butch. We were essentially wearing the same outfit when we were at that show together. Like suit, tie. And she did it at a time before it was kind of cool and hipstery to do."

Paula once joked that "Joan of Arc and I actually have a lot of similarities. When she was twelve, she began to hear voices which she believed to be angels of God talking to her, telling her to crop her hair, don armor, and go into battle to restore the king of France to his proper throne. I, of course, didn't do that. But God did speak to me once, I'm pretty sure. I believe he said, you're wearing that?

"I bought a black chiffon spaghetti-strap shirt and jacket once. The salesperson told me I couldn't wear it with corduroy. There was a sense of danger in her voice. It didn't sound like merely a 'fashion don't,' but rather a word of serious caution, as though the combination of the two fabrics might result in an explosion. She repeated the warning as she bagged the garment. She was troubled by an uncanny sense that I owned a lot of corduroy. The military must have bunkers full of carefully separated corduroy and black chiffon secreted away somewhere in Nevada. It's one of those tigers we hold by the tail, like the A-bomb. I never wore the black chiffon shirt and evening jacket. Too risky. I buy impulsively sometimes, totally forgetting what I look like and how I spend my time. Amazingly, the fantasy of going out someplace kind of fancy, on a night when I wasn't wearing corduroy and had shaved, lasted long enough for that shirt and jacket to make the cut through three moves and countless closet cleanings."

I'm struck by Paula's impulse buy because, in a rare moment, it seems as if she bought something that made her either look or feel more traditionally feminine. Did this clothing cross some unseen line between fantasy and reality?

Between society's expectations of a woman and the audience's expectations of a comedian?

For this reason, Eliza Skinner "spent like a year performing as a garbage bag. I would wear layers and layers and layers of clothes and pull my hair back and just turn myself into a weird little gremlin on stage—and audiences loved me so much," she said, snapping her fingers for emphasis. "But while audiences love that, if Industry was there, they'd be, like, 'She's funny, but I can't put her in a show; she's disgusting.' So, when it was time for me to maybe try to get cast in something, to have a career beyond just the stage, I went in the other direction and tried to put myself together. To dress a little bit better. To put on makeup. To do my hair. And then audiences were like, 'Who the fuck are you?' Or, 'Are you trying to date my boyfriend?' Or, 'Would you want to go out with me?' Even while I was performing, they were a little bit on edge. They were far less comfortable, so I had to find a way of breaking that down."

Wendy Hammers, who cut her teeth in comedy in the late '80s, claimed that current comedienne-ballerinas absolutely can be pretty *and* funny. They don't have to assume the T-shirt-hoodie-jeans-thick-glasses combo unless that's truly how they feel comfortable. They can come out in stilettos and hot pants if they feel so inclined. Anything goes today, as opposed to the days of *The Tonight Show with David Letterman*, when "it used to be against the law to be pretty and funny. I used to come on stage in sexy outfits because I just liked to dress that way—I'm very girly—and the people could not hear the punch lines over the cleavage. It was *an issue*."

New York–based stand-up Bonnie McFarlane agreed. "There was a time when people didn't think being both cute and funny was possible. Now, the pendulum has swung to the other extreme, where you'd *better* be cute if you want to be a female comic. A lot of women have really played into that. They're dressing sexy or their album covers are just naked pictures. Which, okay, is a certain kind of freedom, and a certain kind of power, but I don't know if you need empowerment to be naked as a woman. I feel like people aren't going to stop you from doing that."

Have we come full circle? What is the true relationship between being pretty and being funny?

In the beginning, it's true—you couldn't be both. This is what Phyllis Diller had to deal with: *If you're pretty, you can't be funny.* If you were pretty, you were the object; if you were funny, you were the subject—the one making the jokes and taking action.

Off stage, on film, there were some exceptions to this dichotomy. Actresses in screwball comedies, like Carole Lombard and Barbara Stanwyck, were certainly funny and pretty at the same time. But overall, women were always judged by their appearance. That was the only thing that mattered at the end of the day because, according to this belief system, outward appearance was the only thing that men were going to see, and since men were making all the decisions, a woman's appearance was the deciding factor. As a result, it became the only thing that some women could see, as well. No matter how funny Lucy may have been, audiences judged her and excused her antics because she was really trying to be beautiful.

Later comedienne-ballerinas would move in the opposite direction, either hiding their attractiveness or donning a form of manliness to "trick" audiences into laughing at "non-male" comics.

When asked whether she wore boxers or briefs, Paula Poundstone responded, "What an excellent question . . . because this is really going to get us to the bottom of so much.

I wear a thick, high-waisted cottony brief that I purchase in bulk every eight to ten years at Sears. And I find that the elastic goes out at about seven years but you can still cut it and tie it and get another couple of good years out of it. It's an attractive image, isn't it? You know, I'm actually recognized when I go into Sears, because they say, 'Aren't you the girl who buys her underwear here?' and I say, 'Yes, I am.' I think they have that one rack, it's just for me."

Johnny Carson once said, "It requires a lady not being a lady for a little while to make it in show business." Perhaps the idea that comedienne-ballerinas should (or must) leave behind their femininity expands beyond comedy to succeeding in general. Maybe this explains why, in American culture today—and perhaps in other developed parts of the world—there's a growing movement away from either/or identification and toward Both. Unfortunately, in terms of beauty culture, this can sometimes translate into a newer, even more impossible standard.

The standard today, it seems, has replaced "can" with "must": Women must fulfill the ideal standards of beauty no matter what else they identify as—politician, doctor, actress, writer. It doesn't seem to matter. Everybody should be as beautiful and glamorous as a model in a magazine. And that's a whole new game that women can't possibly win. For example, acclaimed comedian, actress, and writer Laura House asked me, "How's my hair? My face?"

"Terrible," I told her.

"Oh good!" she said, expertly hiding her initial shock. "Thank you."

"Why thank me?"

"Because I feel like when people say, 'Oh, you look great!' you should never really believe them. So 'terrible' becomes either refreshingly honest or easily reversed."

"Reversed? As in reverse psychology?"

"Yes. I can say to myself, 'Oh, she probably didn't mean that!' I'm always doing reverse psychology on myself. Comedians do that all the time."

"So whether I'd said 'beautiful' or 'terrible,' you wouldn't have believed me, either way?"

"Probably. I guess everyone already *knows* what she looks like, but she asks anyway. If someone reacts with, 'Hey, it looks like three of your teeth are missing,' then you can go, 'Oh! I guess I'll go fix that!' Otherwise, it's just your normal state of affairs, you know? It's what your head looks like, so there's not a lot you can do. I didn't wear makeup when I was younger, and I would say this to people as a child: 'If you're pretty, you're already pretty, and if you're ugly . . . makeup is not going to help.'" Then she laughed at her own joke, realizing. "What an asshole I am!"

I laughed too. I couldn't help it. Laura was (and is) the exact opposite of an asshole. But her comment about beauty was so painfully true that it became funny, which immediately made me wonder: is this correlation or causation? If it's true that a ballerina's body shows what's right with the world, while a comedian's voice shows what's wrong, how does a performer who embodies both *do* both? How can she best use those burdens?

Susan Rice answered by veering from beauty into size:

"I learned a long time ago that if you want to have anything to say you have to get the painful crap out of the way first. And that's basically what I do as soon as I go on stage: acknowledge it. I try to take a dump, *really loud*. That's what every fat person does. We get on stage and we go, 'Here's the obvious, folks! Now, here's a joke. And here's another joke. And here's another joke. Now let's move on, okay?'"

Gilda wrote that she'd once been scapegoated because of her weight. She didn't have any friends. As a child, her parents sent her to summer camp every year, where the other girls "wouldn't let me play with them. In 'the princess game' there would be controlling girls and pretty girls. The controlling girls would make a pretty girl the princess and the controlling girls would be advisors to the princess. The fat girl would be the servant or something, and that would be me. At night, I'd be in my bunk sneak-eating Tootsie Roll Pops and pistachio nuts that my mom had sent me and thinking about how to belong. I couldn't be as pretty as the pretty girls and I couldn't be as controlling as the controlling girls. It wasn't in me." Her babysitter, Dibby, tried to save her from this by telling her to "say you're fat before they can. Make a joke about it and laugh. Let them know that you are fat and *you don't care*." This idea coached Gilda through her teens, when humor became her tool for handling life: *I'm going to keep talking anyway.*

Today, we see the same attitudes in supposedly "women's places," which are, in reality, extremely anti-women. Women's magazines routinely feature images of women that have been, according to LA-based stand-up Virginia Jones, "so overzealously Photoshopped that they look like smooth rubber masks stretched over an armature. It's that rich Uncanny Valley flavor!" And she's right—it is uncannily true that women's magazines are always the worst for telling women what to do, and for helping us to develop terrible body dysmorphia and eating disorders.

But here's the thing: We help them destroy us. Women still write those magazines. Women still make their living selling fear and insecurity and self-loathing to other women. And most of them go through life wondering why bad things happen without ever holding themselves accountable as part of the problem. Until comedienne-ballerinas started calling people out for systematically categorizing and then either benefiting from or discriminating against individuals based solely on their physical appearance, there seemed to be a sort of obliviousness to this widespread practice, which I refer to as "Lookism."

Up until recently, comedians have failed to publicly acknowledge the many callous ways that our culture has used Lookism—one of which being our insistence that girth is diametrically opposed to attractiveness (meaning, more specifically, that one is mutually exclusive of the other). Because comedians failed to acknowledge this opposition, no one was poking fun in order to stop it. In fact, many comedians still very much considered this opposition to be true: fat women could, perhaps, be funny but never sexy. That older women, and especially mothers, could never be whores (I guess their children were the presumed fruits of immaculate conception?). That women of color could only be either lusted after or laughed at, but never taken seriously.

All of this began to change with the self-proclaimed Red Hot Mamas—Sophie Tucker, Belle Barth, and Pearl Williams—who fought ardently against their era's strain of mental illness by suffering no fools, brooking no dissatisfaction, and not allowing themselves to be dismissed as "too big and ugly" to sing about sex.

Choosing to fight the negative effects of Lookism by putting size at the front and center of comedy was Sophie Tucker's favorite tactic. Instead of making herself the butt of her own joke or pretending she didn't care about the audience's jeers, she commanded an entire attitude readjustment. Her looks

were specifically aimed at getting both men and women to recognize the sexual needs of the overweight, and Sophie went out
of her way to make it clear that her huge bulk corresponded
with a huge sexual appetite. Her overtly sexual, risqué, and
equally hilarious song routines *demanded* that her audience
recalibrate its expectations for how funny "should" look.
This was during the 1930s and 1940s, when beauty ideals and
women's magazines were focused on slimness and perfection,
as detailed by *Seventeen*'s 1948 story, "The Fattest Girl in the
Class," in which a young girl struggles for male attention.

Sophie refused to be ashamed of her two-hundred-pound
figure. She belted songs like "I Don't Want to Get Thin," and
the loudly tongue-in-cheek, "Nobody Loves a Fat Girl," featuring lyrics that insisted "a fat woman is a better lover, has
more to give, and requires more than thinner women." Amy
Schumer hardly invented the idea of telling her audience, "I'm
about 160 [pounds] right now, and I can catch a dick whenever I want." The Mamas were doing this long before her, and
they created the air space for her to follow.

To Amy's credit, however, she and other comedians today
are taking this celebration of the body, this idea of owning
yourself no matter what size you are, to the next level by refus-
ing to pretend that women should be grateful for men finding
them attractive. As opposed to the Mamas, who insisted that
men *include* them in their fantasies, today's comedienne-ballerinas seem to be saying *I couldn't care less whether you include
me at all.*

Lisa Lampanelli, Lena Dunham, Amy Schumer, Lindy
West, Bri Pruett, and Bridget Everett (to name only a meager
few) all refuse to dismiss their size, to hide behind it, or to
make excuses. Their bold-faced demand has caused contro-
versy for television viewers who still adhere to beauty culture's

motto: *Thin is in.* But that's slowly changing, especially with the influence of transgender performers and comedians of color, whose body types have inspired modern notions of what constitutes "beautiful." This new era of altered thinking, this shift in women's mindsets, is exciting and represents a new step for liberating our subconscious bias against women who live outside of the traditionally thin, white, petite, feminine beauty paradigm.

This is not to say that these comedians have completely escaped all aspects of Lookism. In Schumer's sketch, "Twelve Angry Men Inside Amy Schumer," for example, the baseline assumption underlying the debate over whether she's hot enough to be on TV rests on whether she even cares what these twelve men think at all. Still, she and others have created work that moves farther away from the notion of caring than we've ever been before—and they've taken up the Mamas' mantle. Whereas Sophie, Belle, and Pearl demanded men's approval, today's comedienne-ballerinas know better than to waste time seeking permission, for you'll never get it. Both were and are revolutionary for their respective eras.

Can we ever stop participating in Lookism? Can we just . . . stop playing the game? Or refuse to engage? Comedian Bri Pruett thinks this refusal is unlikely to ever occur because "if you're getting up in front of people and telling jokes, you're already in it. You're participating in a medium where there's a male gaze."

I asked her, "Is there a female gaze?"

"I think the female gaze is adopting the male gaze—even when it's done by an all-female audience. The audience members reflect everything they've watched back onto us, just like we say everything we've heard back to them. It's a conversation. Even with a female comedian and an all-female audience, we're all still trying to escape . . . and we're trying to do it together . . . but we don't even realize we're trying."

"So are we using our appearance as a prop?"

Angelina Spicer answered that: "You have to. That's what people see. You can't ignore it; you can't deny what people see. It's very much a part of the comedy. If you don't address what people see, your first three minutes will be crickets because people are trying to figure out what this is . . . I'm less bothered by it because I feel like it's a part of my job. To just accept it and to make it work. I feel like CEOs of corporations and people who work in corporate America don't like certain aspects of their job, and they just deal with it. Because they like what they do, or it's a means to an end. If it's something you enjoy doing, something you're passionate about it's just like, 'OK, I dislike this part of it, but there's so much more to it that gives me gratification and a sense of purpose that, whatever, I'll just deal with it for now.'"

"How long is the 'now' in 'for now'? We've been waiting for gender equality since the beginning of time," I said.

"But we're getting there. It's evolved. And I feel like women have been getting many, many more opportunities to create, to write, to bring our voices to the forefront. I feel like once the perspective changes that the dialogue will change. I don't feel like the 'now' is forever, because we're not dealing with the same gender issues that Lucy and Moms Mabley were dealing with. They've transformed."

But just because the surfaces of a problem have changed doesn't mean that the problem itself has changed. To look at a thing is not necessarily to see it. Certainly, over time, the prices that women have seen fit to pay may have changed, but the menu of limited choices paired with maximized expectations has stayed the same. And although gender inequality's various symptoms, including Lookism's double-edged sword, fluctuate wildly across generations, its essential, underlying causes remain as they were. This particular "ism" (like all other "isms") is resilient, and thus its effects are as keenly felt today as they were for Lucy and Phyllis and Moms and every other comedienne-ballerina. Outside of the obvious body shaming, Lookism has changed shape, making it slightly less recognizable, but the fact that we can't spot it as easily makes it even more dangerous. We are no more separate from the past than we are separate from each other. Right now, in this very moment, we are linked together by shared experience that, while different in many details, nonetheless remains human.

Subconscious, hidden, and thinly veiled in the form of everything from EmpowerMint Ben & Jerry's ice cream to Dove soap's "love the skin you're in" commercials (but, of course, make sure it's supple and soft and beautiful at all times), Lookism is a powerful tool of Patriarchy and is extremely effective at undermining our self-confidence. We must work harder than we used to, in many ways, to recognize these systems of oppression and prevent ourselves from internalizing them. Women who don't learn how to ignore, block, or unlearn these messages end up being very mean to themselves and even meaner to other women.

As LA-based stand-up and comedy writer Laura House said of fellow comedienne-ballerina Kira Soltanovich, "I was so dismissive in my head. 'Oh, she's probably just a pretty girl.' But she's *so funny*. And when I heard her, and I saw her, I apologized. I actually had to say . . . well, I didn't have to, but I *chose* to say, 'You don't know me well, but you're so funny, and I just assumed you were too pretty to be funny.' Isn't that awful?"

It is, and yet it isn't. Laura is a kind, loving person, who would never act intentionally Lookist. But the issue is one of our collective unintentionality. Our nonobvious reactions. Our unconscious behavior, programming, and default settings. Being injected with all this isn't in any way Laura's fault, but it is our problem, as a whole, to recognize and fix by raising our expectations, opening our eyes, and learning to see that sameness over separateness is one of our most powerful tools.

All of this circles back to Lucy.

Life magazine published their issue on Lucy the same week that the episode "The Ballet" premiered. Their article was entitled "Beauty Into Buffoon." Its cover featured a glamour shot of Lucy alongside pictures of her wearing a few crazy get-ups, all clearly intended to communicate the message: *Here's someone who is so beautiful, who was a Ziegfeld girl, who could fulfill the standards of beauty as defined by Hollywood, but who also chooses to put on crazy wigs and horrible outfits and act in all these crazy ways. To participate in beauty culture, which is both feminine and glamorous, and yet to be a buffoon for the laughs.* The article doesn't obviously point out this mixed message, but it certainly conveys the curiosity of Lookism: even Lucy, as powerful and as successful as she was, still metaphorically broke herself in half, assuming two seemingly different Lucys who were expected to play two very different roles. While many claim this was Lucy's conscious choice, I wonder if it might have had much more to do with her unconscious behavior in response to a lack of true choice.

To this conversation, Wendy Hammers added that her own personal heroes, like Lily Tomlin, reinvented themselves within the confines of Lookism, in an attempt to twist the mirror, if not to breaking, then at least to a different angle. "She just did her own thing. And Bette Midler, who really was just Sophie Tucker and Belle Barth, she was brash and she was outspoken and she was saying, 'I am who I am. I look how I look.' The old saying, 'I am woman, hear me roar?' Hers because, 'I am woman, hear me joke.' And we still have a right to do that!"

"'I am woman, hear me joke.' That's great!" I said.

"It is, isn't it? And also: 'Hear me joke, and know that I have an opinion.' Because stand-up is showing others how to see through your eyes. You know when you can't remember the words to a song and you say, 'This is how it goes,' and then you hum a few bars? Stand-up is just like that. We get up there and we say, 'This is how it goes. This is how I see the world.'"

And yet, as Judy Carter aptly pointed out, part of the duality of being a comedienne-ballerina is pursuing Both-ness: Light/Dark. Man/Woman. Seeing/Listening. Truth/Character. Singing/Speaking. Showing what's wrong with the outside world/showing what's right within. Reaching for and grasping two seemingly conflicting goals, all to trick the audience into love *and* laughter.

Being a comedian is, at its core, *needing*. Desiring to be vulnerable in front of someone to be loved in return. That's what it really comes down to when you're on stage. When you're showing your worst side, whether you realize it or not, you still want the audience to love and agree with you—and yet laugh at you. That's the duality within every comedienne-ballerina: wanting perfect strangers to show up so they can laugh at you, and through laughing at you, affirm that they love you more than anyone else in the room.

Yet we have to start from a place where women are "allowed" to be funny—and not just funny, but both pretty *and* funny—in order for anything to be funny.

"Absolutely," Wendy says. "Because when you're on stage it's you and the audience . . . it's a partnership . . . But if you're too far ahead of your audience, you're not going to be able to keep going down that track. You got to kind of pull 'em. They can't be so far away that you can't reach and pull them along with you. They have to be within reach so you can be like, 'Come on. Come this way. Let's go.'"

In "The Ballet," when Lucy begs Ricky to let her into the show, Fred points out that she does have "nice stems," and, like a "cool girl," Lucy expresses appreciation for this unsolicited male opinion about her body and says, "Thank you." Despite this moment of temporary insanity, Fred's actions and Lucy's reaction represent a kind of Lookism that resounded through the echo chamber of the mid-twentieth century. Two generations later, Joan Rivers's last interview with Howard Stern carried her era's coming of age into the present.

According to Emily Nussbaum, writing for *The New Yorker*, Rivers asked Stern, "'Lena Dunham. Who I think is, again, terrific. How can she wear dresses above the knee?' Stern said that what he loved about Dunham was that 'she doesn't give a shit.' 'Oh, she has to,' Rivers insisted. 'Every woman gives a shit.' When Stern and his cohost described funny scenes from 'Girls' of Dunham in a bikini, Rivers nearly sputtered: 'But that's wrong! You're sending a message out to people saying, 'It's OK, stay fat, get diabetes, everybody die, lose your fingers.' In a passionate rasp, she made her case. Dunham was a hypocrite for doing *Vogue*, she said, because it showed that she cared about being pretty. Stern was another hypocrite, for his 'tits and ass' jokes, for his hot second wife—would he have married Dunham? Stern said that he thought Rivers would 'rejoice' in the younger woman's freedom. 'But don't make yourself, physically—don't let them laugh at you physically,' Rivers pleaded, sounding adrift. 'Don't say it's OK that other girls can look like this. Try to look better!'"

Comedian Eliza Skinner, who once worked for Joan Rivers, added that, in her experience, Joan's generation had so adopted the male gaze that few, if any, other women could measure up. "I was the only woman who worked for her, who wrote for her, and who lasted on her staff. I saw her fire other women who were *so* funny, and we would try to figure out why. Maybe this is crazy thinking, but I think it came down to whether or not she liked their reflection. All the women who got fired reflected something she didn't like, that made her think, 'That's not what a female comic looks like. That's not how a female comic acts.' So I really made sure I always dressed well and wore something interesting and that I was polite and on time—along with, of course, writing good jokes. She didn't like it if you were too crass. She didn't like it if you were sexual. She especially didn't like it if you were sloppy. I would really try to stay on my toes to continue reflecting what Joan wanted to see, and how Joan thought a female comic should look just so I could keep my job. She didn't have protégés. There are people that probably think, 'Oh, she's a Joan Rivers protégé.' No, I'm not. She didn't like anybody. She had bad things to say about *a lot* of people because she had gotten knocked around a lot, and yet she'd kicked open doors for the same people she didn't like. So yeah, she was a bag of knives. But that's not a secret. That's clearly why audiences loved her."

According to Nussbaum, Joan's act "was like a person trapped in a prison, shouting out escape routes from her cell." It's indeed true that Joan's obvious self-loathing bleeds into her body-shaming assessment of first Elizabeth Taylor and then everyone from Christie Brinkley to Madonna to Jane Fonda to Fourth Wave exhibitionist Feminist Lena Dunham. But for all of Joan's sound and fury, she signifies nothing of her subjects and much of herself. Her insisting that Howard Stern would never want to marry Dunham because of her weight seems naive in the face of Dunham's sex- and body-positive Feminism, and for that matter, as Nussbaum rightly asked, why would *she* want to marry *him*? Joan's presuming that Stern's wishes would dictate Dunham's marital options reveals much more about the prisons of the mind in which many women of Joan's era found themselves. The bars, it seems, were sometimes of their own making.

For Joan, the rule was that looks mattered, first and foremost. This rule constrained her entire life, and her comedy seemed to rail against its harmful double standard, and yet in the end, she (like Lucy and Maddy and many others) didn't know any better than how she'd been raised. But why? In her earliest years, Joan didn't take potshots at real women, only imaginary "sluts" like her fictional character Heidi Abromowitz and abstract rivals, who, as Nussbaum wrote, resemble "airline stewardesses who . . . cater only to men."

At some point, it seems, Joan found that punching down—or sideways, really—at other women was profitable, even if, ultimately, her entire gender would also pay the costs. Sadly, perhaps the best analogy here is that she began punching *herself* for the sake of fame. Once she'd started down that road, there was really no going back. Later, when she tried to cut out the punching, the audience got mad at her.

In her 1991 memoir, *Still Talking*, she claimed that these jokes were a form of catharsis, that she was mocking celebrities rather than women as a whole, and that the ultimate point was to educate her audience about the "dangers" of investing in inner beauty. But her own words reveal the sad depth of the Stella Syndrome's hold over Joan, who (like many of her generation) found herself caught between following and flouting Lookism's rules: "If Blanche DuBois took stock and said, 'This is where it's at, and I'm going to get rid of these schmatte clothes and get me a nice pants suit, and look smart here, with a pocketbook and a hat'—she would have been all right."

Is buying into beauty culture just like getting a seat at the table or joining the boys' club? Is it a form of protection from Patriarchy? From Male Supremacy? Does beauty actually *help* a comedienne-ballerina (or any woman, really) to feel any safer, happier, or—perhaps most importantly—free?

Since Lucy's and Joan's time, yet another wave of back-lash to our progressive fight against Lookism has rolled in, spearheaded by those whom it most clearly benefits: attractive women. I find this new phenomenon increasingly curi-ous. Much like the strange feeling of disorientation Feminists encounter whenever we see white, cisgender, heterosexual men argue against Patriarchy (much to their credit—you'll get no arguments from me about that), it seems that in the 2010s, beauty culture had begun to eat its own. A lot of really nice-looking, fit girls began talking about how "gross" and/ or "fat" they were. When viewed in terms of the reverse-psy-chological effect that can occur whenever an attractive woman hears the word "terrible" in response to "how do I look?" that Laura House mentioned, I can understand that some inter-nal revisionism may be at work. In a way, perhaps inside our minds, we're justifying our own self-loathing by responding with, "Oh, I'll bet she didn't really mean that!"

There's been some doubt as to how well this reverse psychol-ogy works on others once it's left our own inner monologue— and it doesn't seem to work particularly well on coed audi-ences—but this equal and opposite reaction only proves that Patriarchy's symptomology is rising to an unexpected surface. Until now, many of us have assumed that only women who fell outside "classic" or "traditional" beauty norms felt like shit. Apparently the disease of Patriarchy is more contagious than we originally thought, and now we *all* feel like shit. Maybe we're all a little bit sick in this respect—even (maybe especially) the ones who seem to be benefiting most from their sickness: the skinniest, prettiest, straightest, cisgender-est, whitest, and/or wealthiest ones of us. These are, increasingly, the poster children for Lookism. These are the women who seem to be the most truly worried about either becoming or staying beautiful. They are, for the most part, already beautiful. The rest of us are busy eating our Big Macs, drinking our full-calorie margaritas, and taking naps. We don't own much makeup. We think Spanx are a waste of money. We prefer flat ballet shoes. We're content with being largely ignored by DudeBros. We would make the best NPR hosts (outside of Terri Gross and Diane Rehm).

As some of my conversations revealed, these victims of their own prettiness are not only tormented by maintaining said prettiness but also routinely manipulated by those seeking to exploit it. Some only pretend to be interested in victims' comedy in order to use them for sex. Others presume that they have little to offer other than their attractiveness. Even those who aren't victims of their own prettiness at all—who aren't tormented by keeping track of what they see in the mirror, but who just happen to have hit the biological jackpot—still suffer for what they can't control, forced to waste time convincing both men and women alike to take them seriously beyond their surface.

Janet Varney is one of these lucky jackpot winners who, during our conversation at iO West, seemed totally free of Lookism. She only wishes that (1) she didn't have to give a shit about being judged as either pretty or funny anymore, and that (2) we'd all stop mistaking attractiveness for actual accomplishment. "People ask, 'How did you get to be so funny?' as if being funny is only something you do as a backup to being pretty," she said. "As an actress, it's hard to read a role that's described as a 'funny woman,' and then she turns out to simply be supporting a funny man. I get that network television is reflective of society . . . but shouldn't it reflect *actual* society?"

Co-creator of *The Daily Show* Lizz Winstead added that "people look at 'classically attractive, beautiful' people as people of privilege, and so I think they do make an assumption about them, like, 'Oh really? Are you going to give me some observations about how life works? Am I supposed to go along with your self-deprecating, "I am just fucking too much, and I can't find enough time to go shopping!" routine of what it must be like to have "attractive person" problems?'"

Angelina Spicer added that "pretty women"—she placed the words firmly into air quotes—are doubly burdened, and must often choose whether to be either pretty or funny, since they can't truly be both. For Angelina, this choice is often determined by who's in the room. Since women are already plagued with the presumption that they're not funny, anyway, "if you throw in a good set of boobs, a flattish stomach, and a perky ass, you are *losing*. You walk into a comedy club, or you try to get into a sketch thing, and you look halfway decent? Honey, your work is cut out for you. So, as one of these women, I downplay. It's sort of like how my mom taught me: You're one way when you're free, or at home, or in your comfort zone . . . and then another way when you are out in the world. When I'm auditioning in front of a bunch of men who need a sexy girl, I play that up. But if I'm in a room full of women, and I know that they're not interested in that, I can *really* bring it."

"Do you feel like you bring it less for the men in the room?" I asked. "Or for those who might want a sexy girl for a role?"

"Absolutely not. It's just a different set of characters and energy that you bring when you're auditioning for a room full of women versus a room full of men. I think that it's important in a room full of men to play to the pretty for a short period of time, but then strip all that away and show, 'Listen, I'm so much more than that, and I'm fearless. I don't have to *rely* on this. This is fluff. This is to make you feel good. But, trust me, there's way more to this than that.'"

"Will we ever get to the point where we don't have to do that?"

"No. In this business, I don't think we'll ever get to a point where looks don't matter. It's too much a part of what people want to see on TV and in films. Lucy led with her looks, I think . . .

"I wonder if things will change. I know the *Broad City* girls, on Comedy Central, are making huge headways for women who are just funny. Who don't play up their looks or hyper-sexualize anything . . . I just know how I feel when I go into these rooms. But I also know also that when I do stand-up, I also have to pull back on the sexy."

"Is it because of the women in the room?"

"Yeah. It *is* because of the women in the room. They're just not on your side immediately. They're kind of distracted. I don't think that they're judgy necessarily, but they've kind of . . . when you go in front of an audience, I think they kind of believe the hype of women not being funny. And then you throw on a flashy outfit and six-inch stilettos and boobs, and it's going to take them a minute or two to get on board. And you *have* to be self-deprecating. Your work is so much more cut out for you if you go up there confident. You have to be nice to them in that way—make them feel like they're better than you so they'll believe what you're trying to get your comedy to really *say.*"

For white male–dominated culture, "beautiful" has long been defined as whatever appears the frailest, weakest, and generally least threatening to "masculinity," which has long been defined as Male Supremacy over everything "female," which has long been defined as legal, financial, physical, intellectual, and emotional inferiority. These definitions were so prevalent that First Wave Feminists even had to combat the widespread belief that women had smaller brains based on their gender alone. Still, there are many equally ridiculous beliefs we cling to today. Male Supremacy has convinced white women, for example, that thin equals healthy and/or feminine and big equals unhealthy and/or masculine. Male Supremacy has convinced nonwhite women that gigantic curves and tiny waists are the ultimate symbols of fertility (the only true purpose a woman's body serves). Both have, together, convinced women that the only reason any man would ever approve, have use of, or take any interest in her is to promote his dominance. Thus, the only reason she exists is to affirm it. To appeal to him sexually. To serve his reproductive purposes. To obtain his permission to exist.

This is all especially true while we are young.

When we are young, we are such strangers to ourselves. We think that the only reason anyone likes us (or would ever like us) is because we're beautiful. Or we think that the only reason life sucks is because we're not. We have to go out into the world and react to it before we can even begin to discover who we are or what we want. If we make it through this time alive, instead of looking afresh and for ourselves, we hold our bodies up to the light, checking for cracks along our surfaces. Instead of congratulating each other and reveling in our survival, we train our eyes and minds to *care what they think*. For some comedienne-ballerinas, this push-pull between survival and emancipation translates into inspiration. Ask Naomi Ekperigin. Ask Gilda. Ask anyone—she'll tell you what Judy Carter told me: "I've spent the last twenty-five years of my life trying to get over the *first* twenty-five years of my life."

Gilda sang about all of this during her *Gilda Live* performance as the leader of an all-girl group named Rhonda and the Rhondettes. Their biggest hit was entitled "Goodbye, Saccharin!"

"Tonight I would like to sing a song with a very socially relevant message," she tells the audience. "I know I speak not only for myself but also for my closest personal friends in the entire world, The Rhondettes. Up until now, I never really felt the need to protest. I mean nothing in the '60s really bothered me. None of the guys I knew went to Vietnam; they went to law school. And, um, actually I've always found protests kind of pushy and whiny . . . until recently I read in *The National Enquirer* that the FDA was considering banning saccharin from the market. I nearly died." She then insists that it's un-American to turn her favorite dessert, Mocha Frost Dream, into something that contains 810 calories per serving. "I'm sorry about lab animals, but statistics prove that most guys prefer skinny girls with cancer over healthy girls with bulging thighs."

When the music starts, Gilda croons a sexy love song to her favorite sweetener. As the music continues, Rhonda and Rhondette #1 have a spoken interlude, where #1 keeps passive-aggressively pushing Rhonda to reveal her *true* weight until finally, at the end of her rope, Rhonda calls #1 a "bitch!"

Only a year after this performance, America entered the 1980s, stifling much of this comedic honesty and forcing us all to, once again, remain as sick as our secrets. Susan Rice commented that being pretty today doesn't bear the stigma that it did during that decade.

"It used to be really hard for really pretty women to be stand-up comics and not to be booked *because* they were pretty and they might put out," she said. "I had so many very funny friends that really were fearful on the road. And kept having to re-prove themselves, and re-prove themselves, and re-prove themselves. It was hard for them to find a place to be *both*." Perhaps she's right. These chauvinist suggestions have been happening for decades and continue to happen, even today.

From 1950 to 1954, another famous Second Wave comedienne-ballerina, Imogene Coca, faced the same ridiculously one-sided scrutiny—only she and Sid Caesar used their national platform to put this kind of hypocritical treatment of women on full blast. According to the *New York Times*, in one sketch from *Your Show of Shows*, Imogene played a wife "posing for her amateur photographer husband, who could not quite satisfy himself about her face. Poking here, pushing there, he kept rearranging her features, which froze where he put them. Finally, he got it right: her left eye shut in a grotesque wink, the right following him around the room like a searchlight," metaphorically revealing the true purpose behind beauty culture's scrutiny: to focus women's vision solely on and around men.

By 1975, Gilda Radner faced the same challenge: how to appear funny enough for audiences to both love and laugh at. Modern-day comedienne-ballerina Sara Benincasa, who shares Gilda's "fuzzy hair"—which, as she put it when we sat down to talk, "I have attempted to beat into submission today with limited success"—empathized with both Imogene's and Gilda's struggle to change—or rearrange—themselves into the preapproved image of comedy. In Sara's opinion, "women with fuzzy hair are regarded as wacky and suspect, whereas a woman with hair that is under control, in some fashion, is regarded as sophisticated and having it all together."

"It's important that women have it all together?" I asked.

"Women *must* always have it together, because women are so often branded as 'crazy.'"

"What does 'crazy' mean?"

"'Crazy' usually just means 'acting in a different way than a man in the same situation might.' It's very important that men regard women as rational and reasonable—which, of course, they interpret through their *own* lenses of 'rationality' and 'reasonableness.' So before I came to do this interview, I strapped my hair under control, I got my makeup done, I got it together."

"Was that very important to you?"

"*Very* important."

"Did you think I was going to think you were 'crazy' if you had fuzzy hair and no makeup?"

"I thought about what it would look like if a woman showed up to talk about 'female comedians,' or about Gilda Radner, or about comedy in general . . . and didn't look nice."

"What would be the reaction there?"

"It would not be good. It would make people think that women who do comedy don't look nice. This is, of course, the crazy, narcissistic, psychological thing that's happening in my head—and I call it 'crazy' not because it's different from how a man would think, even though it is, but because it's ridiculous to me that I even think this way."

Like Laura House's comments on her own reverse psychology, Sara's painful honesty made me love her even more. She's both right and wrong. It both is, and isn't, ridiculous. Few of us mind thinking about ourselves at length. Thinking we're "crazy" for doing so may be another story. "I, I, I all the time

. . ." as timelessly brilliant Feminist author Fay Weldon once put it. "Mother always said never to begin a sentence with 'I.' In the end, that's quite true." But in my opinion, "I" stories are some of the best. They're also usually the ones we could be disowned for telling.

Molly Shannon says that doing character-based comedy frees her from "I" stories and caring how either "crazy" or "together" she might look: "I just don't think about what I look like. I don't give a shit. I don't care what my body looks like. I just want to *be* the character."

I'd always assumed that, because they speak directly as themselves as opposed to speaking as characters, many stand-up comics don't enjoy that same freedom. Paula Poundstone, for example, claimed she dyed her hair because HBO wanted her to. Steve Martin, on the other hand, says that comedy isn't pretty (we should therefore assume that no one's asked *him* to dye *his* hair for a comedy special). But over time, it seems, comedians are getting better looking—either because they're allowed to be or because they *have* to be. This appears to be the real conversation for today's comedienne-ballerinas.

"It bothers me," Laura House said of this trend toward better-looking comedians. "And models are getting smarter. Like, wha . . . ? I always felt like you had to choose, when you were little. But maybe you just have a way of being that suits you. I feel funniest when I'm the buddy or the friend—when it's not about my looks."

Laura's hardly alone in this. Many comics who happen to be female simply don't feel comfortable appearing on stage in anything that might emphasize their femininity. Wearing a skirt on stage runs the risk of treating the first few rows to an extra show. This possibility makes some women feel vulnerable. For women who aren't accustomed to wearing uber-feminine garb, attempting to do so can be draining. In one of her first tele-vised specials, Laura was transformed from her usual T-shirt-and-jeans self into a glamorous vision in heels, makeup, and wearing her usually cropped hair in long, wavy curls. As a result, she said, she performed badly. It just freaked her out too much, seeing herself in the mirror right before going on stage. It made her feel less in control—less commanding, perhaps—and certainly less confident . . . which is so odd, considering our entire society is geared toward insisting that women feel confident when they feel beautiful.

Maybe this doesn't work for all women. Maybe some need to feel less beautiful to feel more powerful. Or perhaps beauty is tied to femininity, which is tied to weakness, which is appar-ently the opposite of what an audience wants from whoev-er's standing on stage. Certainly, few of us have ever paid to attend a show where we, and not the performer, are creating entertainment. We walk into the room expecting to be led into laughing. Whereas in Chaplin's day, all that comedy may have needed was a pretty girl to play the object of a funny man's affections, women have *become* the funny ones. In so doing, we've also inherited comedy's presumption of masculinity. We've taken on the audience's expectation of strength, includ-ing the idea that the only kind of woman you should *ever* be is a strong one. What if this either/or exists only for the skinniest, prettiest, straightest, cisgender-est, whitest, and/or wealthiest comedienne-ballerinas?

looking and seeing

A s a cisgender, white, and truly beautiful woman, Portland-based stand-up Bri Pruett may initially seem to fall into some of these aforementioned categories, yet she now occasionally dresses as a man on stage, a persona she calls Bro. She does so not as an essential part of her gender identity but as a way to explore new material and connect with her audience as a man rather than as a woman.

According to Bri, her audiences "want me to be bulletproof. I feel like they want me to be really strong . . . but I think sometimes I'll do a set where it's, you know, there's a little bit more vulnerability, a little bit more insecurity and the right audience can get behind that. But if I'm at a club, someplace where there's going to be a lot of different experiences, I do just want to be just one note: strong. And whatever message I have for them it's going to be from a place of a lot of strength."

"When you perform, are you invulnerable? All-powerful?" I asked.

"I *pretend* to be, yes."

Bri wasn't sure how to prepare for her first night as Bro. She didn't exactly know what to expect, but with a theater background, she wanted to go for it—and she was excited about an experience that would likely challenge her beliefs about the relationship between outward appearance and inner confidence. Still, the practical implications of convincingly taking on the appearance of a man for an entire audience, a room full of people with their eyes trained on her every move and their ears listening to her every inflection, became problematic. "I had this experience of trying to find a pair of men's slacks to fit over my gigantic caboose, which is really hard . . . Before I began shopping, I thought, 'Oh my God, I'm going to be so relieved when I'm up there! I'm going to be so free of all the Patriarchal expectations of what I should look like and blah, blah, blah.' But when I put on those boy's clothes, I was just as insecure as I'd been dressed as a girl. I looked at myself and thought, 'Oh, I'm just some fat, soft bro,' when I thought I was going to be this cute, hunky boy. I was still plagued with the *exact* same insecurities! In fact, someone told me, 'You look just like Kevin Smith,' and I was like goddammit! I'm not going for fucking Kevin Smith! And when I got on stage, I immediately realized that the audience also read me that way: as a soft, nerdy boy. So when I told my regular jokes about women's bodies, only as Bro Pruett instead of Bri, I asked them, 'Oh women's bodies, why do we got to shame women's bodies?' And I got a totally different response this time. Now, I was coming from a place of authority in their eyes. Instead of being just another woman complaining about men objectifying her, I was a *man* pointing out how unfair this is—and somehow the audience was much more willing to go along with me, in a new direction."

The newfound sense of authority inspired Bri to explore more jokes and different topics with a sense of freedom. Even though Bro may not have relieved Bri of *all* her physical insecurities, he did give her an entirely different kind of security on stage.

"I wrote this joke about how men keep their sexual relationships with big women secret—especially from their other male friends. It's usually a masculinity performance. So when I dress in drag, and I'm talking about that as a man, it feels like I'm telling the other men, 'You can be free!' But when I tell that joke as a woman, it's sort of shedding a light into a lot of women's real-life experiences, so it just feels very personal and very serious instead of funny and liberating. It's fascinating. As a man, I was like, 'Break the shackles! You're free! You can date whomever you want! *You can sleep with whomever you want*!' And while I didn't talk to any of the audience members, their reaction was definitely like, 'Whoo! Yeah!' I'd never gotten that reaction when telling that same joke as a woman—in fact, the women in the audience didn't laugh *unless* I was telling it in drag."

Bri wasn't sure if this happened because she was dressed as a man or because her appearance of masculinity served as some sort of silent cue. Her costume must have worked, because few (if any) of her audience members guessed her true gender. Instead, they saw and heard her only as Bro. Bri feels that this allowed the women in her audience to get behind her other jokes, too. It was as if her appearance somehow gave these women permission to become objects. Bro made them feel psychologically comfortable with this objectification, and they allowed him to speak to and about them in ways that they might have rejected, coming from Bri. "When I was Bri, it felt as if they didn't want to laugh because that might make them appear to be complicit in keeping someone else's secret or agreeing to be a part of someone else's dirty laundry," she said. "But as Bro, they laughed just as hard as the guys. It was eye-opening."

Keeping a secret—yours or anyone else's—has long been the tie binding cisgender and transgender women together. "It turns out that one of the least attractive things in terms of attracting women is being a guy who's clearly hiding something," comic Riley Silverman said of dating during her pretransition days. "The thing is, when you're in your twenties, and you're obviously very uptight about something, most women aren't going to go, 'Well, I'll bet he's actually a woman.' No. They're thinking, 'I'll bet he's got a basement somewhere that I don't want to find out about.' And that was before *50 Shades of Grey* made having a 'Red Room of Pain' a cool, cutesy thing. Back then, it was just plain old terrifying."

Riley spent many of her younger years looking the exact opposite of who she was. Her eventual transition involved changing her appearance from traditionally masculine to more traditionally feminine. She got new clothes. She wore shorter skirts. She invested in more makeup and grew her hair out and chose a new pair of glasses from the women's side of the optometrist's selection. She wore gowns to public events and even attended the premiere of *The Danish Girl* in a lovely calf-length tulle and chiffon cocktail dress, posing alongside Rachel Bloom from *My Crazy Ex-Girlfriend*.

"I've found that the element I have most in common with other girl comics is the idea that you have to prove yourself more to the audience from the very beginning than a male comic does," she said, echoing Susan Rice's exact sentiment from the 1980s. "When audiences see most straight, male comics, who look how I used to look—jeans and T-shirts, hoodies, and thick glasses—there's a default approval. They subconsciously say, 'This is the preapproved image of comedy, so we know this guy's going to be funny because he *looks* like a comic.' Whereas people don't really ever think that a girl looks like a comic unless she *also* has on a hoodie, T-shirt, jeans, and thick glasses. They won't laugh unless we can trick them into thinking we're men."

The burden of keeping secrets has weighed down every artist since Oscar Wilde, but one of the most touching stories of the sometimes equally devastating effect of revealing them belongs to Marga Gomez. Over the past three decades, Marga has come to be known as a phenomenal stand-up and solo performance artist who was also one of the first openly lesbian performers in the nation, not to mention a member of the Latinx community.

"There was this thing when I was growing up—and I'm not quite sure it still applies because I think people are more hip to it now—but back then, no one knew about lesbians, so girls could do anything, and people would react with, 'Oh, they're just *girls*! They're naked and playing with each other's titties, but they're just experimenting with how to please a man!'"

In Marga's house, growing up, her room had a single bed. Her girlfriend at that time, whom she describes as a "taller Joni Mitchell," would come and stay with her during the summer, and they would sleep together in that same bed. They would get stoned, apparently, and engage in a lot of 69s because "it was very equal and Feminist and just—and very politically correct," Marga said. Her father, also a comedian, would come home around four thirty a.m., right around the time that Marga herself was also coming. One night, Marga and "Joni" were being exceptionally loud. The next morning, he was angry—scary angry. He suddenly knew. Marga's parents had been divorced for six years and had never spoken until that morning to compare notes about her behavior. Marga claims that "I brought my parents together through their homophobia." They were so furious, in fact, that Marga and her girlfriend left New York altogether and moved across the entire country. "I wound up in San Francisco because my parents couldn't handle the truth."

I can hardly imagine how difficult it must have been for Marga to simply come out during the early 1980s, let alone openly discuss her Both-ness on stage in front of thousands of strangers. Comedy writer and performer Janine Brito, who looks up to Marga, describes her as "not a household name, but she was 'out' on stage way before Ellen—*ages* before anyone else. She's this comedian who came up in the ranks with all these other comedians who are famous now, but because she was out, was never given that push from Hollywood to get on television."

At Comic Relief VI in 1994, Robin Williams introduced Marga's performance at the Shrine Auditorium. "Thank you! Thank you! I feel so . . . unknown . . ." Marga told the crowd, before labeling herself as "half–Puerto Rican, half-Cuban, and half-lesbian." She's clearly dressed up for the event. "She's in makeup and a pantsuit . . . but a very feminine pantsuit," Janine said, "so she looks the part of a street woman, but then she starts talking about being a lesbian, and I think *that's* the difference. The audience at the time was confused about that male-female combination. There was a disconnect for them. A 'we can't put these two together' sort of thing."

Fast-forward five years, to Eddie Izzard's *Dressed to Kill* tour. American audiences absolutely adored this sexy British comic who also happened to be a man, dressed in a similarly feminine, bedazzled pantsuit, matching heels, and peeking out from behind a Bob Mackie–inspired mask so thick and deli-cious that I'm still convinced he swiped his makeup from Joel Grey's *Cabaret* closet. Audiences went wild.

So why didn't they embrace Marga the same way?

Aside from the obvious differences in their levels of celeb-rity, Marga may *dress* in a masculine style, but she identi-fies as a woman, whereas "Eddie Izzard actually identifies as transgender, so Eddie is kind of in the same boat as I am," Riley Silverman explained. "When I first saw Eddie, he was on *The Tonight Show with David Letterman.* As I watched him, I remember thinking, 'Wait, there's this guy who dresses in women's clothing but it's not as a gag? It's not another Monty Python thing?' I get that there's a lot more cross-dressing in British comedy, and that cross-dressing is kind of a British comedy mainstay, but Eddie's act wasn't like that. It was just a person who wants to wear his clothes and is going to wear them . . . full stop. This was, in the back of my mind, how *I* wanted to be. I'd always had transgender-type thoughts as I kid. I never understood why I just couldn't simply *be* a girl . . . I wanted to dress and express myself how I felt I should be. And the first person I really saw do that in a comedy setup was Eddie. Eddie wasn't playing a character of a woman; he was playing *himself* in a dress, heels, and makeup. And that made me go, 'Oh, wow. That's a thing you can do? I get it now.' That realization definitely helped me to come out. He called himself a male lesbian at the time—in fact, he said he thought of himself as a whole man and half a woman—so, in that way, Eddie was one of the first people to really show that you could just be *yourself*, which really helped me to realize I didn't have to wear wigs or fake breasts. The idea of stuffing a bra and putting it on as a costume just never rang true for me. I don't like to feel like I'm in a costume. I just want to feel like myself in my own clothes."

Still, as author Fay Weldon said, "men can turn themselves into women, and women can turn themselves into men—not literally, but simply through their preoccupation and what they do." Her idea is relevant to a discussion of the ways things have (and have not) changed since both Eddie and Marga began performing in the 1980s. "It doesn't affect their gender, you see," Weldon explained, "but rather the effect that men and women have on each other as they try to adjust but continually fail. What men and women are is different from what they do—or can be. People don't marry in the same way in which they used to, but when you did, as a woman, you took on the male's world: his friends became your friends, his way of life became your *whole* life, and his way of thinking and behaving became your way of thinking and behaving. If he played hockey, you'd play hockey. That was how women bettered themselves at that time—by becoming certainly attached to, and very much a part of, a man. It was almost as if you'd put his skin over yours and disappear into him. But that would have never, ever happened in the other direction, where a man sublimated himself and became a part of a woman."

Perhaps this is, again, why male-to-female drag is considered humorous while female-to-male drag is considered serious. The former (when done by a cisgender male as ladyfacing) is almost always used as a way of either ridiculing women or emasculating men by making them take on female characteristics, which most audiences are terrified to see men do.

This theory continues to permeate a number of other, less obvious contexts. Insults, as I mentioned, and cursing have their own unique way of ridiculing women. Lingual associations between femininity and negativity permeate our culture. This is why so many of our most common insults spring from a deep-seated distrust of women. We insult someone of the male gender by either comparing him to a female, calling him a derogatory name for female anatomy, or downgrading him from his superior male status to an inferior female status:

Don't be a pussy!

Stop crying like a bitch!

We also insult men by comparing them to either their own anatomy or to anatomy that both genders share:

You're such a dick!

Asshole!

The reverse never happens, however, when we insult women. We don't compare them to men, or call them derogatory names for male genitalia—and using nouns to change their status from traditionally female to traditionally male becomes complimentary.

Hey, chief!

She handled that shit like a boss.

Instead, to insult a woman, we emphasize (rather than change) her gender. We highlight her inferior status, which is inherently tied to her genitalia. We drag to the surface what's lurking beneath language: our subconscious loathing of female sexuality.

What a slut!

Whore!

Cunt!

These insults, much like cisgender men dressing up in female garb when there are no actual gender identity issues at play, exist because we, as a society, hate and distrust women.

According to writer Natalie Abrams, writing for *TV Guide* in 2012, since comedians reflect society as a whole, in many ways, when comedians like Adam Carolla insist that they "don't hate working with women," the opposite message comes through (which was always intended). It worsens when he insists that networks "make you hire a certain number of chicks," and then claims that certain well-known comedienne-ballerinas are only famous *because* they're women. This is one of the same kinds of arguments that have been leveled at people of color by affirmative action opponents, who similarly claim that employers and universities "have to" hire and admit women and minorities, and that this therefore makes such women and minorities less qualified for these positions as compared to white males, which results in discriminatory paranoia about the "others" who "take" jobs and positions at top universities away from "real" employees and students. The implied (and again, always intended) message here is that this "realness" lies primarily in white, male, heterosexual, upper- to upper-middle-class Christian capitalists, and that employers and schools that look elsewhere in the name of curing our nation's racist past are, in fact, promoting racism—especially if they can't cure all racism quickly and with as little inconvenience to the majority as possible. Welcome to Gas-lighting 101, wherein those who seek solutions to a problem are then rebranded as the problem itself.

In terms of sexism, the same gas-lighting effect occurs when those who created sexism in order to benefit from sexist policies seek to rebrand Feminists as the "real" sexists. When women buy into this calculated strategy, infighting results, forcing women to attack themselves and each other rather than those who actually lit the gas. This can occur without women ever realizing it's happening. When we hear these insults—sometimes open and sometimes cloaked in protectionist language—for years at a time, we absorb the insults' implied message of hatred and distrust. Then we project this message on each other. We start to distrust each other. We start to distrust our own instincts. This makes it easier to attack "the other woman" instead of a man, for example. Or to dismiss a rape victim as "asking for it" or "obviously exaggerating." To call each other "gold diggers" or "dumb blondes." To watch the *Real Housewives* catfight and feel better about ourselves. To cling to our double standards, "holding our noses" for "crooked" Hillary, while ignoring other candidates' even more glaringly obvious corruption and smug indifference toward vast swaths of urgent suffering.

It's almost like we've absorbed the messages of our oppressor.

During this current resurgence of ultraconservatism, there's a certain blowback when performers even attempt to confront the harmful effects of beauty culture and Lookism. When they push further into issues involving cross-dressing, transgender identity, butch femininity, and sexually fluid lifestyles, they're often threatened into silence. When audiences saw Kate McKinnon imitating Justin Bieber, for example, she experienced pushback by many who would prefer women to stay in dresses and men in pants. These are the same viewers who viciously attacked Leslie Jones simply for appearing in a modernized, all-female reboot of *Ghostbusters*. These elements within our society don't care to live in the present, nor do they care to see anyone on television who doesn't perfectly mirror their American mythology of a country filled with white, male, heterosexual, upper-middle-class Christian capitalists.

Despite their attempts to silence her comedy, the Justin that Kate McKinnon depicted remains interesting and smart.

Similarly, though some objected to her playing the role, Melissa McCarthy's Sean Spicer galvanized his weaponized hostility and seemed to capture the growing possibility of a dictatorship-in-progress.

Both Kate and Melissa were able to look well beyond their subjects' gender and assume their unique characteristics—and, through their embodiments, nail something about both men that audiences found universally funny. I believe that this universality comes from their poking fun at particular individuals' characteristics rather than attempting to lampoon all men as a whole. For a while the tradition of ladyface has focused on poking fun at femininity, Kate McKinnon's dressing up as Justin Bieber is poking fun at his celebrity—not his masculinity—and Melissa McCarthy's roasting Sean Spicer's rageaholism has little to do with his gender. It's not about making fun of men or making fun of Justin's or Sean's maleness; Kate's performance mocks any celebrity who also happens to be regarded as a lazy, all-around douche, and Melissa could choose literally any member of Trump's cabinet who happened to display the same distaste for a free press. Kate could be dressing up as a female celebrity, and the impression would still be just as funny. Melissa could lampoon Kellyanne Conway's so-called "moxie" and call her "conservative Feminism" out for what it is—a refusal to challenge male dominance—and still create the best parody in recent *SNL* history.

There are comedians who also happen to be ladies who consciously go out of their way to maximize (rather than minimize) their gender and emphasize (rather than de-escalate) their gender-based experiences. And there are comedians who also happen to be ladies who don't necessarily want to be seen as women *at all*. They minimize and de-escalate to the point of near eradication, because they don't want to be "othered." They don't want to be victimized because they no longer fit within the mainstream, where there's safety in much greater numbers. They fear being vulnerable. Who can blame them? Writer Carol Diehl perhaps put it best in her moving poem, "For the Men Who Still Don't Get It."

What if
all women were bigger and stronger than you
and thought they were smarter

What if
women were the ones who started wars

What if
too many of your friends had been raped by women wielding
    giant dildos
and no K-Y Jelly

What if
the state trooper
who pulled you over on the New Jersey Turnpike
was a woman
and carried a gun

What if
the ability to menstruate
was the prerequisite for most high-paying jobs

What if
your attractiveness to women depended
on the size of your penis

What if
every time women saw you
they'd hoot and make jerking motions with their hands

What if
women were always making jokes
about how ugly penises are
and how bad sperm tastes

What if
you had to explain what's wrong with your car
to big sweaty women with greasy hands
who stared at your crotch
in a garage where you are surrounded
by posters of naked men with hard-ons

What if
men's magazines featured cover photos
of 14-year-old boys
with socks
tucked into the front of their jeans
and articles like:
"How to tell if your wife is unfaithful"
or
"What your doctor won't tell you about your prostate"
or
"The truth about impotence"

What if
the doctor who examined your prostate
was a woman
and called you "Honey"

What if
you had to inhale your boss's stale cigar breath
as she insisted that sleeping with her
was part of the job

What if
you couldn't get away because
the company dress code required
you wear shoes
designed to keep you from running

And what if
after all that
women still wanted you
to love them.

The point isn't to shame these women or label them "bad" for wanting to minimize their female gender to escape all of these physical and psychological dangers. Instead, we should try to determine why and how this situation arises wherein women who also happen to be comedians very much *want* to become "one of the boys." This is different from cross-dressing, and although it's certainly not a transgender issue, it does bear a resemblance to "passing," as it's commonly known within the gay community. This term usually refers to a person's ability to go through daily life without others making the assumption that this person is gay; however, according to GLAAD, the term itself is problematic as it implies "passing as something you're not." When transgender people are living as their authentic selves, and are not perceived as transgender by others, that does not make them deceptive or misleading.

Cisgender women don't become "one of the boys" in order to literally "pass" for a biological male—they simply want to receive the same sense of equality, social protection, and professional respect that so often accompanies this gender—both from other men and from women. As a result, they often attempt to take a place within the boys' club by surrounding themselves with men, claiming that they "don't like" or "don't trust" other women, by putting down other women while in the presence of men, or simply by failing to defend a woman as she's being ridiculed based on her gender alone.

This choice is largely subconscious, and almost entirely motivated by a deep unhappiness with gender constraints and an even deeper desire for safety—physical, emotional, mental, and financial. It's a kind of camouflage that recalls the many centuries of history where women practiced the art of dressing as men to avoid rape, to escape oppressive domestic roles, to enjoy basic everyday liberties like voting or driving or trans-acting business without fear of reprisal, or even to go to war. To express, in essence, their innermost selves apart from the trappings of their outer appearance.

Again, this doesn't mean that they wanted to literally tran-sition, but they did desire the safety that society attached to men as the "superior sex." Perhaps, even more keenly, they craved other men's acceptance. They wanted to know how it felt to finally take a seat at that table. They wanted to join the club, at least for a little while. I know what that temptation is like. Getting a seat at that table is just like getting to sit with the popular kids in a high school cafeteria. It's still desirable to sit there because guys are still more powerful than women in our society. If we get to hang out with them it's *really* cool, and so, for women who are allowed into the club, there's this gleeful sort of feeling: *Oh wow! They think I'm worthy of attention now! I must not be as inferior to them as I thought! Look at all those other, uncool girls down there, on the floor! They aren't sitting up here, are they? I must be so much better than all of them! And because the guys invited me up here, they must believe it, too! I definitely won't be raped or condescended to or grabbed by the pussy now! In fact, I bet they'll even start paying me the same! Right?*

This especially happens to newer, less well-known comedienne-ballerinas. Doubly so when the ones inviting those women to the table happen to be men who also happen to be older, better-known comedians. And it happens to women everywhere, in all industries, when you want to be cool, and sometimes being cool means putting yourself and/or other women down or pretending to love misogynistic shit that turns women from three-dimensional characters into mindless fuck puppets. This longstanding phenomenon is frustrating because there are so many positive aspects of femininity, so many more women who want to trust and be trusted. Whose voices—like their appearances—display an attempt to dispel fear. One of the most basic principles of improv comedy is centered on embracing and supporting our fellow comedians in their acts by saying "yes" to a partner's idea and then adding your own. Not at all coincidentally, "Yes, and" is also one of the main tenets of Feminism. Feminism itself is one big "Yes, and," since both this ideology and this improvisational method—when practiced by and among comedienne-ballerinas—are rooted in the belief that female collaboration, rather than competition, is and always has been the starting point for power, and that trusting ourselves and our partners, both on stage and off—especially when those partners are other women—creates superior comedy and a safer world.

part five

"YES, AND-ING" THE F-WORD

"You should never say bad things about the dead, you should only say good. Joan Crawford is dead. Good."

—Bette Davis

does millennial = feminist?

I ALWAYS THOUGHT OF MYSELF AS a Feminist, but I used to be the worst kind," Riley Silverman said as she sipped from a half-full cup of coffee in her living room. "I was the kind who said things like, 'Well, it's not really Feminism, it's humanism.' Which is kind of like saying, 'All Lives Matter,' because it negates the history of the original term. I didn't understand that, at one time. I didn't understood why Feminism *has* to be called Feminism, and why it's about breaking down hurtful gender roles that have *specifically* disadvantaged women—not *all* humans. Once that unlocked for me, I was able to start identifying as a woman. I was able to start saying that and owning that. And I became proud to stand up beside all these other women who are such powerful figures, and to openly say: 'This is who I am. This movement is what I want to be a part of.'"

In standing up beside her fellow women and Feminists, Riley actively engages in a rewiring of her default settings: turning away from all the discouraging information about gender roles, continually embracing the positive aspects of femininity, and supporting other women in their performances and choices. Like a true Feminist, she sees other women—whether trans- or cisgender—through her own eyes rather than through the cars' windows; using her own instincts rather than seeking permission from Patriarchy. She has let go of Male Supremacy's divide-and-conquer technique. By letting go, by endeavoring to trust and be trusted, other women have become sources of collaboration rather than competition. This fundamental shift in perspective—from "The Rule of Two" to "Yes, and"—is as important to many modern comedienne-ballerinas as it is to millennial Feminists. This is why Riley also noted how much it disappoints her when women shy away from the term Feminism, which for Riley encompasses both comedic and personal freedom.

"It's an entire mindset about yourself, your self-worth, and your value—both in and to the world. It's an incredible movement to associate with, and I think that most women *and* men in modern society have benefited from the advocacy of Feminists in the second half of the century. That's why, in my act, I always point out that women who reject Feminism are intrinsically selfish, because they are. Their slogan might as well be, 'I'm not a Feminist because I like it when others do all the heavy lifting for me.'"

Livia Scott agreed, describing herself as a woman who "very consciously supports the sisterhood of Feminism, which is essentially the same as supporting civil rights. Feminism, like civil rights, means that we *all* get to be here. We *all* get a place at the table. We *all* get to be treated with respect. And comedy is just the most rock-star, fun, powerful way to express Feminism."

When a comedienne-ballerina "Yes, ands" another's idea, this collaboration not only reinforces (and possibly improves) her own comic effect but also commandeers and neutralizes

Male Supremacy's attempts to divide and conquer women. Feminism and comedy work together to empower women who engage in both, whether they do so on stage or off. And when women join forces, their power is multiplied—power that they might not have in other careers and especially not in everyday life. By making an audience member laugh, these women create a physical response based on *their* choices: their words, their presentation, their inflection, their tone, their facial expression, their entire appearance . . . yet they haven't made physical contact. They've made that person respond—sometimes even against his or her will—and forced a reaction from that person's body and mind with comedy alone. This can be unsettling for those who are largely unaccustomed to—and unwelcoming of—females retaining any power or control at all, especially over men. This upending of power can create fear in those who oppose gender equality. Many fear the powerless suddenly gaining power. This fear is evidenced by the deeply entrenched social structures that still so clearly favor men over women, and it feeds back into the old claim that women aren't funny— because a woman who can exert that level of control has a great deal of power over the one who's listening. It's a very scary thing for some people of any gender to admit that a woman can provoke such a response, especially in a man. Perhaps even scarier is the idea that he can't necessarily stop her.

As a transgender woman who has lived on both sides of that power structure, Riley explained, "I would never go back to living as a man because it made me unhappy and miserable . . . and yet I definitely see how much easier it was for me then. Some people question whether it's harder for me now because I'm female identified or because I'm seen as queer, but I think it's all part of the same problem—and that Feminism is our attempt to address the problems that both of these two communities face.

That's why, in my opinion, most of the attempts to discredit Feminism are not really reacting to the basic idea that men and women are equal and should be treated accordingly."

Riley's astute comments touch on yet another domination technique: confusing the chicken with the egg, which seeks to confuse both women and the LGBTQ communities as to the causes of their struggles versus the effects; Patriarchy's actions versus Feminists' reactions. Those who seek to discredit Feminism—and by so doing, dissuade both women and the LGBTQ population from "Yes, and-ing" each other toward collective equality, ultimately resulting in empowerment—want to make sure that both communities remain confused as to what is causing the discrimination they face and how to address it. The more confused we all are, the more divided we are from one another, the more we see each other as competitors rather than collaborators, the less likely we are to join forces and attack the real cause of our suffering: Male Supremacy's near-total dominance over all legal, financial, and political structures.

Most people believe in the basic idea that women and men are created equally (although not identically). The basic assumption is enshrined in our founding documents and underlies all of our civil liberties and unalienable rights. As a result, most people also believe that women should be treated as equally valuable to men in a society created and sustained by both genders. This belief is exactly why most people believe in equal pay for equal work, and thus why President Obama signed the Lilly Ledbetter Fair Pay Act into law in 2009, extending the protections already guaranteed to historically marginalized and oppressed groups who (like women) have traditionally lacked substantial political power to overcome this oppression through voting alone—either because they're outnumbered or because they're socialized into remaining silent (i.e., victims of the Stella Syndrome).

This new Act was Obama's attempt to correct some of the generations-old wage-based discrimination that women routinely face—for example, the presumption that they'll be less ambitious than men; less hard-working than men; or that they'll quit their jobs, or prefer part-time work, or shun promotions, all because they're presumed to remain the primary caretakers of children even while working. Many employers even assume that a woman will take a job and then quit the moment she becomes pregnant, and so they will offer her less money, assuming she'll be a less committed employee.

This 2009 Act, much like the Civil Rights Act, attempted to counteract employers' sexist presumptions—not by changing their minds (since it's impossible to legislate conscience) but to constrict their ability to act on those presumptions. Whereas the 1964 Act prevented differences in compensation based solely on race, color, religion, national origin, age, disability, genetic information, and/or retaliation, the Act of 2009—also called the Equal Pay Act—prohibited "sex-based discrimination between men and women in the same establishment, who perform jobs that require substantially equal skill, effort, and responsibility under similar working conditions." However, let's be clear: This Act should never have been necessary. We should always have been paying women equally for equal work, and the 1964 Act that protected other groups should have protected women, too. Unfortunately, it took us that long to actually acknowledge what women routinely face. Even today, we don't have the same workplace protections in place for members of the LGBTQ community, who can be fired in many states based on their sexual orientation alone. Obama attempted to sign these into law as well, but his work was stalled by conservative members of Congress and then killed by President Donald Trump who, within two hours of swearing into office, deleted all information regarding important policy changes for gay and transgender citizens from the White House's website.

This history, and more like it, continues to confuse people about what caused the discrimination they continue to face: Patriarchy or Feminism? In order to get many women and members of the LGBTQ community to reject Feminism, critics of Feminism like to switch those two around. They like to make it look like Feminism caused the problems facing both women and the LGBTQ community rather than admit what Feminism truly is: an antidote to those problems, a reaction to Male Supremacy's actions, a defense rather than an offense. They would prefer that we all believe that the Civil Rights Act and the Lilly Ledbetter Act caused inequality, rather than learn the history behind the truth: they were reactions to inequality. The unifying, collaborative concept of "Yes, and" ran through both, which is why for a brief moment—while the truth was still fresh in our minds and not relegated to history—true equality seemed on the horizon. But time passes. The details get fuzzy, and the "rebranders" get to work, labeling our attempts to "Yes, and" one another as "executive overreach" or dismissing it as the work of "activist judges" pushing a "radical Feminist agenda" on Americans . . . 51 percent of which, they conveniently neglect to mention, are women: the exact same group this Act protects.

This rebranding sometimes works. It confuses people about where the problems really came from, and Feminism becomes a loaded word. It becomes all the things to which it's reacting. Ironically, in this way, it absorbs the messages of its oppressors, too. Instead of working together, we work against one another. We grow suspicious, once again. Instead of "Yes, and-ing" the F-Word—Feminism—we edge backward toward the "Rule of Two," insisting, unfairly, that all women who enter male-dominated spaces are "asking for" the discrimination they then receive.

The same kind of one-sided response can apply to men who enter traditionally female-dominated spaces as well. During the 2016 Olympics in Rio, opportunities for media exposure and product endorsement by male gymnasts fell far below that of their female counterparts—a sexist response that, ironically, could be cured by ending the media's preoccupation with sexualizing young girls' bodies.

Let's turn to another exercise. Take a look at a few online photos of most Olympic athletes who also happen to be female. What's usually in the forefront? Could it be their asses, perhaps? So the very forces that are objectifying these women are also ignoring the men who compete in these same events. According to online writer Jeff Eisenberg, corporate America bears much of the blame, for while Title IX "created more opportunities for female gymnasts at the college level and began the gradual process of cash-strapped athletic departments axing their men's programs," it also inspired a new trend: younger, tinier athletes than were ever seen before. This extreme tininess created an all-new, often impossibly skinny standard for girls who both watched and engaged in the sport. When fourteen-year-old Nadia Comaneci scored a perfect 10 (the first girl to do so) and won three gold medals in 1976, "she quickly became the darling of that Olympics," according to Eisenberg. "Young girls identified with Comaneci's small stature, vibrant personality and remarkable athleticism. Parents began enrolling toddlers in tumbling classes and more gymnastics clubs began popping up nationwide to satisfy the growing demand." Other girls and even grown women suddenly endeavored to look like Nadia. Her body type became so popular, in fact, that an emaciated Gilda played her in an *SNL* sketch in 1977.

After (and perhaps in response to) Nadia, there came a string of noticeably more fleshed-out gymnasts, including Mary Lou Retton in the mid-80s and Shannon Miller and Kerri Strug in the mid-90s, at which point audiences (ironically) began taking to the Internet to address the media's obsession with "female athlete" bodies. To their credit, these athletes have begun pushing back at the media's hypersexualizing their bodies while undermining their credibility by pointing out how photographers capture their male counterparts in positions displaying skillful prowess while females are often captured in positions that emphasize only their sexuality.

Meanwhile, this inequality is exacerbated by ever-shrinking talent pools of male gymnasts. In the US, this pool is apparently much shallower for men than women. Fewer boys sign up for gymnastics at young ages, and when schools experience cutbacks, they usually address the problem by ending under-enrolled programs. The more schools that justify ending their gymnastics programs for men, the fewer men who *can* enroll, feeding yet another self-fulfilling prophecy: Where schools do not build, athletes cannot come.

When applied to women, this is the same old chicken-and-egg argument: there won't be many bicyclists when the roads aren't built for them. In this case, while the genders are reversed, the problem of inequality remains.

In order to combat our collective forgetfulness—to avoid any further confusion—we must remind ourselves that we are the cure and not the disease. Put more poetically: We must learn to exit through our wounds, for we are the true magic-makers and dreamers of dreams. But we must also confront an uncomfortable question: Are all Millennial comedienne-ballerinas inherently Feminist? And, by extension, should we assume that millennial women in general are also Feminists?

I think we assume the contrapositive: That all *Feminists* are *women*—period—and that all Feminists are exactly the same. Part of this is our overwhelming need for labels (which isn't inherently a bad thing—our brains have been categorizing our world since the dawn of mankind as an evolutionary tactic developed to help us survive all kinds of present, physical dangers), but today, anytime you subscribe to a particular "ism," there will always be a spectrum of opinions within that group. So, yes, there are going to be some humorless Feminists, just like there are some humorless comedians and humorless Republicans and humorless Democrats and even some humorless horticultural activists in the city of New York. And then there are people who are hilarious and delightful. And then there are people in between. It's really hard to say exactly what Feminism is other than its two key ideas:

#1: That women and men (while not identical) are equal.

#2: That, because they're equal, society should treat men and women as equally valuable, and it should endeavor to afford them equal opportunities for full participation in all areas—political, legal, financial, and otherwise.

This includes opportunities for full and equal participation for those who fall outside—or simply don't participate in—the gender binary. Some call this the Fourth Wave, but I would respectfully rename it Millennial Feminism: the inclusion of gender differences beyond the binary in our conversations about equality, and the use of comedy as a method of mocking (and thereby undermining) those differences in order to create Both-ness (or even Sameness, if more than two categories apply) across all sexualities, races, socioeconomic classes, religions, and cultures.

While some critics might claim that Feminists center Feminism around "having a vagina," this is a basic misunderstanding of the F-word. Feminism is a belief system, not a reproductive system, and like any belief system, it's rooted in personal conviction—more specifically, that all genders are created equally, for better and for worse, and that this equality of creation should extend to equality of opportunity for full and equal participation in society. Feminism's center can expand, certainly—as it should—to include others who share this belief. But anything that lessens or negates this core conviction is simply a tactic to—once again—derail, divide, and conquer, for (much like any members of a faith-based community) while no two Feminists are identical, we are all believers. It is not our differences that divide us. It is our occasional inability to recognize, accept, and celebrate those differences that may be used to divide us.*

Mocking those who would use our differences against us isn't punching down. Pointing out the sinister corruption of those who seek to transform beautiful diversity into divisive tactics, and then laughing at the attempts to use those tactics to conquer social movements (like Feminism) by causing the movement's members to attack one another instead of the true source of their discrimination, isn't bullying. And this is because punching down and bullying aren't the same as creating comedy. Neither of these tactics is comedy at all, in fact, but simply weak people's imitations of strength. And although some audiences may enjoy watching a certain kind of comic bully the marginalized and long-oppressed, (or anyone else on the sole basis of their immutable characteristics, rather than their character as individuals), doing so doesn't make comedy. It makes misery. In some cases, it justifies war. And, eventually, it helps to create a very unfunny world.

Comedienne-ballerinas are the antithesis of all this. By mocking dividers, comedienne-ballerinas are punching up. Feminists and Feminist-allies should always feel free to punch

---

* An ode to Audre Lorde.

up, using their comedy to mock the power structures that either empower the undeserving or disempower the desirable. Obviously, this is subjective and will expand and change over time according to basic social mores—and it is far from an attempt to flatten diversity. Rather, mocking those who attempt to hurt us is a way to bring us all together for one big, heartfelt, much-needed, contextual laugh. To give us a purpose other than gritted-teeth rebellion. Or, perhaps, to give our rebellion a new purpose: When we laugh, that is *life itself*. That is freedom. That *is* Feminism. Which is why Feminist comedy is the essence of Millennial Feminism.

However, until the pendulum of time swings back once again toward progress and ultimately reaches the zenith, "one does feel that women are their own worst enemy," said Fay Weldon. "I mean the whole sort of insistence on being slim and beautiful is mostly, I've seen, imposed by gays and other women. Straight men created the expectations of being beautiful and available to them sexually, of course, but the rest of us have sort of fallen for it, in a way. And we sometimes remain competitive over attaining (or keeping) those standards of beauty because they provide access to men, and through them, power. It reminds me of how it was before Feminism, and what we were trying to combat. You see, pre-Feminism, women were very, very competitive, because you *had* to be competitive to get a good husband. You *had* to compete with other women, and you *had* to put other women down, and women were very catty about each other. They competed for men the same way men competed to climb the corporate ladder, you could say. Well, when Feminism became popular, this sort of thing ended. Those problems slowed for a while, and women weren't so desperately in need of a man, so they stopped being so catty . . . but that may be coming back now."

Both women and members of the LGBTQ community can sometimes become our own worst enemies. We have been so influenced by Patriarchal expectations that we serve as our own judges, jurors, and executioners. That's the thing about oppression: It makes instruments of its victims.

This has been true throughout the ages. Though the Romans oppressed, marginalized, and persecuted Hebrews, some agreed to collect taxes from their own people in exchange for special treatment. Centuries later, in the antebellum South, groups known as "house slaves" (who worked for their owners inside the home) often degraded "field slaves" (who worked the land). The former looked down upon the latter, and even mocked them for the master's entertainment—all as a form of survival, to remain inside the house, closer to food and warmth, and closer to the center of power.

Today, we sometimes see the same antagonistic behavior between married and unmarried women, with members of one group denigrating the others' choices in order to feel superior in their own. This rationalizing of discrimination—this choosing to see only difference and not similarity—echoes certain aspects of the Stella Syndrome. It also sabotages any progress toward true equality by rejecting "Yes, and." Women and LGBTQ citizens remain divided and conquered through their suspicions, their judgment, and their intra-group competition. In the case of married versus unmarried women, the "Rule of Two" can morph into the "Rule of One," where the divide-and-conquer technique is ultimately the most devastating, creating the impression that a married woman—because she has "secured" a husband—is more valuable, more stable, happier, healthier, and better fulfilled than an unmarried woman, who is cut off from the source of social, legal, financial, and political power—a man—and subsequently has less "security." This technique thereby encourages women to fight one another for the proverbial "ring to rule them all." The same can often be said of mothers versus non-mothers. Each group feels its choice is superior and thus seeks to make the other choice seem inferior, twisting any relationship between women who have children and women who haven't into a tenuous stand-off. But in the end we are all women, and in attacking each other, we all suffer. Male Supremacy can be the only winner.

The way to prevent this is by embracing "Yes, and" both in our comedy and in our everyday lives. Competing with other women divides us all, forcing us to fight for access to benefits rather than claiming them as our own, which conquers our collective power, which saps us all of strength and robs us of comedy. Collaboration with other women, on the other hand, creates unity, which leads to strength, which ensures power, which inspires comedy. For this and so many other reasons, we need to stop all the infighting. The best way to do that is to stop fighting ourselves. The woman we see in the mirror each day. But if collaboration with other women creates unity, which leads to strength, which ensures power, which inspires comedy . . . what about competition with ourselves? And what happens when we compete with one another for success, rather than over men or access to Patriarchal power? Is that when, per Feminist author Audre Lorde, we can finally use the master's tools to dismantle the master's house?

When we take those same competitive forces, those anti-Feminist techniques, and turn them inward—or upside down, using them to become more successful outside of rather than within the domestic sphere—is *that* when enforced competition becomes empowerment? Can Patriarchy's rules backfire and break the invisible cage? And, if so, *how* can a comedienne-ballerina transform all that was designed to confuse and destroy Feminism into a primary and supremely powerful Feminist force?

i have met my enemy,
and she is me

A SUDDEN NEED TO COMPETE INSPIRED late-night tele-vision writer Laurie Kilmartin to perform her first set of live stand-up comedy. "I remember being in fourth grade and I was sort of on that perimeter. You know, there was like the cool group and I wasn't a part of it."

"Why weren't you part of it?" I asked her, feeling sudden pangs of sympathy.

"I don't know. I just was never, and am currently not, cool. It's just never anything I've been able to pull off. And the girl who was in sort of the center was named Jackie and she was always just nasty to me. And we had to write these stories and read them out loud, and I read my story, and she laughed. And I was like, 'I fucking got you.' And then I didn't care that she didn't like me after that, because I felt like I won. Years later, I got that same feeling while watching another woman doing stand-up, who wasn't particularly funny. I remember thinking,

'I can be better than her.' Which is weird. I think I needed to believe that I could be better than the person I was watching."

As a former writer for Joan Rivers, Eliza Skinner said that Joan's outlook toward other women of her generation who also happened to be comics—much like female competition itself—became a kind of metaphor for capitalism: *I'm going to do what's best for myself, and that will make me more successful. If we all do that, then everyone's doing her best for her own purposes, and everyone's going to be successful.*

Yet Eliza also made clear that Joan didn't think of competition as a form of Feminism—and she certainly didn't think of competing with her peers as a form of "Yes, and-ing" their jokes, or collaborating with them in any way. Maybe that's why for many Gen-X women, Joan—at first glance, anyway—resembled an anti-Feminist, a Stella, who was now hypocritically supporting the double standards she'd railed against during the 1960s—not to mention double-crossing the Feminist movement that had created her career in the first place.

"When I first noticed Joan Rivers, she looked like the enemy," Emily Nussbaum wrote of Joan's raw, gritted-teeth, GI-generation comedy during "the early eighties, at the height of her fame. She was Johnny Carson's permanent guest host at the time—warm to his cold, abrasive yet charismatic, with a brash engagement with the audience. (Her trademark line: 'Can we talk?') I was a teenage comedy nerd, into *SCTV* and Tom Lehrer, obsessed with Woody Allen and David Letterman. I was eager for female role models, of whom there were only a handful, other than Gilda Radner and the mysterious Elaine May, no longer on the scene. Yet Rivers terrified me. Glamorous in her Oscar de la Renta dresses and her pouf of blond hair, she was the body cop who circled the flaws on every other powerful woman—she announced who was fat, who had no chin, who was hot but, because she was hot, was a slut or dim. She made it clear that if you rose to fame the world would use your body to cut you down. The fact that she was funny made her more scary, not less: 'What's Liz Taylor's blood type? Ragú!' I laughed, then hated myself for laughing."

But at the same time, Joan's jokes were lateral punch ups, aimed at A-list celebrities—not horizontal jabs at women in her same position, or whose work paved the way for her own. Although these women—few as they were—likely became Joan's "competition," she seemed to use her competitive nature to better herself rather than hurting others. In this way, it's perhaps true that competition among her peers inspired her to make better comedy, and that this competition generally— when used by all women to better their own individual talents rather than to attach themselves to sources of Patriarchal power—does ultimately serve the cause of Feminism, whether they meant to do so or not.

Meanwhile, voices reinforcing the idea that women should compete with each other rather than support each other continued, notably in the advice column Dear Abby (Abigail van Buren, the longtime pen name of Pauline Phillips). Abby spent decades delivering a mix of black comedy and pure tragedy to her readers in the form of sexism—the deep inferiority of wives to their husbands—and a general sense of seething self-hatred among women. Her excerpts from 1958 and 1962 show in stark relief what many women unfortunately continue to believe. As bestselling author Therese Oneill reported in 2016, "Abby" once advised a woman who was complaining of her husband's infidelity to, "Sit him down and say quietly,

'What does she have that I haven't?' or 'Where have I let you down?' This approach is magical. He'll be so stunned by your compassion and understanding that I'll bet he'll start remembering why he married you.

"This above all: If you're entangled in a triangle, consider 'her' as a rival for his love and devotion. You're in deadly competition. So think of what you would do if you weren't married and had to win him all over again. Then do it!"

The problem isn't that forgiveness or compromise between married people is wrong—it's that all of the apologizing and compromising comes 100 percent from the wife, while the actual cheater, her husband, is treated as a big dumb child, unable to exercise any amount of self-control. "Remember, you are dealing with a little boy in long pants, who is short on will power," Abby goes on. Apparently, if he cheats, you should apologize. If he cheats again, it's probably because you "made a scene." Oh, and remember, cuckolds, to level all your ire at the "other woman," as if she held a gun to your dude's head and forced him to cheat. Because, really, she's the one you should be mad at. Not the one who promised to be faithful and then, you know, wasn't. Right.

Abby goes even further, claiming that if you don't follow her advice, and keep insisting on having a say in where your man spends the night, you might as well resign yourself to dying alone. "The so-called 'emancipated woman' who regards her marriage as one of those 50-50 deals is weakening her own marital security. As a husband's sense of obligation is diluted, so is his sense of responsibility to his family. He feels less bound to stick with his wife and children through trials and unpleasantness." That's apparently why "all important family decisions should be fully discussed by both partners. But on day-to-day matters involving the well-being and security of the family, the last word belongs to the Old Man." You should also be sure to devise a spending system that "provides that the husband give his wife a checkbook so that she may pay all nonpersonal bills. There's only one catch: He has to sign them. That way, the Little Woman is actually running things, but the Big Man still feels he has final control!"

But wasn't he just "a little boy in long pants, who is short on will power"? I'm totally confused, Abby.

The list goes on and on: Don't pay too much attention to the kids, or he'll cheat. Don't get fat, or he'll cheat. Don't drink in public, or he'll cheat. Don't let him see you with all that moisturizer on at night, curled up with your laptop, watching *Revolutionary Road* or any such "femi-nazi" nonsense, or he'll cheat. "Women, like sausages, are best enjoyed when one does not witness their making."

And the kicker?

"There are marriages where a woman will irritate her husband deliberately until he finally lets loose and takes a poke at her. The psychiatrists have a nine-lettered word for this, and it is not considered normal. But if she likes it (and doesn't mind having her teeth replaced) they could be enjoying a successful marriage."

All of these not-so-subtle methods of gas-lighting the female population into willful submission make Joan's and Phyllis's comedy more understandable, and they highlight the psychology behind it. According to Emily Nussbaum, "Joan Rivers was a survivor of a sexist era: a victim, a rebel, and, finally, an enforcer" whose mentality, common for many women of her (and our) era, may be boiled down to gender-based economics: "If you got cut off from access to men and money—and from men as the route to money—you were dead in the water. Women were one another's competition, always. For half a century, this dark comedy of scarce resources had been her forte: many hands grasping, but only one golden ring. Rivers herself had fought hard for the token slot allotted to a female comic, yet she seemed thrown by a world in which that might no longer be necessary. Like Moses and the Promised Land, she couldn't cross over."

To put this in perspective, Tina Fey was born in 1970, only a few years after some of the aforementioned Dear Abby advice was circulating and Joan Rivers's comedy was taking off. Think about how it might have influenced her own comedy, growing up surrounded by all this "sound advice" on womanhood. Then think about how many women you know today who still blame either themselves or the "other woman" who "took" their man.

Go a little further. Maybe count how many times you've said "I'm sorry" today when you didn't do anything wrong. When you apologized for things like speaking, or asking questions, or taking up space. Think back to earlier—maybe toward the beginning of this book—when you automatically moved out of the way to let others have . . . almost everything. Think about how many times it's been assumed that you'll move to avoid colliding on the sidewalk. Think about all the times when you've been biking along and a car cuts you off. Try to remember how it felt to take your anger out on another cyclist instead of slamming both of your bikes through its driver-side window.

Think hard for a second, and then ask yourself, *why?*

It's because this kind of internalized suspicion, this divide-and-conquer technique that's been used to pit women against each other forever, really works.

If you think about the logic behind all of it, it's the same kind of emotional warfare that oppressors use to distract and neutralize: "Don't look at me, shutting down all the Planned Parenthoods in your neighborhood while paying you 21 to 66 percent less than your male coworkers—look at *her*! Yeah, her! The one who might be trying to steal your man! She's the *real* problem around here!"

It's also the same kind of delusion that the oppressors themselves emotionally invest in. Every bad guy believes he's the hero of the story, remember. It helps you to feel justified in, say, revising history to make your side look like the true victim. Sexism, like all other "isms" and phobias, brainwashes both oppressor and the oppressed.

Still, we must contextualize Dear Abby, just as we contextualized Lucy's and Maddy's writing of the *I Love Lucy* pilot—not to excuse them, but to better understand.

Therese Oneill wrote, "As much as a modern reader might want to spit venom at her," referring to Dear Abby, "one must consider the social climate in which she wrote. Compared to now, life was rigid and rough in midcentury America. Abby knew her readers lacked something more than ideal husbands. They lacked options.

"What if 1958 Dear Abby had advised an abused woman to take her children and leave? What then? What sort of safeguards were in place to protect her? How would she keep herself and her children off the streets? What if she'd told fat women to love themselves and concentrate on health not thinness? Those women didn't want self-actualization, they wanted to feel normal walking down the street at a time when as much as twenty extra pounds could steal that from them. So Dear Abby was harsh, blunt, and never coddled. To Abby's credit, she acknowledged much of her advice was flippant and chosen to entertain readers. She tells us in *Dear*

Abby (1958) that there were other letters, a large pile every week that she marked 'not for publication.' Those letters contained what she called 'genuine human suffering,' and she answered them personally and at length. It's terrifying to think of what was in *that* pile, if rampant abuse was in the jollies and jokes pile.

"Perhaps those letters made the ones complaining about drunk wives seem particularly deserving of snappy one-liner replies. That, combined with the rigid social structure of mid-century America, could have been what fueled a lot of Abby's 'bad advice.'"

What wave of Feminism are we in now? Where are we going? What are we subconsciously saying to ourselves and to each other? When we look beneath the surface, we can see the thread binding us all. What Tina and Amy went through is what Gilda went through and Whoopi Goldberg went through and Moms went through and Lucille Ball went through. And now we're painting a portrait where we are all carrying on these great traditions and passing the torch to each other and elaborating in our own ways. We're showing how similar we are in our collected humanity—even as competitors.

That's the thing: You must *become*. It takes a long time. That's why it doesn't happen often to people who break easily, or have sharp edges, or who have to be carefully kept. Generally, much like a Velveteen Rabbit, "by the time you are Real, most of your hair has been loved off, and your eyes drop out, and you get loose in the joints and very shabby. But these things don't matter at all, because once you are Real you can't be ugly, except to the people who don't understand." Did Phyllis ever become Real? Did she ever truly surpass the rules so often forced upon her generation? Did Joan?

When Phyllis passed away in 2012, Leslie Bruce wrote for *The Hollywood Reporter* that, in her own way, Joan revered—and perhaps even loved—her competitor, whom Joan supposedly described as a "pioneering stand-up comedian who paved the way and never had the attitude of, 'Poor me, I'm a woman.'"

"When I was just starting out," Joan wrote, according to Bruce, "I did a routine at the Bon Soir nightclub in New York . . . I was really shaky and on the bill with a girl named Barbra Streisand. And Phyllis Diller was in the crowd—one of the first great stand-up comedians. She sat there and applauded and laughed the absolute loudest. Believe me, we weren't bringing down the house back then.

"She was wonderful and encouraging to the young comedians—everything I'm not. After I got friendly with her, I told her what that meant to me. She broke the field for women. She didn't sing. She didn't dance. She would come out, say wonderfully funny things and go home. Phyllis said, 'This is what I am: I'm a funny woman, I'm a funny housewife, and I need a job.' That's why she started in her late thirties—and she worked like a man. She didn't ask for help and didn't complain . . . I was always in awe of her. If something happened that afternoon in politics, she already had a comment about it. I would go see her and say: 'Oh, shit! Why didn't I think of that?' Take away the wig, the stupid dresses and just listen to the lines. She was smart, smart, smart.

"I had brunch with her not even a month ago, and she didn't miss a beat . . . She was all there. She had a great life. She was in her own home and had lots of friends, and she even had a beau—how about that at her age? So I'm not upset. She wasn't sitting around being forgotten."

The bite does come back around a bit toward the end:

"We exchanged necklaces that day. She was wearing a very pretty necklace, and I was wearing one of mine, and we exchanged. So, now I'm really excited to have her necklace—but it's not as pretty as Joan Rivers's jewelry. She got a better deal on the necklace."

However, this bite can also backfire—for example, when especially selfish individuals seek to use Feminism itself as a form of competition rather than allowing Feminism to remain an inherent undercurrent that's ultimately pushed along.

To this, Eliza added that "there are a lot of people who say things like, 'I'm a Feminist; put *me* in the show.' And so the real questions become: Do you want women in this? Or do you want *you* in this? Do you want women to have it easier? Or do you want *you* to have it easier? And that's true for all the 'isms,'" meaning all the various forms of activism. "It's very tempting to become the cause that you're fighting for rather than to keep your focus *on* the cause. Specifically, with Joan, because she was so competitive, fewer people had to be. But I don't think that any part of Joan did so intentionally. She never thought, 'This will be good for the other women.' No, she was like, 'This is going to be good for *Joan*. And, okay, if this leaves good stuff for them, too, that's great—but I hope it doesn't leave more good stuff for them than it does for me.' So thank God for Joan . . . even though she didn't mean it."

Her seemingly selfish individualism and competitive nature translated into a mental toughness that lasted for decades and affected nearly every part of Joan's offstage life. Even after her husband Edgar killed himself, she went back to work, using her pain for laughs. Oz Scott, director of 1994's *Tears and Laughter: The Joan and Melissa Rivers Story*, which chronicled

Edgar's suicide and its aftermath, said, "Many of the reviews asked, 'Why is Joan doing this movie?' Joan would answer the question by saying, 'I'm an actress. Why would I give a good part to someone else?'"

"Do you think comedians are just inherently competitive?" I asked LA-based comedy producer Charlene Conley.

"Always. Always! I'm sure that's not a popular opinion. In fact, that's definitely *not* a popular opinion. But if you have your eyes on the prize and you have to get to this point and you have to do these three things to get there, and these three things are things that are acceptable to you to do, why not do them?" she asked.

"Do you think men have done the same?"

"Oh, of course! They're much more proficient at it, but equally harsh when it comes to competing for career success," she said. "In a way that really speaks to our equality: Equal for better *and* for worse. I think when women are in competition with one another to be the one girl who rules them all, I think Feminism can fall apart. I'm not someone who thinks all women should love each other just because we're women. Some women suck. Some men suck. Some gender queer people suck. Some people who don't participate in the gender binary suck. Some *people* suck."

What's equally fascinating is how—relative degrees of suckage aside—those same people (meaning all of us, as a society) haven't yet progressed to the point where competition itself, whether between women or between men and women, fuels Feminist comedy. Joan didn't compete with comedians who happened to be men, regardless of their age or celebrity status or whether she considered them her peers, but with some comedians—Billy Eichner, for example—things seemed the exact opposite. Perhaps the difference was his gender; perhaps his sexuality. Perhaps they connected on a professional and personal level that she didn't find with many women who looked to her for similar support. Whatever the case, though he claimed that Joan had been "wonderful and encouraging to the young comedians—everything I'm not," Billy described a very different kind of Joan when they met in 2010, "right before I went to Funny or Die and was trying to sell [the TV show] *Billy on the Street* . . . I was really down on my luck. I had no money; I had credit card debt and no health insurance. I was turning thirty, so it wasn't that cute anymore. It was the first time I thought, 'What am I doing? I'm going to keep doing YouTube videos until I'm forty years old for no money?' I emailed Joan—it was right before she started *Fashion Police*—and told her I was stuck. She was doing her stand-up gig in midtown Manhattan, and she set me up with tickets, and we sat upstairs and had martinis. She told me, 'I came up with all of them. I saw Billy Crystal, Robin Williams when he was starting out, and Howie Mandel, and you can run with those guys—but you have to stick with it.' I went home and called my dad, who was a big fan of hers. He knew I was starting to panic, and I told him what Joan said. He said, 'If Joan is saying that, I think that too.'"

"Maybe it goes back to what I was saying before about pitching in the room," original *SNL* writer Rosie Shuster said. "Guys are conditioned to play team sports. And back then, comedy was even more of a team sport. There was more passing the ball. There was sort of a power in their numbers. And women, because we didn't grow up that way, weren't automatically conditioned to play with and inside of a team the same way. We were forging new ground. We really were at that point in time. There wasn't like a lot of precedent. I didn't know any other female comics like us, and while some of the guys had grown up with male role models—sometimes even their own fathers—our mothers had never done anything like what we were trying to do."

This psychological phenomenon—a mother's projecting her own oppression (and its accompanying resentment) onto her daughter—is hardly uncommon. The question underlying many of these projections seems to be *why should you shine when I wasn't allowed to?* The thing about forty thousand years of women putting up with everything from minor condescension to unequal pay to flat-out rape is that it creates a history of internalized, unexpressed anger. That anger infects all women, regardless of their color or religion or creed. We all have that in common. We were infected with it against our will as little girls, and we grow up and infect others with it. We were injected with it, and we inject our daughters, too, without even knowing. It's like we're all carriers of the same contagious disease. *We can't help it.* Oppression makes instruments of its victims. The symptoms of our collective disease come out in the most seemingly insignificant ways, like when women started harping on each other's "vocal fry." Or when we married women try to "help" single women get married, as if attaining the honorific of "Mrs." somehow gives anyone a true purpose or in any way justifies a lifetime of existence. When we insist on turning "married" into more than what it is: an adjective like "pink" or "hollow" or "fattening." None of these serve any purpose alone; they exist simply to better illustrate the core noun, in the same way "married" is one of many ways to describe a woman but can never *be* the woman. Competing for "the ring" really makes no sense, since it will never determine a woman's worth or provide her with a real identity. Only her true sense of self can do that.

During our conversation in Boston, Professor Landay explained one way in which this woman-on-woman battle first permeated televised comedy, growing like a psychological parasite over time, pushing itself through everything from *I Love to Lucy* to today's nauseating, cat-fighting *Housewives*. "For the most part, every encounter [Lucy] would have had in her professional career was sexist. And that would have been true of all the women. They would have been belittled and demeaned and made to feel like they were not fully capable, even at the same time that people were praising her for the good things she had done in the larger context, it would have been in this idea, well, yeah, but in the end, women aren't making decisions, and she wasn't making decisions."

"And men weren't the only people saying that," I said.

"No, no, it was just the whole context. So even when women did have some sort of power or control they still were a part of and immersed in the overall thoughts and ideas and stereotypes surrounding that power."

"They were internalizing the sexism and then expressing it themselves."

"Yeah, they couldn't help it."

Two waves of comedic Feminism later, the progress has finally become clear. But it still took Lucy and Maddy until they were well into their forties to recognize their own self-sabotaging. As Gloria Steinem put it, "women radicalize with age," slowly growing to understand all that we've internalized—and finally gathering the strength of conviction to reject that internalized oppression and begin to reclaim our own power, apart from Patriarchy's rules. Apart from Male Supremacy. Apart from the expectations of what it means to be someone else's wife or mother or daughter. Apart from those labels, we have to be okay with being ourselves. We have to be fearless—for when we are unafraid, we can be anything we want, including the kind of women who "Yes, and" one another in true solidarity and who, in turn, reap the benefits, both in comedy and in life.

Still, as Saint Cynthia Heimel tells us (please turn to page 199 of your *Sex Tips for Girls* bible), the fear of defining yourself as simply *your* self is real. Because it's so scary, we tend to either let others define us or use others to help us create a definition. The only problem is that this definition will inevitably be based on that other person.

After a few years of allowing others (or using them) to define her, the average single person may very well go through the following narrative on a near-daily basis:

Will I ever find another man? Am I going to die cold and miserable and lonely? There are no men out there anymore, right? All my friends say that all men are either gay or married, and they're probably right.

So what are you going to do? Who's going to love you? You're not so special, are you? And you're certainly not as young as you used to be. Do all men only want nineteen-year-olds? What if you're too smart? What if you're too stupid? What if you have bad breath . . . you must be unlovable, right? How are you going to spend tomorrow night? How about the night after that? What if you never again meet anyone? WHAT IF YOU NEVER AGAIN GET LAID?

Conversely, the average married or long-attached person might very well go through the following alternative narrative on a near-nightly basis:

I love you, and it's lovely to be in a relationship, and it feels good and all . . . but I'm slowly losing my identity. I'm torn between my love for you and my love for myself. I don't even recognize myself anymore sometimes. My personal autonomy feels almost gone! There is no part of myself or my life that I even like, let alone enjoy, and I don't think you know how that feels. I feel like I've accomplished almost nothing that I originally set out to do, while the one goal you've ever had you're currently achieving. Not me! Oh no! I don't even know who I am anymore. I am a maker of lists. A runner of errands. A planner of finances and meals. And this just feels like one more thing that I'll end up doing instead of all the things I ever wanted to. Enough. At the end, I don't want my life to feel like a consolation prize!

Sound familiar? Your plan to be all things to all people at all times while ignoring your own need for support is backfiring, and yet we still can't—or won't—have face-to-face conversations about our disillusionment with isolation. Some of us are afraid of judgment. Others want to avoid the temptation to judge others. Why do we carry around these silent, menacing anxieties? Because there's still no good way to fully champion other girls in an honest, open, emotionally secure way. Very few of us know how to be truly transparent, supportive, and happy for someone else's success(es) without bringing in our own agendas, and we all have to deal with that. But while we're attempting to escape from this hideous self-fulfilling prophecy that the Patriarchy first created and we seem doomed to perpetuate, let's at least try to define ourselves with and for and using *our* selves instead of allowing others to do it for us. Women like Phyllis Diller never had a chance to control their own narrative in the way that we now do, so let's take advantage of the spoils of her generation's war. She had to watch Sid Caesar, Milton Berle, Morey Amsterdam, Jonathan Winters, and other men on TV in order to learn the craft of stand-up comedy. She had no other choice but to try and channel her voice and experiences through theirs. Those were the only voices women like Phyllis got to hear, and she grew up hearing them define her (and all comedians at the time) using men's reflections. But now we have other influences. Even better, we have each other. We can model our entire lives, if we so choose, around the voices and experiences of those who reflect *us*.

"There were nineteen of us that started out in 1983," Susan Rice said. "I was one of the only three women comics working in Portland in 1984. Think about it: There were only *three of us* then. But it was great! There was so much work in town that I could work every night for a month, then start over . . . I got hired but I noticed I was getting hired and being billed as 'the girl' or, you know, 'the female comic,' or 'the comedienne.' You just took it. You knew it was kind of wrong but you took it 'cause you were having a good time and learning your craft. But when I got to LA . . . that's when I realized there was a big difference."

"What was the difference?" I asked.

"You were singled out. It was the belly room for women. It was the all-girl, girls' night out. I worked with Paula [Poundstone] one time on the road, and there were only a few people, and she refused to do 'women shows.' And it wasn't because she wanted to be exclusive. It's because she didn't want to be a part of the freak show. . . . She said, 'Take the money but don't believe the pattern,' because it *shouldn't* have been that way, but she was right: It was a pattern. But still, you had to do it to get ahead. So, you took the money, and you did the gigs, all so you could move up fast."

In this way, "Yes, and" became the idea of women supporting each other to combat the narrative that women are each other's competition. An idea that really started with Lucy and Ethel. Two best friends who were also neighbors.

we're all in this together

W<small>E CAN TRACE THE PROGRESSION</small> of female friendship as a basis for comedic Feminism from Lucy's friendship with her landlady/neighbor, Ethel, to Mary Tyler Moore's friendship with her neighbor/coworker, Rhoda, on *The Mary Tyler Moore Show*—two iconic sitcoms that enshrined "Yes, and" as the source of timeless entertainment. More would follow: *Laverne & Shirley*, *Kate & Allie*, *Sex and the City*, *Broad City*, and many others where female friendships formed the basis for comedic situations and social commentary. *I Love Lucy*'s emphasis on female friendship remains one of its most lasting elements, inspiring much of today's current Millennial Feminism.

When we spoke from the stage at the Magnet Theater in New York's theater district, Abbi Jacobson of *Broad City* said, "Without a doubt, I feel like I'm a Feminist. I hope that our show is definitely identified as a Feminist show as well. It's something I feel strongly about, but at the same time, we don't ever sit down and say we want to push these ideas. I think it's an inherent thing that comes across in the show because of our belief system, if that makes sense. These values come across. It's never something that we're like, 'I want to make sure we put this in.' I think our Feminism is more subconscious, and I like it even better that's it's subconscious rather than the blatant mission statement of our show. It just is because of the way we are, the way that our writers are, and the way that our cast and crew operates. So, I hate when people say, 'Well, they talk just like guys,' because, no: This *is* how women talk. Maybe men talk like that, too, but we're women, this is how we talk to each other. And that's what we're examining and observing and putting on the show. Because of the way we talk, we're always compared to male-driven shows—some people even call us the female version of *Workaholics*. But again, no: We're the version of *us*. That's where the Feminist point of view comes in. We don't need to be compared to a male-driven show; we're *our* show."

Abbi's show isn't identical to other female-driven shows simply because they all involve females; these shows can all be equally different and yet, because they share certain important traits, equally funny and, as a result, profoundly effective. And shows like Abbi's are indeed so incredibly effective because: (1) female friendships are given equal weight to situational humor and (2) both are developed in direct proportion to one another, forming yet another kind of "Yes, and" between storyline and character development. As a result of these shared traits, it's consistently clear that the former—female collaboration—creates the entire basis for the latter—effective comedy.

Further, because these shows portray how female friendships so often work in real life, including emphasizing women's need for continued support from one another (especially with regards to relationships), their undercurrent creates yet another "Yes, and" to combat the Patriarchal narrative that a relationship (usually marriage) should be a woman's sole goal. A narrative that encourages her to either separate herself from other women in order to "get a man," or (even worse) to use women as "fillers" (temporary stand-ins until they enter into marriage, at which point their female friends are left behind as no longer servicing a Patriarchal purpose). Either way, she's left isolated and dependent on her partner for the support her friends could provide.

This narrative clearly recalls Sophie Tucker's description of First Wave women growing up with the idea that they should "cling like a vine" around a man's neck. Two waves later, Abbi and Ilana embody an entirely different mindset shared by many millennial Feminists like LA-based stand-up Brandie Posey, who celebrate this shift, even if remnants of the old rules remain.

"A lot of women were—and still are— raised from little girls to be in competition. And I do feel that when I'm on stage. When you're the only woman in the lineup, all the women in the audience are sometimes projecting this negative energy. They put a wall up. They cross their arms and lean back in their chairs, which so often translates to, 'What are you going to say? Are you going to be with me or against me?' When I see that, I can't help but think, 'We're not in competition with each other. I just want to exist with you in this world.' But it's a mindset—almost anti-Feminist belief system—that has to be slowly overcome.

"Alternately, they get tired of dick jokes, and yet they laugh along politely at them simply because they don't want to look like prudes. But when *you* get on stage, they're like, 'Give me something. Oh, you're not giving me exactly what I want in this moment? Well, then, I'm gone.' And they turn off from you. That happens all the time, when you're the token in a lineup where (whether you like it or not) you speak for everyone in the room who happens to look like you. There's extra pressure to overcome that implicit, subconscious sexism that women in the audience have absorbed for so many years and that they're now projecting onto the stage—and onto *you* specifically—without realizing.

"And yet, if you say something funny, and their boyfriends are laughing too hard, it's weird for them. Then their vibe changes to, 'Who is this that's making him laugh? Should I feel threatened?' And conversely, if a guy sees his girlfriend laugh too hard at my joke, he'll project the vibe of, 'What's so funny? Is there a secret language going on here? Should I feel threatened?' So it comes from both sides.

"I know that I was raised this way, too. I had to re-train myself to *not* want to be 'one of the boys.' And I've always had good girlfriends my entire life, and I'm still very close with a lot of them from all different walks of life . . . but there's still that thing that was in my brain from a young age, telling me to discount my female friendships because if I focus too much on females, I'll never get married to a man. Because *that's* supposed to be my true purpose and ultimate goal, rather than simply being happy with whoever makes me happy. It wasn't until maybe my early twenties that I was like, 'That's bullshit. I love guys and all—and I also love my guy friends—but men serve a different place in my heart than my girlfriends do. It took me that many years—which, if you think about it, is still so much better than earlier generations had it—to overcome everything I'd seen and everything I'd learned. For such a long time, *every* TV show involved women hating on each other over a guy, either directly or indirectly," Brandie went on to explain, "and you still see women fighting on TV all the time. How many dating shows are based on nothing more than fifty women fighting over some boring loser, right? And all these guys; they just look the same. They're all just boring, fratty dudes, but these women are still clawing each other to death because a man is still their status symbol. But that's not actually true of most women that I know," because, as we've mentioned, these shows, unlike *I Love Lucy* or *Kate & Allie* or *Laverne & Shirley* or *The Mary Tyler Moore Show* or *Broad City*, aren't based on female friendship as they exist in real life.

Which is not to say that infighting and conflicts aren't a part of real friendship. There can be lots of conflict in genuine friendships—since genuine friends care enough to get upset with one another and actually, honestly say so.

These shows wouldn't be realistic if they portrayed female friendships as perpetually sunny and harmonious. But the key differences between "Yes, and" shows and "divide-and-conquer" shows are (1) how often conflict occurs; (2) the source of that conflict; (3) what methods the women use to "fight" one another; and (4) how long the conflict(s) last before sincere support is reestablished.

The answers to these four factors really determine whether the show is combating Patriarchy's narrative about competition or reinforcing it.

On *Broad City*, Abbi and Ilana are very different, in many ways—much like real-life friends—but they acknowledge these differences. No one's trying to make anyone change. They don't try to impose their individual personalities on one another, to silence one another, or to homogenize one another. They're secure enough to be unique. Because they're honest about those differences, they truly know each know other and so they can call each other on their flaws in a comedic way.

This ability to securely, calmly, and lovingly "Yes, and" one another ties back to Lucy and Ethel, who refused to let any conflict go on very long before the bedrock of their friendship reestablished itself in a comedic way.

"There's a great episode where they buy the same dress, and they've been fighting over stuff through the whole episode," Dr. Landay said, "and they sing this song 'Friendship,' and they rip off parts of each other's dresses, like the flower decorations. And it's very, very funny, of course, because it goes against everything they are singing, and it's not feminine in that way at all. They are being competitive and conflictual, but in the end of course their friendship is more important to them than that. But they're not cajoling and tricking and trying to go around each other in the same way that the women do with the men. It's a very different kind of conflict and then a different kind of resolution. Certainly Lucy gets a different kind of support from Ethel than she does from Ricky. The same occurs between Mary Tyler Moore and Rhoda. Rhoda starts off as this kind of satellite character on the show, and then their friendship gets to the point where it becomes the central emotional bond in that show. Because women respond to that, and men do, too—but the dynamic is written mostly for and about women."

"Why do women respond to that?" I asked.

"Because it's *real*. That's the way that women have friendships, and our friends are important to us in that way. Those kinds of friendships often outlast marriages and even family relationships."

Perhaps this dynamic is why, in July of 2011, Phyllis Diller appeared on *The View* and seemed to snidely criticize Joan Rivers. However—in print, at least—it doesn't seem that Joan felt the same way about her predecessor-turned-competitor.

Maybe it all boils down to the evolutionary timeline of Feminism: Phyllis got her start with the help of Groucho Marx in 1958 and Jack Paar in 1962, right as the Second Wave was really taking hold, whereas Joan cut her teeth a few years later, when it had already taken hold, and women generally—and comedienne-ballerinas specifically—were becoming more of a "real" presence outside the domestic sphere.

In the beginning of the *I Love Lucy* series, the general theme of the show was, *Let's watch silly Lucy try and have a job outside the home and continually fail and come back to Desi where she belongs.* By the end of the series, times had changed, and the theme of the show became, *Well,* of course *she's able to have a job outside the home. What's the problem with that?*

"I wonder when that mindset shifted?" I asked Dr. Landay.

"The culture *itself* shifted," she answered. "By the time *I Love Lucy* was over, so many of those things were over as well, and there were things that had just changed so much by the time she had her first solo show in the 1960s. That character's a widow, but of course she was divorced from Desi Arnaz. Even though the comedy could go on without a husband figure, without Ricky, it couldn't go on without her best friend, without Vivian Vance, and the 'Viv' character that is revealed as one of the real central aspects of *I Love Lucy*, and that friendship. What we see is that kind of duo, of Lucy and Ethel, and how important that is to comedy."

This theory plays out in Lucille Ball's spin-off series, *The Lucy Show*. Even though *I Love Lucy* began after Ethel and Lucy had already met and married their husbands, when Lucille Ball got divorced in real life and went on to make *The Lucy Show* (where there was no more Ricky), she couldn't do so without Vivian Vance returning to play Ethel. Lucy also brought in other real-life friends, such as Carol Burnett, to play foil characters—but the reality of Lucy and Ethel's friendship remained, allowing them to transcend the "buddy" element of a traditional "buddy comedy."

Whereas *I Love Lucy* occasionally promoted the idea that the true basis of women's happiness is at home, with a male partner, *The Lucy Show* made clear that their friendship alone made Lucy and Ethel happy. As a result, their relationships with male romantic partners outside of that friendship could come from a place of *wanting* rather than *needing* men in their lives. "She always had her best friend with her, and I thought that was always wonderful," Dr. Landay said. "It was always she and Ethel against the world. That really brought me a lot of comfort as a kid, thinking, 'You and your buddy can take on the world.'"

This later series also allowed Lucy and Ethel to escape another conciliatory narrative: that women manipulate to get what they want. "For example," Dr. Landay said, "I was teaching a lesson on the *I Love Lucy* episode entitled 'The Freezer' to my students. The premise is that Lucy wants a freezer, and she tells Ethel—in a normal, straightforward, open way—exactly why she wants one. But when it comes to talking to Ricky about getting the freezer, she's manipulative. She maneuvers and whines and cajoles. She uses all of these machinations to trick him into buying what she wants, but she can't simply *talk* to Ricky and openly, honestly, ask for what she wants (let alone go out and buy it herself). There's no way she can do that in that context. With him, there's always an angle. It's only when Ethel and Lucy are alone together that those two characters can actually be themselves. You see this over and over and over again: Ethel and Lucy can talk to each other and expresses themselves openly, but when they are trying to talk to their husbands, there's always a setup."

It really comes down to whether someone's comedy is intended to be conciliatory, emancipatory, or demeaning. Lucy and Ethel's comedy is never demeaning toward women or female friendship—it emancipates women by not only allowing but actively encouraging them to treat one another as friends rather than frenemies. Not that they don't have fights and disagreements and jealousies and competition in a way that speaks to real relationships. In fact, their personalities constantly conflict, and they bicker back and forth because of the very nature of their intimacy, but they do so without painting yet another detrimental portrait of women working against one another. Their intentions are clear: They're in this together. They're engaging in every conflict with each other's best interest in mind. They never make their audience suspect, for even a moment, that they might not be in it for the long haul.

When I read things that Tiny Fey and Amy Poehler have said about each other, and when I look at how long their friendship has lasted and watch the ways in which their own work has intertwined, this same theme of "we're in this for the long haul" emerges. Their work seems to yell out what Lucy and Ethel's could only whisper: There's enough for everybody, and we need to make sure that there continues to be enough for everybody, and *that's* how we combat this competitive model. All of this is a very meta way of "Yes, and-ing" "Yes, and." They start with the baseline assumption that there's enough to go around, then they expect both themselves and us to contribute to making more than enough to go around until this concept of contribution expands to include everyone within the entire scene. *That* then becomes the new model by which the future is shaped: building comedy around collaboration rather than competition.

Lucy and Vivian and Maddy—and many other future creators—helped create this new template for the modern-day sitcom: Women sincerely supporting each other, even when various comedic situations successfully, but always temporarily, disrupt that support. This became a new way of doing things, and it paved the way for comedienne-ballerinas treating each other as collaborators rather than competitors. Still, this was new—and therefore dangerous—at the time. While each episode of *I Love Lucy* could explore this liberated point of view and embrace "Yes, and," at the end of the day, Lucy and Ethel still had to go home to their husbands. They still had to demonstrate their loyalty to the Patriarchy. They still had to be corralled into passive acquiescence, sending out the message, *This is all just an experiment. No need to be threatened. We're still happier with our husbands at home than we would be out together alone, working and single.* So as Feminist as it becomes during that time period, it ultimately had to end with this note of, "Yes, but" rather than "Yes, and." Until *The Lucy Show*, when Lucille Ball was actually single, her freedom had to remain painted as merely a comedic ploy.

Thankfully, later shows no longer required so much outward display of loyalty to the rules. *The Golden Girls* exploded the 1980s by portraying an all-female, all-forty-plus cast that returned home to one another at the end of each episode rather than constantly ruing their lack of romance. By the 1980s, it seemed, there was less of a need for ploys. "It's so funny because I remember being a kid and thinking, 'My guy friends are the best. I love being one of the guys!'" Brandie Posey said. "But when I grew up, I knew I still wanted to be a Golden Girl . . . It sparked this new voice in my head that asked, 'Why am

I supposed to be in competition with these people? I love these people! I just want to hang out with a bunch of Rue McClanahans until I die! It's the dream!'"

The Golden Girls's success was followed up by yet another popular hit, *Designing Women*, which portrayed female friendships in a workplace comedy. But while the characters on these shows remained in loyal friendships, the women who played them couldn't seem to escape infighting when the cameras stopped rolling, leading to persistent rumors that they actually hated one another, and that Delta Burke made her costars' lives miserable off stage.

Unfortunately, we see these rumors borne out in other types of comedy—especially when gatekeepers cast members of sketch comedy teams or lineups for stand-up shows, where women were (and still are) kept away from each other, which seems to serve a sabotaging purpose: *Keep them separated, because when they get together, they find like-minded, funny people, and that might really explode into something.*

"When I first moved to New York, I started writing with a sketch group where I was the only girl," Eliza Skinner said. "We used to have actual, literal rules against having more than one girl in the show, and so me and the other girls who worked for the same company would never get to tour together. We never got to be in the same shows. The other members of the teams would compare us to each other, too. I remember being on tour one time. We were in Florida. Me and four guys who were in the show were sitting around in some bar, and they were just ripping into the new girl, who wasn't there. Then they started ripping into the second-to-newest girl. Finally, I was like, 'Hey guys, do you guys notice that you only say this about women? You only complain about the women.' And they were like, 'No! It's just those two and they just happened to be the worst.' And I was like, 'Well, there's only three females who are even allowed to be in the whole company so . . . I doubt that's true.' They got *so* pissed at me. Speaking up like that gave me a reputation for being such a hard core bitch for so many years. And at the time, I doubted myself, and wondered, 'Was that a bitchy thing to say?' But now, when I look back on it, I'm like, 'Good! I'm glad I said something, because it was true, and I was right!' I'm still glad that I spoke up for those other girls. I hope they would have spoken up for me."

Even in the relatively emergent field of comedy podcasts, these limitations sometimes seep in, as Brandie Posey later explained.

"There's this weird thing where, as a female comic, you're given more responsibility other than just being funny. Which in itself is sexist and ridiculous. And women even do it to each other. With our podcast we have . . . every once in a while we have women write in and they're just like, 'I didn't like the way you said this.' They nitpick what you say as opposed to understanding that progress works by imperfect things building on each other and like evolution over time."

"They don't 'Yes, and' each other? Even in this brave new world?" I asked.

"No, they don't. They want you to be perfect out of the gate and that's it. And yes, be funny but also say the truth all the time. And it's like, 'Well no, it's a comedy show.' Sometimes I'll catch myself doing it too, at live shows. I'll see another girl I've never seen before, and then I'll sort of want to size her up, and she'll just jump out to me more by virtue of the fact that she's the only other girl. But then I'll sort of check myself on those thoughts and be like, 'Well why are you feeling this way?'"

"Do you think that might be part of the narrative?"

"Yeah. Like, they've decided, whoever 'they' are, that there will only be two of us. And thus they're going to allow us to duke it out with one another. And then we're fighting each other as opposed to wondering where that rule came from. Right? We're fighting instead of questioning *why* there's the 'Rule of Two' and *who* it was exactly who created the slots that we now have to size each other up for. And that's bullshit. But it still works, and it always will . . . until *we* stop working it. You know? Until we start truly working with rather than against one another. So, I guess my point is: Give each other a break. Feel compassion for each other. This doesn't mean that you can't get mad at or be hurt by other women, and it doesn't mean you have to give them an automatic pass. But if anyone has been where you've been, if anyone has had the problems you've had, *she* has."

Brandie's sentiment recalls Emily Nussbaum, who wrote of this intrinsic need for compassion within "Yes, and."

"There's a poem by Sharon Olds called 'The Elder Sister.' In it, the narrator talks about how much she used to hate her sister, 'sitting and pissing on me.' But then she learned to see that the harsh marks on her older sister's face (her wrinkles, the frown lines) were 'the dents on my shield, the blows that did not reach me.' Her sister had protected her by being there first—not with love," but as a kind of human shield, whose sacrifice allowed the younger sister to escape similar wounds.

"Maybe that's true of Rivers," Nussbaum said. "Her flamboyant self-hatred made possible this generation's flamboyant self-love, set the groundwork for the crazy profusion of female comics on TV these days, on cable and network, cheerleading one another, collaborating and producing and working in teams, as if women weren't enemies at all. (Everywhere but in late-night TV: decades after Carson, there are still ten men on that list.) Rivers came first—and if her view darkened, if she became an evangelist for the ideas that had hurt her the most, she also refused to give in, to disappear. 'I would not want to live if I could not perform,'* she once said. 'It's in my will. I am not to be revived unless I can do an hour of stand-up.' That's its own kind of inspiration. We can celebrate it without looking away."

"If you're watching a show, and there are only two women on it, and one of them has being doing comedy for a long time and is really polished, and the other one is maybe newer . . . an audience's interpretation of that is going to be something along the lines of 'very few women are funny,'" NY-based stand-up Aparna Nancherla said. "Maybe it's more subconscious now. And maybe that's a harder target to hit than something that's so explicitly obvious as, 'the law needs to change.' Now it's our thoughts that need to change. And people get very defensive about that stuff."

"Why do you think they get defensive about their thoughts?" I asked.

"Because they think that nobody wants to be seen as sexist, or racist, or homophobic."

"Do you think they have more of a problem with the label or the actions that underlie the label?"

"Definitely the label."

Which speaks directly to Kate Harding's now famous quote: "We live in a country full of racism, but no racists; rape, but no rapists. And the common denominator is power. To believe

---

* Seemingly channeling the spirit of iconic (and deeply tragic) French singer Édith Piaf, who famously answered the question, "What would you be if you weren't singing?" Simply: "Dead."

a rape survivor's word over that of her male classmate, colleague, teacher, or superior officer is to upset the natural order of things, privileging the voice with less cultural authority over the one we expect to have all the answers."

Similarly, we live in society with sexism but no sexists, which allows many of us to continue investing in the comforting but ultimately self-destructive mantra, "I know this exists but it's definitely not me," which, Aparna said, "is such a strange thing to cling to because—while I understand that admitting it is scary because it requires facing the fact that *we're* the problem—we're all in this together. And that means *we* can also be the solution."

"And yet, it's important to avoid being mired down in the obvious. I mean, obviously, sexism still exists. We *know* there's still sexism—*of course* it still exists everywhere," Rosie Shuster said, to which I responded:

"I agree. You're right: It is important not to simply repeat the obvious. But I also think you may be coming from a place of acknowledging the problem—of saying, 'of course'—which is a baseline assumption that not everyone shares."

There are still a lot of people—both men and women—who think sexism isn't an issue and rape victims are exaggerating their claims in order to extort and victimize men. Even Attorney General Jeff Sessions has said he doesn't believe that women and the LGBTQ community face discrimination. People like that think that we're post-sexism, post-racism, post-homophobia. Others won't admit that those ever existed at all.

"That's true," Rosie said. "It kind of reminds me of a real great quote I heard recently: 'These days, it's worst to be *called* a sexist than to *be* a sexist.' You know? I thought that had some depth to it, that comment."

Perhaps because of this current glaringly hypocritical mindset, the mid-1970s and early-2000s casts of *Saturday Night Live* remain seeming oases in a long history of Male Supremacy's rules. "Jane Curtin and Laraine Newman and Gilda Radner were such supportive people in real life," Dr. Landay explained, "and that season became spectacular because of that." Years later, Amy Poehler and Tiny Fey were even better, closer friends, both on stage and off—and once again, *SNL* became brilliant. As women have gained more control over the production of comedy and as they've taken positions of power within the media, they've been able to combat that competitive narrative by supporting one another's work. "By the time Tina Fey became head writer, the whole environment had shifted, and a lot of that has to do with improv's cooperative technique of saying 'Yes, and,' rather than, 'Nope, let's do it my way and forget about you,'" Dr. Landay said. "And that wasn't just about the women on *SNL*—that idea was encouraged by the men who were also involved in improv."

Real progress necessitates not only activism on the part of the oppressed but support from their allies. Both must work together to make change. "In a way," Dr. Landay said, "improv, although it was originally established by men, remained based on women's theory. So it had something that was going on there from the very beginning that was really different, and that difference filtered into other aspects of comedy—into television and film and stand-up, as well—at the same time that more women were joining the industry. And so, as all of these things start to come together, the mindsets change for new improv performers who embrace the idea that women don't have to compete against each other."

By the mid-2000s, this allowed even more women to join the cast—Maya Rudolph, Kristen Wiig, Rachel Dratch, and many others—safe in the knowledge that things had changed. They could be friends and do wonderful things both for and with each other, but never in a way that suggested that there was only room for just one or two of them at any given time.

When even younger men joined the cast during this time, they saw this, and it gave them a progressive, gender-inclusive mental picture of how to work together with the "girls" in the show. Unlike previous generations who trained under Del Close's model, they no longer believed that women were relegated to costarring roles. They could actually be the main character who carried a scene. This progress opened up all-new avenues for creating bigger, better comedy. It also made improv creatively safer for women to bring in new and exciting ideas.

"It's a *great* feeling," Livia Scott said, "to feel safe and included and supported by your teammates. That's why I love Amy Poehler, specifically, *so much*. I saw her at UCB one time . . . I don't know how many years ago it was. Maybe it was like 2006 or something. It was the UCB 4, and the cast was doing a scene, and she just sort of stepped out of the scene and started singing, 'I Wanna Dance with Somebody' by Whitney Houston. The audience loved it. It made us feel like 'We're all here. We're alive.' We all got to experience that joyfulness and generosity of spirit. Because, you see, there are usually two different kinds of performers: The ones who project to their audience, 'You're here for me.' And the ones who project, 'We're here together.' The latter is what Amy gave to me and to all of us."

"Do you think Gilda gave that to her?"

"Yes! Gilda *was* that. Gilda was so beautifully and exactly that. She was like, 'We're all here. We're all in this together.'"

safe spaces

WHY?

Why do "the rules" still exist?

Why haven't we totally done away with divide and conquer and replaced it with "Yes, and"?

Why do so many women still flock to shows like *The Real Housewives* or *The Bachelor*, where they witness other women verbally—and sometimes even physically—fighting one another and tearing each other down? Why do women watch those shows—and why do they sign up to participate in, certainly encourage, and maybe even expand their own inequality?

"Some women maybe flock to those shows because they haven't found a way to be fulfilled," Brandie Posey said. "If you haven't found that, and you're stuck in an older mentality of waiting around to be fulfilled by having a man or defined by somebody else, then those shows become very important to you. It's a distraction, while you're waiting. It's a train wreck for you to watch that will make you feel superior, since you have nothing else to make you feel that way. These shows allow you to tell yourself, 'I'm not happy with what I have going on, but at least I'm not getting my hair pulled on national television.' It's a way to be a mean girl, only passively and from afar."

Our mothers may have been passive-aggressive—battling each other silently, stealthily, not through open war but rather a series of secret raids, nonconfrontations, and near misses—but their daughters have split apart to become aggressively passive. Our mothers embraced the old adage that there are but two strategies in life, force or guile, the latter being more feminine and therefore socially acceptable. Today, we are perhaps less overtly "feminine" and, as a result, perhaps less openly closed (talk about a mind-fuck), but we haven't yet gone the way of force, either. We haven't crossed over to that oneness with the traditionally masculine. We reject both, in many ways. We abdicate. We avoid the topic. We don't talk about Feminism except when it concerns motherhood, wage inequality, and/or abortion. We timidly avoid labeling anyone a Feminist without her prior informed consent. We have left the room of our own that Virginia Woolf once proclaimed necessary for putting pen to paper and voicing our own, true opinions, the room outside of the common areas paid for and thus controlled by men and dominated by the needs of growing children. We have withdrawn, in some ways, and many more of us aggressively defend our right to speak no evil, see no evil, and think no evil.

It's not Feminism, it's humanism.

It's not Rape Culture, it's just [BLANK].

That's not today, that's yesterday.

It's not his fault, it's yours, really, because you misunderstood what he truly meant, and after all, I know him so much better than you do, and that means you should know that I know that he's really a very nice guy. So back off. Or I'll block you on Twitter.

Welcome to Rape Culture. Simmering beneath a rape apologist's diatribe is usually something along the lines of:

"She got raped because she [BLANK], but I didn't [BLANK], and I'm not a [BLANK], so that will never happen to me."

Or:

"She got raped because she [BLANK], but my mom/daughter/sister/aunt/coworker/best friend/podiatrist/etc. would never [BLANK], and plus she's not a [BLANK]. So rape will *never* happen to her."*

Sometimes, women don't talk about these things. Other times, they wait until they get into a safe space—like Joan Rivers talking about Woody Allen to Howard Stern: "I think he's brilliant. What Woody does in his private life is his private life. You want to be a pedophile, be a pedophile. I like . . . what's her name? Ping-Pong. The wife. She wears yellow too much. Too matchy-matchy." Loyalty always seemed to elude Joan, and perhaps that's why she never offered much of it to the younger females who looked up to her.

Or, rather than women of Joan's (and our) generation simply feeling the overwhelming need to compete with other women, perhaps the issue is two-fold. Maybe it also involves our finding the right kinds of safe spaces. Sometimes, when

---

* Part of the problem is our Patriarchal legal system. Under English common law, derived from a cool combo of William the Conqueror, Ancient Rome, and the Talmud and then handed down in the form of the Fourth Amendment, a cop can perform what's called a "Terry Stop and Frisk" if he feels you may have a weapon, but he can't go into your pocket to search for items that aren't weapons. Why? Because therein you have a "reasonable expectation of privacy."

we feel physically threatened by the real world, that space can only exist on the Internet. Sometimes it takes us three weeks to write the following for fear that our career opportunities will come to an end:

"I have a lot of concerns," wrote a well-known improv performer who asked to remain anonymous. "When I was raped in college by my friend from HS [high school] I told a few friends and when I went home to my HS thanksgiving football game people were throwing things at my head and calling me a slut. He won, he won big time. I stopped attending any [after-school] events after that. When I got into the comedy scene in NYC in 2001, I was propositioned for sex by three different higher ups that are still very much involved in the comedy scene.

"After the first one I repeatedly said no to, I was then somehow not allowed to be a teacher at a certain comedy theatre even though I had been being prepped to do so and even coached the class outside of the class. Another higher up propositioned sex to me and I again said no. I was then let go from my job at a certain comedy theatre. Another higher up at a comedy theatre propositioned me. I respectfully declined and our friendship suffered and consequently I was not allowed to do anything at a comedy institution. All of these things have the same thing in common: I was abused, my career has been compromised, and my friendships with certain people have been compromised. When people make jokes about 'you didn't sleep with the right people,' it stings because I didn't. I did not sleep with certain people and my career suffered. And when I did, my life suffered.

"For a long time I was told to shut my mouth and carry on. I used to scream and shout about these kinds of injustices and it literally dug me deeper. For the past five years I have really just kept my mouth shut, and low and behold my opportunities got better and better. I am in no way telling anyone to keep their mouth shut; I'm telling you all of this because I am incredibly grateful that there are now more than a handful of woman speaking up about this. I don't know what will happen in the end but I do know that this type of thing has been happening as long as I have been around and of course since the beginning of time. I'm not sure how it can change but I am hopeful that with numbers it may. I am scared for those who are taking a stand because even if you are not a victim of sexual assault and have had experiences like me it still can affect your overall career as a comedian in this community. I have no solution ultimately, only respect for the growth in numbers and voices."

"I don't know if this is useful, but I have a tiny, tiny definition of Rape Culture . . ." Portland's Bri Pruett added to this discussion.

"Yes, please. Go on," I said.

"Okay, so. I go on blind dates, from time to time, with people I meet on the Internet because I'm just not really scared. I don't know why. I definitely should be. So I went to this date, and we were kissing a little bit, and I told him, 'I'm not trying to have sex.' But then he put a condom on, anyway, and he got a little rough . . . so I had to kick him. I left the apartment immediately, and it was not the scariest thing in the world that has happened to me, but maybe it should have been."

"Did this experience define Rape Culture for you?"

"Yes, in a way—but not because of what happened. My definition came about because of people's *reactions* to what happened."

"Could you elaborate on that?"

"If someone reacts by telling a woman, 'Well, maybe you shouldn't have gone over to that person's house,' that's Rape

Culture. If there's an assumption that my safety is *always* compromised, that's Rape Culture. A lot of men don't realize until they hear it. My guy friends will say, 'Oh, my God, I can't believe you went over there.' But when I follow that up with, 'So, you agree that Rape Culture is real?' They'll answer, 'No.' But they've just made their baseline assumption crystal clear: Simply by my being alone with any man, it's very probable that I could be raped. The assumption is that, because we live in a Rape Culture, I am in danger pretty much *any* time I'm alone with a man. I'm presumed to be a victim, regardless of the actual circumstances. A woman can go on a date with someone, and it doesn't go well and something terrible can happen, but that doesn't necessarily mean that she was the victim of something—we simply assume that she is and always will be. So, whether or not someone actually *knows* you're in danger, you're *presumed* to be in danger, simply because of the culture that women live in."

"Did they also assume that you should've known better? That it was your responsibility to stop him, rather that his responsibility to stop himself?"

"Exactly, they assumed that his actions were in *my* hands to stop. There's implicit victim blaming. An implicit onus on me to not *be* raped. It's the language our society uses: 'women *get raped*,' not 'men *rape* women.' Or 'men rape *men*' in many cases. And they'll make this guy exceptional almost immediately. They 'other' him right away. They immediately say things like, 'We could never do anything like that. He is separate from the rest of us men. *We're* great.'"

Today's growing conversation around rape jokes in particular has made a lot of comedians who also happen to be men realize the existence of Rape Culture. Before this realization began in earnest, nearly every mention of Rape Culture segregated this problem into the subcategory of "women's issues." Many Internet comment threads went something like this:

Woman: This is a problem for women.

Man: No, it isn't.

Woman: Well, it may not be for most men, but many women face this issue.

Man: No, they don't. If it were a real problem, you'd tell someone about it.

Woman: We're literally telling you right now.

Man: But this isn't even an issue. I've never experienced this problem in my entire life.

Woman: That's because you are a man, and this is an issue that primarily affects women.

Man: That's sexist.

"A lot of these guys just didn't know what they didn't know. And they didn't know because they never saw it—they're not rapists, nor are they friends with rapists, nor are they interacting with Internet trolls," LA-based author and stand-up comic Jane Borden said during our talk at Second City Hollywood. "A lot of misogyny isn't even seen or recognized by most men. I think it's rare that people set out with malicious intentions . . . but most people don't even recognize the bars of the cage until they're locked inside."

While I don't think that any subject matter should be off-limits and I don't think anything should be censored—even rape jokes—there's always a way to turn it around and make the perpetrator the butt of the joke. *The Onion* did this brilliantly with one of my favorite headlines ever: "Pope Forgives Molested Children." If we were to decide that child molestation should be off-limits, then we wouldn't have that wonderful "fuck you" to child molesters.

To this end, Abbi Jacobson added that "we [*Broad City*] had an episode where we tackled rape, and it was something we were nervous about. It was a conversation about a point of view that we didn't think was really addressed that much"— specifically, Abbi's character "accidentally raping" a guy she's seeing by continuing to have sex with him after he falls asleep. "It was coming from this naiveness; the character's ignorance. Some people were not so happy about it, but it came from a place where we were trying to explore a different point of view through a situation. We didn't sit there in the writer's room, going, 'We gotta talk about rape and make it funny!' No. It came from a story where that filtered in organically. But I learned, through that episode, that you have to be careful with what you're doing when you have a platform. It makes me so upset when people get upset with what we're doing," she said, covering her face with frustration. "But I think enough people got it, what we were trying to do, and so I still think there's always a way."

"Do you think Gilda might have felt the same way when people misunderstood her comedy?"

"Totally. The only difference is that there was not social media then. I don't know if she could even get a sense of what the feedback was. If there *was* negative feedback. I think people were just at home, like what were they going to do with it? Maybe they wrote letters? Now we get it right in the old Tweet. You get it right away. You get a quick reaction *now*. I don't know if that's good or bad. It's both good *and* bad. It makes me so upset. We try to never let it affect the comedy. I would never go in and be like, 'These people hate this thing. We can't do it.' We can't let that affect it. But at the same time, it affects my outlook on what my job is. It's a bigger-picture reminder of the fact that I have this amazing job where what

I'm trying to say and my observations get to be seen and heard by a lot of people, and how powerful that is. It's a responsibility to think about what you're saying before you say it."

In turn, an audience bears the responsibility of thinking about what's being said before laughing. Some would argue this is an unrealistic expectation to place on an audience, while others would argue that an audience should raise its standards if it expects better comedy and wait for a rape joke that's both funny and enlightening. While perhaps rare, such a joke is certainly not impossible—and the patience may be worth the wait. Most comedienne-ballerinas I interviewed felt that, either way, the audience should decide. However, this topic of safe spaces—both physical and comedic—has become so contentious in recent years because of these kinds of jokes. Many who rail against the creation of safe spaces as "too politically correct" also support the kinds of rape jokes that mock victims rather than perpetrators. Comedians who fall into this category then argue that their jokes were, after all, just jokes, but many audience members counter this argument with silence. If a comedian chooses to make a rape joke that "punches down," he or she should be prepared for silence. But whether an audience cheers or protests, the idea that comedy circles should ban outright all taboo topics that could potentially trigger discussion stifles our ability to "Yes, and" the *ways* in which we want our comedians to approach these topics. If we want to encourage comedy to "punch up," we must allow it to punch at all.

"I'm glad that all these rape jokes were happening because it pushed the topic to the forefront. These jokes have revealed a lot about some fans and some audiences—especially online audiences, which always include the most hideous trolls," Jane Borden said. "A lot of abusive, anti-woman trolls have been given a voice through social media, but conversely, a lot of sensitive, intelligent men have also been given the opportunity to read those trolls' comments to women. When these sensitive men read all the threats that women receive online—everything from calling someone a 'cunt' to threatening to rape and murder her—they can see, for maybe the very first time, that Rape Culture exists. In my opinion, as terrible as this online abuse has become, the silver lining is that Rape Culture is showing its true colors. So, in a way, all of these terrible rape jokes opened the door for a greater conversation, and I think that conversation is changing a lot of minds."

"Is that the ultimate point—to change men's minds? Or to unite women against Rape Culture?" I asked Eliza Skinner.

"Both, really," she said, "because one should help the other—kind of like another version of 'Yes, and.' Because nobody, women or men, is going to survive in this world or make any positive changes without help. So you don't want to shut down these bad, dumb, punching-down rape jokes as much as change them for the better so that the punch line lands where it will have a positive impact. You don't want to kill these trolls; you want to open their eyes, because nobody knows until he knows. We all *think* we do, but we have no idea."

"That's sort of the essence of privilege, isn't it? Thinking that if something doesn't affect *you* personally it doesn't affect *anyone* personally," I said.

For example, if you're a booker at a comedy club, and you're only making room for one girl in the show, you don't realize there's only *one* girl in the show. And as long as there are only one or two girls, then the ouroboros continues feeding back onto itself, reinforcing the idea that there *can* and *should* only be one or two in the show. And that everything those women do will represent all other women. And that if *you're* not the funniest comedian they've ever seen, then *no* women are funny. "It's just one of those burdens on the girls in the show, or any women stand-ups, really," Eliza said. "It's not just 'Is *she* funny?' Instead, it's a test: 'Are *any* women funny?' And if you fail the test, then all of us do, too."

"Our idea of what's funny versus what's offensive—the boundary between humor and taboo—is always moving," NYC-based stand-up Ayanna Dookie said. "There's that line of things that are funny and things that aren't funny and things that are too serious or unfair, or unjust or wrong, that you can't make fun of. Then there are always people saying there is nothing off-limits and that kind of thing. I always wonder: What are their motivations? Are they trying to be the person who is getting the attention for being outrageous? Or do they really not care? Do they *really* think that's funny even though it's so obviously sexist or racist?"

As our culture changes the ways in which it deals with, treats, and thinks about rape, what does that mean in our comedy? How do we joke about a topic during periods of change? There was a period of time—and certainly this was the case during Lucy's First Wave—where topics like rape weren't considered funny at all, regardless of whether they punched up or down. Jokes about this topic were simply not to be made. During that same era, not coincidentally, forcible rape (or what the law refers to as "legitimate"—as opposed to "statutory"—rape, partly because of our biased language of consent) was much harder to establish. The fact that a victim had been coerced, for example, wasn't enough in many states to establish that she had been raped—there had to be suffi-cient force involved, which usually meant physical violence. In some states, a victim had to prove she physically resisted her rapist. And if she were drunk or asleep at the time, and therefore couldn't physically resist, rapists often went free because no "force" was present. Clearly, these laws were written by, for, and to support Male Supremacy, but during the Feminist movement of the 1960s, they began to change. It wasn't until 1993 that states such as North Carolina finally agreed that husbands who raped their wives were guilty of a crime. Until then, your husband could pretty much do anything he wanted to you, sexually speaking, simply because you were married. Upon marriage, a husband and wife became "one people" in the eyes of the law, and so he couldn't be prosecuted for raping "himself." Our society no longer supports such legal fictions that allow rapists to escape on cleverly worded technicalities.

At some point in the future, perhaps we'll have figured out the very best methods for joking about rape. Perhaps this will happen when we, as a society, feel safe enough about this issue to no longer worry about its victims. Perhaps by then we'll no longer subject women to living in Rape Culture—where they must live in a near-constant state of safety concerns. (*Do I know this guy well enough to go out with him? Should I bring a friend? What should I wear? Will I look like I'm "asking for it"? Did I bring my mace? I definitely shouldn't have stayed out so late because now I have to walk through this darkened parking lot . . . Oh shit, is that a windowless van?*)

When there is no rape, in some ideal future—when these jokes are about our distant past—we won't have to worry about which way we're punching. By then, comedians will simply ask audiences to try and imagine such a crazy, backward time when we actually made some women feel like rape was their fault. Society placing the burden on the victim rather than where it belongs—on her rapist—will, perhaps, be the punch line. Perhaps we will have evolved beyond all of Male

Supremacy's rules to reach that point. It's not such a crazy idea, considering how far we've come from the "physical-resistance-required" days. After all, we don't defend murderers by suggesting that the victim's clothes justified her death. It's not like we ask someone who's just been robbed, "Hey, I know he took your money at gunpoint and all, but didn't you just lend that guy a dollar yesterday? Maybe he thought you wanted to spice things up!"

Unfortunately, we're still nowhere near this future ideal comedy scene. Right now, we're still trying to get women to support each other enough to go to each other's comedy shows, much less consistently back each other up over rape allegations. We're still very much in the process of changing, and society itself will have to change the way it either prevents or responds to rape in order for there to be the possibility of such jokes truly creating (or reflecting) any positive change.

As LA-based comedy producer Charlene Conley said, "A trigger is a trigger. And, when you start talking about rape, that's a huge trigger for a large percent of the population, both male and female. And most rape jokes are not funny. But does that mean that they should be off the table completely? I don't think so, because I think a well-constructed joke is a well-constructed joke. If you can pull it off, God bless you, because you've done something that most of the population cannot do. And you gotta have to respect that. But then there's yet another problem: If you tell that joke, there's a nearly 100 percent chance that at least one rape victim will be in the crowd. And then what? Then you're in trouble. If people catch on that you've caused real pain, in that moment, the moment itself will be gone—you'll lose the room and any chance you might've had to make *any* kind of a point."

"I was just recently watching *The Unbreakable Kimmy Schmidt*," Dr. Landay said, "which is all about a woman who's survived abduction and rape for the past fifteen years. I can't imagine anything like that existing on television at any other time than the present. To be able to poke fun at subjects that are so shocking and potentially hurtful to so many women, and yet doing so in a way that never seems to hurt anyone at all . . . I don't know how they managed it."

"I wonder, too. How did they pull it off so well? Beyond societal changes in terms of how we legally respond to abduction and rape, what makes that kind of comedy so effective today?"

"Well, what makes *anything* funny is really good writing," she said. "And, of course, doing it from a place of sympathy." This struck me as, perhaps, the entire point. "Yes, and" is essentially just another form of sympathy—a branch of the tree of human compassion. If a rape joke expresses sympathy and human compassion, it's "Yes, and-ing" victims, and providing them with support through laughter. Laughter, in this way, becomes an entirely new wave of change—and that proverbial spoonful of sugar. You can't help but want comedians to succeed in getting this wave going. When we think of comedians in this way—with motives coming from a place of compassion—it becomes clear that very few are actively trying to impose the rules onto others or punch down at victims. As Lyndsay Hailey once said, "If you're going to act like a stripper, strip to the best of your ability, because you're a human being, and you're not a stripper, and you're going to fall short. And falling short, unapologetically, is where the comedy comes from." Perhaps the best method to combat victim-shaming punch downs is to laugh as loudly as possible—not at the joke itself but at Patriarchy's failed attempt to punch.

What also makes things funny—which is always the distinction—is whether the comedian's point of view is, at its core, an underdog's. Many of the issues that comedians face today in deciding whether or not something is funny (or "too soon") comes down to power. The beautiful, elusive power of humor and how best to wield it. It's well accepted (or, at least, should be) that more politically, legally, and economically powerful individuals (i.e., white, middle- to upper-class, heterosexual men) have a responsibility to keep their widespread power in mind when performing and to avoid implying that they are somehow victimized by a system that they, and their ancestors, created specifically for their own benefit. Conversely, when a comedienne-ballerina chooses to wield her humor in accordance with her vulnerability, she turns this system on its head. When any woman speaks her truth and backs it up with humor, she reclaims the power that Patriarchy specifically endeavors to deny her, and she replaces "divide and conquer" with "Yes, and." In this way, the ability to mock is truly the ability to destroy.

"So including yourself in the joke is the key?" I asked Susan Rice.

"Exactly. Plus, it helps all of us come to a social understanding. At first, most of us women are railing. We're trying to strive. For me, personally, I was always clear that I wouldn't make jokes that hurt other women. I was always clear that I would fight for them and for things like *Roe v. Wade.*"

But down the line, Susan discovered that you have to be willing to mock everything. Even your own militancy; Feminism's constant striving for more/better/equal/both. You have to make fun of yourself in order to make fun of anyone else— and that can include making fun of all the times you've been victimized by sexism. You've been victimized, but you are not a victim—you're punching up at the process rather than down at yourself. This can become a way of extending empathy to everyone who's also experienced this pattern. "That's what Carol and Lucy and Moms and Gilda did," Susan said. "They never ran away from that, and neither will I."

This kind of in-depth consciousness-raising is important for all women, especially comedienne-ballerinas, especially in terms of understanding what sharing our stories and experiences means in both a constitutional and political context.

running from *roe*

S INCE SUSAN WAS KIND ENOUGH to bring it up, I will go ahead and admit that, as both a lawyer and a fervent historian, I consider *Roe v. Wade* one of the most important decisions in our constitutional history. As my dear friend Professor Shannon Gilreath of Wake Forest University's School of Law once wrote, "At its core, *Roe* realizes that women cannot exercise any constitutional right, not free speech nor equality nor any other right, without first having an absolute integrity of the body."

The holding of *Roe* established a pregnant woman's right to choose abortion within the limitations of the "viability" standard and reinforced the heteronormative paradigm of a married couple's right to privacy.[1] The right to choose abortion has, since *Roe*, been considered a component of the constitutional "right to privacy" guaranteed by the Due Process clause of the Fourteenth Amendment. Privacy itself involves "two different kinds of interests. One is the individual interest in avoiding disclosure of personal matter, and another is the interest in independence in making certain kinds of important decisions."[2] Thus, the right to privacy includes the state's interest in keeping things out of public view of the majority—such as, in *Roe*, abortion and, in other relevant cases, homosexual activity—and also the individual's right to choose whom she marries, and whether or not to bear children. It is important to note that these definitions of privacy are all based in heteronormative standards of what should and should not be considered parts of the greater "right to privacy."

But it's also arguable that both the wording and structural arguments within *Roe* hurt our efforts at "Yes, and-ing" gender-based equality by focusing too narrowly on pregnancy as the main source of female identity. Thus, in many ways, *Roe*'s limited, isolated, and divisive central conceit, much like those of its predecessors and successors, reinforced not only this heteronormative paradigm but also America's gender and sexual orientation–based caste systems by pitting women against one another (splitting them into two seemingly oppositional groups—mothers versus non-mothers) and isolating women from one of their main avenues of potential support: gay men.

Due Process itself, as interpreted by the Supreme Court, applies to certain basic freedoms seen as fundamental to our concepts of liberty, freedom, and the American scheme of ordered justice. Essentially, this means that there are certain areas of private life into which the government should not enter, whether these areas of private freedom are specifically enumerated by the Constitution or whether, as the Ninth Amendment implies, there are too many to list and they are ever evolving. Privacy in the home is one of these freedoms.[3] Most people would not think that the government would ever enter a man's own home to arrest him for consensual, adult activities taking place therein, but (as the saying goes) most people would be surprised.[4]

Taken together, it is clear that the Supreme Court has now established a judicial precedent of protecting both the individual's right to privacy in the home as well as her "independence in making certain kinds of important decisions." These aspects of Due Process and "privacy," the court has said, are "where the state should not be a dominant presence . . . Liberty presumes an autonomy of self that includes freedom of thought, belief, expression and certain intimate conduct."[5] Ultimately, because "all of women's aspirations—whether for education, work or any form of self-determination and autonomy—ultimately rest on their ability to decide whether and when to bear children," these, the court says, are basic to freedom, liberty, and our concept of justice. The unfortunate fact, however, is that while the court has a history of protecting the individual's right to privacy in the home and the individual's right to independent decision making, it failed in *Roe* to protect the individual. Instead, its wording reinforced normative gender and sexual orientation systems in such a way that protected only limited groups' (*pregnant women's*) limited rights to choose (*whether or not to beget a child*) within their "right to privacy." This limiting and divisive language was dishonest about the true nature of caste in America, and ultimately separated women from gay men instead of uniting them in support of *Roe*. Had more inclusive language been used to protect the individual's right to equal access to sexual health care, the court would have more honestly revealed the gender and sexual orientation–based caste systems as they existed in 1973 and continue to be reinforced through the Male Supremacy's control over the current health-care system.

During the course of *Roe*, a pregnant woman's right to choose abortion was first debated by the Fifth Circuit and ultimately decided by the Supreme Court of the United States. The court found that (1) a woman's right to choose fell within this right to privacy paradigm under Due Process; (2) because of its inclusion with the right to privacy paradigm, pregnant women had the right to choose to abort an unviable fetus, and finally; (3) the right to abort an unviable fetus was fundamental to the American scheme of ordered liberty and thus guaranteed by the Due Process clause of the Fourteenth Amendment. In subsequent years, however, this already limited and isolating right to choose abortion has been slowly hacked away by diminutive case law and burdensome, anti-choice statutory legislation.

Specific changes in both the wording and structural argument of *Roe* would have allowed women and homosexual men to join together in defending access to sexual health care from anti-choice public policies. The existing, unfortunate wording within *Roe*, which extended its protections only to pregnant women's right to choose whether to give birth, as opposed to individuals' right to sexual health care, effectively reinforced the sexual caste system against women and isolated them from gay men. For these changes in the wording of *Roe* to matter, its structural argument should have been based in a revamped version of equal protection designed to protect the constitutional rights of gender and sexual orientation–based castes as opposed to those of similarly situated suspect classes.

Thus, in order to make the court's holding stronger, the wording of *Roe* should have read, in pertinent part, "The Texas abortion laws must be declared unconstitutional because they deprive individuals of their right, secured by the Ninth Amendment, to equal access to sexual health and to choose whether to have children." This wording would have defined the right to choose based upon equal access to sexual health care as opposed to basing it upon gender, sexual orientation, marital status, and immediate medical condition (i.e., pregnancy).

As a result, the court might not have later diminished this right by reinterpreting the right to choose abortion as simply another judicially imposed extension of Due Process "liberty interests." Had *Roe* used language capable of joining two disenfranchised groups instead of dividing them, the court would likely have faced tougher future opposition to diluting this right. In turn, this opposition might have made future legislation less likely to succeed in imposing burdens on women's access to abortion services. State legislatures would have had a much harder time restricting the right to choose, since both women and gay men would together have opposed these restrictions—one group unwilling to let the other's rights to equal access become abridged lest its own access be targeted next. However, the language of *Roe* isolated instead of united, and the diminution occurred both within the courtroom and without, making the language of modern-day anti-choice advocates seem somewhat prophetic: "*Roe* will be reversed . . . not in one decision but over the course of several cases in which the Supreme Court repeatedly upholds increased state restrictions on abortion . . ." Indeed, many states have already succeeded in imposing burdens upon women's access to abortion that the court in *Roe* likely never intended to be possible, but that the deficient language of its holding was also ill-equipped to prevent.

Roe presented a unique opportunity for the court to embrace the reality of American caste systems. Since its founding, America has harbored an extensive, hierarchal caste system based on gender and sexual orientation. Within this system, heterosexuals are placed above homosexuals, and men are placed above women. As a result, access to sexual health care is regularly used to reinforce this caste system, as health care is most often controlled and regulated by the heterosexual male majority that decides whom will receive this access, when, where, and at what cost.

Protecting minorities based on whether they fall into similarly situated classes is inadequate to address this reality. The current structure leaves women without adequate (let alone equal) protection simply because they are not insular, even though they carry generations' worth of documented invidious discrimination, comprise less than a fifth of our nation's elected representatives, and are generally easily identified by the same physically immutable characteristics on which Male Supremacy bases its discrimination.[6]

The current structure also leaves gay men without adequate protection because they, too, are thought to carry only three of four "I" characteristics* necessary to be considered a "suspect class"** and thereby form an equal protection argument when certain important rights are threatened. As a result, both women and gay men are considered only "quasi" suspect classes; however, this point is a hotly debated one. While they are technically an insular group, the court often does not consider gay men to be as small a percentage of American society as they actually are. Because of this, gay men may also lack

---

* Immutability, Insularity, a history of Invidious discrimination, and political Impotency.

** A class of minorities whom the Supreme Court considers especially and historically vulnerable to the whims of the majority, and whom, as a result of its vulnerability, the Court endeavors to protect against certain kinds of discrimination.

the perceived insularity thought necessary for a serious equal protection claim.[7] While most expert estimates place America's homosexual population at 10 percent or less, Americans tend to guess that the number is higher, around 20 percent. Before the 1980s, the few representations of homosexuality in popular culture tended to consist of potentially dangerous social deviants (think Norman Bates in *Psycho*). Since then, however, portrayals of gay characters in pop culture have become far more numerous and mostly positive. That growing representation may have spurred growing acceptance—and inflated population estimates. From the last part of the twentieth to the beginning of the twenty-first century, the percentage of Americans who considered homosexuality to be an acceptable alternative lifestyle increased from 38 percent (June 1992) to 51 percent (May 2002), but then decreased to 48 percent (June 2008).

Further, the Supreme Court does not often perceive homosexuality as an immutable characteristic. Unlike gender or race, the court observes, gay men may not "exhibit obvious, immutable or distinguishing characteristic that define them as a distinct group." But then again, in today's modern culture, do all people of color "obviously" exhibit "distinguishing characteristics" that "define them" as minorities? Do all women? Not necessarily, yet they are still members of two of America's lower castes simply by virtue of their race, gender, or both.

As a result of their questionable immutability and insularity, the Supreme Court often does not realize that gay men are, like women, in such dire need of protection from Male Supremacy. Further, and again much like women, gay men are generally politically impotent, and have a well-documented history of invidious discrimination. These characteristics are nearly identical between women and gay men, yet they are not considered to be "similarly situated" classes equally worthy of protection under current equal protection doctrine. If this doctrine were restructured to acknowledge the reality that both women and gay men fall into castes routinely relegated to lower positions by the heterosexual male majority, judicial protection might be truly equal.

After noting the existence of these gender and sexual orientation–based castes, it is essential to examine how Male Supremacy used the pre–Affordable Care Act health-care system to reinforce them. Women's and gay men's unequal access to sexual health care, including prevention and treatment for venereal diseases, pregnancy, anal and testicular cancer, and HIV/AIDS evidenced such reinforcement. Even today, because homophobia and other stigmas against gay men persist in the United States, negative attitudes about homosexuality can lead to rejection by friends and family, discriminatory acts and violence that harm specific individuals, and laws and policies that adversely affect the lives of many people. This can have damaging effects on the health of gay men and other sexual minorities. Homophobia, stigma, and discrimination can (1) limit these men's ability to access high-quality health care that is responsive to health issues of gay men; (2) affect income, employment status, and the ability to get and keep health insurance; (3) contribute to poor mental health and unhealthy behaviors, such as substance abuse, risky sexual behaviors, and suicide attempts; (4) affect gay men's ability to establish and maintain long-term same-sex relationships that reduce HIV and STD risk; and finally, (5) make it difficult for some gay men to be open about same-sex behaviors with others, which can increase stress, limit social support, and negatively affect health. Further, gay men who experience homophobia, bullying, and/or rejection due to their sexual orientation were found to be 3.4 times more likely to have risky sex.[8] Because safe sex is one of the most effective ways of reducing STDs, these gay men are especially vulnerable to transmission.

Much like gay men's struggles to obtain access to medical insurance and various sexual health-care treatments, women regularly experience similar difficulties when attempting to obtain abortions. In 1981, the Supreme Court in *Harris v. McRae*[9] ruled that the state could not criminalize abortion but that it also did not have to affirmatively pay for it. This effectively forces lower- and lower-middle-class women who wish to exercise their right to choose to undergo potentially hazardous, low-cost abortion procedures and to bargain for their reproductive freedom. These women must negotiate with their male partners, parents, doctors, and/or HMO representatives for access to the same caliber of sexual health care that has historically been automatically granted to men. In contrast, heterosexual men are highly unlikely to have to negotiate with outside parties—especially of the opposite sex—in order to pay for necessary or elective sexual health care. Further, the social and financial stigma attached to men's sexual health care is far from that attached to women's. Heterosexual men have historically received sexual health care for a variety of conditions regardless of whether their need for treatment resulted from sexual activity or not. Conversely, women often do not enjoy the same equal access. While prostate exams, vasectomies, and Viagra are often covered by most state or employer-sponsored health-care plans, in vitro fertilization is considered unnecessarily "therapeutic" and hardly ever covered, and abortion procedures are only covered by the most expensive PPO option plans, and even this coverage is limited to the first trimester only. Further, according to Peter Williams's *Ain't Nobody's Business if You Do*, anal cancers that affect primarily gay men are usually covered. All of these financial double standards are not only unequal but also potentially unconstitutional, as they ignore *Roe*'s viability standard, which bases women's right to choose on whether their fetus is viable, not on any specific trimester. While heterosexual men enjoy equal access to sexual health care without financial restrictions from the state, women are much more likely to have to negotiate in this way for access to the same medical treatment.

In 1976, the Hyde Amendment further illustrated how health care is used to reinforce gender-based competition. This Amendment prohibited the use of Medicaid funds for abortions and thus, like *Harris*, seemed to suggest that *Roe* did not protect lower-class women, much like gay men. In 1989, the Supreme Court seemed to confirm this suggestion by deciding *Webster v. Sexual Health Services*.[10] In *Webster*, the court effectively reduced federal spending for abortions, thereby limiting free access to sexual health care for poor women and minors, while simultaneously declining to uphold legislation requiring physicians to perform initial viability tests. In effect, after only five short years, *Roe* had begun to create castes within a caste. *Harris* further divided the pregnant women *Roe* was designed to protect into socioeconomic classes, some of which were protected by *Roe* and others that were clearly left with no other choice than to abort by any dangerous means necessary.

The heterosexual male majority's use of the health-care system to reinforce gender-based caste came to a head in 1992 with *Planned Parenthood v. Casey*.[11] In *Casey*, the Supreme Court reinterpreted the right to choose abortion as no longer fundamental but simply a vaguely defined and loosely supported liberty interest. In *Casey*, the court claimed it was upholding *Roe* by retaining its viability standard but in fact paved the way for the heterosexual majority to further control access to health care and, through it, keep women firmly rooted within their lower caste. *Casey* established an "undue burden" standard, holding that states must allow access to abortion before the fetus became viable, but also allowing them the right to impose certain economic, geographic, and emotional burdens on women seeking abortions. States quickly enacted health-care legislation that made the procedure more expensive, forced abortion clinics to relocate to remote locations, demanded that women submit to twenty-four-hour waiting periods, and required minors to provide parental consent. Although health exceptions must exist in situations where abortion would be necessary to save the mother's life, it has become clear through the years since *Casey* that the court is unlikely to consider anything short of criminalizing abortion to be an "undue burden" upon the mother.[12] The court was already aware that this might happen, as *Roe* herself alerted the court to this distinct possibility, both at the time that *Roe* was decided and in the future. An excerpt from Norma McCorvey's (*Roe*) affidavit to the Fifth Circuit read that she had "wanted to terminate [her] pregnancy because of the economic hardship which [her] pregnancy entailed and because of the social stigma attached to the bearing of illegitimate children in our society." Since McCorvey could not afford to travel to another state for a legal abortion, she said, "I fear that my very life would be endangered if I submitted to an abortion which I *could* afford." McCorvey's financial concerns mirror the privacy issues found in *Lawrence v. Texas*, where, in 2003, gay sex was finally brought within the protections of "right to privacy," so long as it was conducted out of sight within the confines of the home. Similarly, the right to abort in *Casey* and *Webster* was still protected as long as it was paid for privately, and thus kept out of the direct sight and economic concern of the heterosexual male majority.

Thanks to the late, dogmatically conservative Justice Scalia, the following portions of *Roe* have not been saved:

Under *Roe*, it's unconstitutional to *require* that an abortion doctor or clinic provide a patient with truthful information designed to influence her choice *before* she can give her informed, written consent to the procedure. Under *Casey's* "undue burden" standard (as applied today, at least) such a requirement is constitutional. As a result, many states have mandated that patients receive ultrasounds, "informational" videos, and other medically unnecessary procedures that anti-abortion advocates routinely foist onto women in an attempt to delay or even block their choice.

In some states, such procedures also include 24- to 36-hour mandatory waiting periods. Under *Roe*, requiring a waiting period between the time the woman gives her informed consent and the time of the abortion is unconstitutional. Under the "undue burden" regime (again, as applied today) it is not.

Under *Roe*, requiring that information be provided by a doctor, rather than by non-physician counselors, is also unconstitutional. Under the "undue burden" regime (again, as of today) it is not. This opens the door for states to attempt to shut down abortion clinics by requiring that they maintain emergency room admitting privileges at a local hospital.

Under *Roe*, requiring detailed reports that include demographic data about each woman who seeks an abortion, as well as various pieces of information about each abortion, is unconstitutional. Under the "undue burden" regime (as applied today, at least) it generally is not. This final change allows others to record and possibly even share details about a patient's private life—strange, considering the entire basis for the freedom of choice lies within her *right* to keep such details to herself.

Other states have proposed legislation seeking to not only restrict but completely defund some women's access to abortion altogether. In 2011, the North Carolina legislature voted to defund Planned Parenthood by statutory amendment. Only months later, the legislature then proposed a statewide Act requiring abortion providers to read booklets full of partisan, legislatively scripted "information" to patients, ironically titling this the "Women's Right to Know." Unfortunately, the legislature did not stop at this. In one of the most extreme attacks on *Roe*'s central holding, the North Carolina legislature went so far as to propose further legislation allowing hospitals the right to deny women access to even life-saving abortions deemed necessary by their doctors. Local legislatures often ride the line between allowable and "undue"; between "informed consent" and "forced propaganda." Much of their medically inaccurate "information" usually insists that life begins at conception and that "the evidence overwhelmingly proves that the morbidity and mortality rates of legal abortion are several times higher than that for carrying a pregnancy to term," theologically and politically biased assertions that directly violate the Supreme Court's holding in *Roe* that this exact "beginning" is debatable at best and go against the American Medical Association's determination that childbirth is, in all cases, far more dangerous to women's health than our current practice of safe, legal abortion. When examined closely by bipartisan reviewers, it becomes clear that such financial, geographical, and consensual requirements are simply Male Supremacy's efforts to dominate women as a lower caste.

Based on the vast pool of empirical evidence detailing women's and gay men's unequal access to sexual health care, including prevention and treatment for venereal diseases, pregnancy, anal and testicular cancer, HIV/AIDS, and instances of sexual assault, it is clear that a gender and sexual orientation–based caste system reinforced in 1973 by *Roe*'s limited, divisively worded protection continues. Prior to the passage of the ACA, numerous studies and internationally recognized authorities cited above support the additional conclusion that Male Supremacy uses health care to further reinforce these castes by denying women and gay men affordable access to coverage and, through it, sexual health care equal to that of their heterosexual male counterparts. This, in my opinion, should be considered a natural right.

In 1973, the Civil Rights Act of 1964 was very young, both socially and legally. Equal protection was a newer concept than that of privacy, and a woman's right to choose was uncertain territory for the plaintiffs seeking federal protection from state action. Perhaps this contributed to the court's determination in *Roe* that the right to abortion—limited to pregnant women and married couples seeking to abort a fetus before it became viable in the womb—should be protected as a right to privacy as opposed to a right to equal protection under the law and thus a right to equal access to sexual health care. Perhaps this was why the plaintiffs in *Roe* eventually abandoned their more radical, more potentially liberating Ninth Amendment arguments in search of firmer, more conservative, and more judicially rooted ground within the Fourteenth Amendment. Perhaps the court felt that society and the legislature was not yet prepared to accept anything more than a limited right, and was not yet willing to further enfranchise women by declaring their right to equality to men in terms of sexual health care. Perhaps they felt their ruling in *Roe* would be better understood and more easily accepted by 1970s society as defending women's privacy as procreators, not radically declaring their equality as individuals. However, as Justices Blackmun and Stevens aptly recognized, abortion is among "the most intimate and personal choices . . ." It is a matter "central to personal dignity and autonomy," and it involves "personal decisions that profoundly affect bodily integrity, identity, and destiny." As a result, "the 'undue burden' standard may ultimately require the invalidation of each provision upheld today if it can be shown, on a better record, that the State is too effectively express[ing] a preference for childbirth over abortion."[13]

By dismissing these justices' warnings that "privacy" and the "undue burden" standard would not be enough, in future years, to protect women from anti-choice legislators—and even the future Supreme Court's own conservatism—Scalia was no doubt attempting to avoid creating a "government of individual men."[14] However, in doing so, he simultaneously created a decision seriously lacking in its support of women and allowed subsequent state legislators—fueled by radical anti-choice advocates—extreme latitude to further erode equal access to sexual health care. In his own words, "*Roe*'s mandate for abortion on demand destroyed the compromises of the past, rendered compromise impossible for the future, and required the entire issue to be resolved uniformly, at the national level. At the same time, *Roe* created a vast new class of abortion women and abortion proponents by eliminating the moral opprobrium that had attached to the act." Exactly who—besides women—had been forced for millennia before *Roe* to "compromise," or whether attempting to do away with the "moral opprobrium" surrounding abortion was in fact a very necessary and noble act, the staunchly anti-choice, conservative Catholic Justice Scalia conveniently chose not to discuss in his otherwise excessive diatribe.

The Supreme Court ultimately decided the fate of women's rights to choose abortion using a "right to privacy" argument under Due Process. Years later, it would establish the gay community's right to privacy in much the same way. In *Lawrence*, the Supreme Court held in a 6–3 decision that homosexual sex was included within the fundamental right to privacy as long as it occurred within the home or another equally private place.[15] The plaintiffs' choice to protect gay sexuality using the right to privacy within the Due Process clause limited, isolated, and defined gay men much the same way as *Roe* limited, isolated, and defined women. Gay sex was now firmly rooted in "privacy"—meaning, implicitly, that it was unsavory activity that should be kept out of sight. This mirrored *Roe*, which implied that abortion was an equally unsavory activity considered fundamental only because it should take place privately, and protected only pregnant women and married couples due to their unique ability to procreate. The plaintiffs knew, perhaps, that the court's interests in these cases would lie in protecting privacy and in shielding the majority from the unsavory actions of the minority, not in establishing equality for either women or gay men.

Understanding *Roe*'s exact constitutional implications (and limitations) is important for women, not only because so many have never read the exact wording of the case that literally gave them any agency whatsoever over their own reproductive systems, but also because this wording relates back to the power of women sharing their truth.

Had Norma McCorvey never shared her truth, we wouldn't have access to many essential aspects of reproductive health care today. Planned Parenthood wouldn't exist, and should it ever evaporate due to the efforts of anti-choice justices, legislators, and advocates, many women will be cut off from not only safe abortion and effective birth control but also life-saving cancer screenings. Abortion itself will not end, of course—instead, it will simply go back to being as it was before 1973: unsafe primarily because it was illegal. We will have succeeded only in endangering women's health by shaming them into secrecy and criminalizing their desire to control their own bodies. McCorvey was hardly the first woman to desire an end to her pregnancy; she was simply the first to bring this desire into the national spotlight. As such, she did more than simply establish a woman's right to choose—she demonstrated how politically powerful women can become by telling the truth.

This idea of the personal being political ties *Roe* directly to comedy, since it hits on the importance of women connecting with other women and puts to use what comedienne-ballerinas have always implied through humor: Women need to talk about their experiences. Women need to listen to those experiences. They need to realize that what's happening to them isn't happening just to them, as individuals. Without this communication, women can become competitive, and competition is a tactic used to separate them from each other so that they'll stay isolated, so that they'll believe that their problems are uniquely their own and give up on ever doing anything politically or legally to change that, so that they'll view Feminism as "whining" and discrimination as something they're doing to themselves rather than something that Patriarchy is extremely adept at doing to them.

When a woman doesn't talk or listen to other women, she can sometimes think that her faults are her fault. That she must have done something to create her own individual problem. That sexism is simply a matter of her personal, skewed perception rather than a legal, financial, and political reality that all women face every day of their lives. "Yes, and" works to counter all of that thinking. When we unite as women and refuse to let our other differences divide us, we're reminded that we didn't create inequality. We simply suffer its consequences.

And those consequences affect us all as *women*, not merely as individuals.

That mindset empowers us by reminding women of the truth that Patriarchy so often hides: The ways in which you are treated and the roles that you are allowed and not allowed to play are linked to your gender . . . and all of this *does* and *should* matter politically. It should become your fuel for change. Comedians who embrace this mindset have always been the source of political change. Shakespeare's character of the Fool, a royal court jester, was tasked with the one job no one else in the kingdom would dare do: tell the king the truth, and in so doing, talk back to power.

Watching and laughing at (or even with) Shakespeare's Fool and his modern-day progeny, comedienne-ballerinas, links us all together through common experience. We feel that we *know* the Fool—now embodied by the comedians we see on TV shows and in movies. We feel we *know* Lucy, or Gilda, or Abbi, or Ilana simply through the shared female experience, comedic or otherwise, that unites us. When we watch them and laugh, we are silently cheering them on. We're on their side as collaborators. When the show ends, this subconscious "Yes, and-ing" can carry on in our daily lives, allowing us to silently (or even openly) cheer on other women in real life and allowing women who don't necessarily feel connected to one another to discover that they have more in common than previously assumed. In this way, shows that portray female characters "Yes, and-ing" one another create connections that allow us to grow close to other women, regardless of race, class, or sexual orientation. This closeness can translate into empathy on a social and political level when discrimination affects those individuals.

Conversely, Male Supremacy–reinforcing shows often destroy such closeness or prevent it from ever forming. These shows depict women of different races, classes, and sexual orientations competing with each other for limited opportunities. When these women experience discrimination based on their gender, these shows make them—and through them, their audiences—feel as if whatever hardship a woman experiences is her fault and her negative experience *alone*. Over time, this penetrates the subconscious and diminishes women's collective agency. There is no commonality among female characters on these shows, and thus the audience absorbs division rather than unity. They internalize the message that there exists no reason to band together to fight back against discrimination. Divided, they remain precious snowflakes that melt separately—but joined together, in large numbers, they become an avalanche.

exploding the bomb

I'T'S FUNNY BECAUSE EVERY THIRD or fourth guest will come on and say, 'Oh, this is so much fun! I don't get to hang out with three other girls that often!'" Brandie Posey said of her popular comedy podcast, *Lady to Lady*. "As a female who also happens to be a comic, you're usually the token in a lineup, so you barely get to do comedy with other females. You don't get the sisterhood like the guys get the brotherhood unless you actively make it a point to hang out with them or like set up brunches. So, for our show, we throw a lot of exercise classes. We're like, 'Hey. We're going to rent out this thing, everybody come do it, and then we'll just sweat together and chill out afterwards and talk about how ridiculous that just was. It'll be hilarious!' So it's really fun to get to just hang out with a bunch of women, simply because that doesn't happen very often. And over the years we've found that—surprise, surprise!—listening to four women talking is just as much, if not more, fun than listening to four guys talking."

"Why do you think that is?"

"Because we're not all trying to win the conversation."

"You think there's less competition between the women who appear on your podcast?"

"Definitely. It's more of a give-and-take relationship. If you're the girl in a group of guy comics who are just talking, in a podcast, everyone is trying to get their lines in, and no one's really listening to anybody else. So as opposed to building a conversation, they're one-upping each other. But in our group, everyone's interested in the conversation *as a whole* being funny, so we let other people talk."

"They have to take over a room, you know," Brandie went on. "When they're with their friends and family, they feel like the star of the show, so some guys feel like they constantly have to compete to feel that way outside of those circles. That's a lot for anyone to take on. It's also what sets *Lady to Lady* apart."

"Conversation building? The four of you actually listening rather than simply waiting your turn to speak?" I asked.

"Yes. Exactly. Women are really good listeners. That's a thing that I've learned."

"Through listening?"

"Yeah." She laughed.

"We have an online group for women comics," NY-based stand-up Ayanna Dookie said, leaning back in her red canvas seat in the audience section at the Magnet Theater. "I remember somebody posting the Comedy Store's lineup and saying, 'Ladies, look at this! It's ridiculous that there's never any women in their lineup!' And then it became a huge deal on social media, with everyone trying to figure out why. But to me, it seemed like a lot of complaining. All of us knew what we were getting ourselves into. This is a male-dominated field. This is going to happen regularly. The only thing you can do is just keep working so that you're undeniable and then you get on this list."

"So you feel that women shouldn't necessarily speak up about the 'Rule of Two' but instead simply focus on breaking it?"

"Absolutely. But, see, I went to school for engineering—so, by trade, I'm accustomed to being around nothing but guys. My experiences in comedy have been the same as my experiences in college. I graduated in December 2005 with a degree in mechanical engineering, and I was the only brown woman in my class, so I'm accustomed to being in that kind of setting. I signed up for it. I didn't walk in there protesting, 'Where are all the other black people?' You know what I mean? I didn't do anything along those lines. And the same thing happened when I moved to New York to do comedy. I didn't walk into this new world going, 'This is ridiculous! There are no women!' Because *that's just what it is.* I understand the frustration, but these are the rules. You don't have to like them; you just have to play by them. You just have to work hard enough and long enough until you get to the point where you're undeniable. And then none of us will have to worry about who's on this list. None of us will have to care about the narrative that 'the man' has written for us: 'Hey ladies, we'd love to have you, but we only got so many spots!' You know what I mean? None of us will have to fight the instincts to size each other up. Right now, we're all silently gunning for each other, thinking, 'No! I'm here! I'm next in line for these two spots that they're going to give us!' rather than seeing another woman and thinking, 'We're kindred spirits, and we should be working together, supporting each other, lifting each other up, and making *our own* stuff.'

"So I think a lesson that more women need to learn is: Stop complaining. Drop the fallacy. Stop looking at other women as your competition. Just focus all of that time and energy into your work. Because the more of *us* who make it and climb up in the ranks, the more likely *you* are to make it."

"Do you feel like you've made any particular sacrifices for your job?" I asked LA-based stand-up Mary Mack during my final interview at iO West.

"Oh, yes! I've made a big sacrifice because I can't have a dog or a cat. And I would *really* like a dog or a cat."

"Okay. Is there anything else you can't have?"

"Sometimes I think about having a baby and dressing that baby up as a service dog so that I could have a dog *and* still get to travel . . . but people are frowning on it."

We laughed. It was the end of the day and getting dark, so I walked her to her bicycle, chained up right around the corner. As we walked, another question popped into my head.

"Do most women find other women funny?"

She took a second to think. "I feel like somebody tried to create a cattiness among women—especially women who also happen to be comedians—but the good ones never participated in it. Those people didn't last. And it's too bad for them, really, because it was such a waste of energy. The good ones, the ones who lasted, cheered for everybody, supported everybody. Even if they didn't like another woman's comedy, if she was a hard worker and trying hard, the good ones still rooted for her. Maybe I'm biased, but I'm always rooting for females."

That made me smile. "Do you think that maybe you express your Feminism by simply not participating in this narrative of cattiness?" I asked. "Is that your way of rejecting this mythology—or this truth, in some cases, since even the most distasteful prophecies can become self-fulfilling? Is *not* competing with other women in itself a Feminist act?"

"I think so," she said. "It's the same way as being a pacifist: you're still making a choice; you're still making an active choice in what's happening." Which may explain why acts of kindness and support are so powerful, and why no amount of love, no matter how small, is ever truly wasted, because in the end, nice guys finish first. If you don't know that, then you don't know where the finish line is.* "Ladies are cheering for each other!" she went on. "There's no reason not to. In fact, I feel like we might be building a bomb."

" . . . You're building a bomb?"

"Not me—*us*," she said. "You know, 'female comedians,' whatever that means."

"Okay," I said. "So what happens when it explodes?"

"Well, I think what happens is that it drops and opens up gently, and there's about four or five—possibly twenty—more female television hosts that come out of it. I'm not quite sure how many jobs there are hosting, but more of those would be great. And maybe Joan Rivers's angel could carry the bomb, and Chelsea Handler could hit it—*whack!*—and crack it open, and that's when all the other hosts will come out."

This metaphorical "bomb" was arguably created by women like Joan and Lucy, but it's now grown to include Rosie and Gilda and Mary and Rhoda and Tina and Amy and Abbi and Ilana and countless others, like the enduringly positive Mary Mack. They now have the power of "the bomb" to carry with them—and though it may sound dangerous, it keeps them safe, and instills them with an inner sense of power. Over time, as more and more women have become powerful in comedy, they've made it safe for us to actually be nice to one another. The popular, cool kids in school aren't just a table full of guys

---

* An ode to Garry Shandling.

with one (maybe two) girls laughing nervously at all their jokes. There are tables full of women to sit with now. In many ways, this girls' club has always existed—from Sarah Bernhardt and Mae West on up to Abbi and Ilana—but now it has its own obvious table. The word has never been quite as out before today.

Today, when I consider all that's changed and all that's stayed the same, I think about Lena Dunham. I think about Amy Schumer. I think about Abbi and Ilana. I think about Tina Fey and Amy Poehler. I think about Sarah Silverman. I think about Ellen DeGeneres. I think about Mindy Kaling and Phoebe Robinson and Jessica Williams and Issa Rae and Aparna Nancherla and Tig Notaro and Maria Bamford and Janet Varney and Mo Collins and Molly Shannon and Naomi Ekperigin and Livia Scott and Marlo Thomas and Laura House and Janine Brito and Virginia Jones and Mary Tyler Moore and Sara Benincasa and Susan Rice and Ayanna Dookie and Eliza Skinner and Angelina Spicer and Bonnie McFarlane and Alison Flierl and Rachel LaForce and Cameron Esposito and Bea Arthur—*all* the other different colors and cultures of cool girls forming their own clubs, who are *all* killing it right now in their disparate yet interconnected ways. My breath stops sometimes with excitement at how connected we all are. That is the absolute best part of it all. It feels really good. It feels like there's a place for them, and us, and *you* in the show.

"So it's more like a funny piñata than a bomb?" I asked Mary Mack.

"Oh, no," Mary corrected me. "It's not a metaphor. It's an *actual bomb*."

"Okay . . ." I said, watching the teasing glint in her eye as we both kept walking down Hollywood Boulevard. As we got close to where she'd parked, I could tell that it was close to six p.m. A man up ahead was walking in our direction—moving fast—clearly trying to get to his car and beat the rush hour, too. He was walking so quickly that I was sure he'd knock us off the sidewalk. I worried suddenly about the three of us colliding; of Mary's riding alone on those roads, bicycling in heavy traffic. Spending more time trying not to get hurt than finding her way home.

"Is the bomb anywhere nearby?" I said.

She nodded again, playfully. I felt myself bracing for impact. But then . . . nothing. No collision at all. The man even smiled for the briefest moment while stopping to share the sidewalk, and we stopped, too.

"Great," I said. "Well, in that case, I hope it explodes the world."

acknowledgments

Molly Shannon, Rosie Shuster, Lizz Winstead, Luisa Omielan, Judy Carter, Janet Varney, Emily Maya Mills, Betty Cahill, Angelina Spicer, Abbi Jacobson, Bonnie McFarlane, Kaileigh McCrea, Alison Flierl, Aparna Nancherla, Amey Goerlich, Mary Elizabeth Williams, Becky Garcia, Christy Stratton Mann, June Diane Raphael, Naomi Ekperigin, Beth Newell, Sarah Pappalardo, Brandie Posey, Riley Silverman, Eliza Skinner, Cody Lindquist, Iris Bahr, Virginia Jones, Ayanna Dookie, Rachel LaForce, Bri Pruett, Jane Borden, Amanda Marcotte, Emily Nussbaum, Lindy West, Charlene Conley, Janine Brito, Laurie Kilmartin, Fay Weldon, Laura House, Mary Mack, Livia Scott, Mo Collins, Lyndsay Hailey, Sara Benincasa, Kristen Bartlett, Shelby Fero, Megan Gray, Elana Fishbein, Susan Rice, Wendy Hammers, Caitlin Kunkel, James Grace, Jana Liles, Robin Hammond, Alex Klein, Iana Dontcheva, Jonathan Groff, Professors Wade Wilson and Nola Schiff of the University of North Carolina School of the Arts, Dara Silver and the Arts Council of Winston-Salem and Forsyth County, Professor Mary Dalton of the Wake Forest University Department of Communications, Professor Shannon Gilreath of the Wake Forest University School of Law, Professor Lori Landay of the Berklee School of Music, and the members and staffs of the Magnet Theater, Second City Hollywood, Second City Chicago, iO West, and several all-girl comedy troupes, including THE STANK, LADY SKETCH LAB, and JUST BOOBS— among others.

bibliography

Abbott, J. (2010). *History of King Charles II of England*. New York: Kessinger Publishing, LLC.

Abortion Facts. n.d. Retrieved February 14, 2017, from abortion facts.com.

Abrams, N. (2012, June 19). Adam Corolla: Women Aren't As Funny As Men. *TV Guide*. Retrieved February 14, 2017, from: http://www. tvguide.com/news/adam-carolla-women-not-funny-1048998/

After Hours Records, LP. (1960). "If I Embarrass You—Tell Your Friends." [Recorded by B. Barth].

Alderman, E., & Kennedy, C. (1997). *The Right to Privacy*. New York: Random House.

Antler, J. E. (1998). *Talking Back: Images of Jewish Women in American Popular Culture*. Hanover: University Press of New England.

Armstrong, K. (2008, March). "My Wish: The Charter for Compassion." *TED Talks*.

349

Baker, N. A. (2016). *Stanton in Her Own Time: A Biographical Chronicle of Her Life, Drawn from Recollections, Interviews, and Memoirs by Family, Friends, and Associates.* Iowa City: University of Iowa Press.

Ballard, K. (2009, January 21). *Kaye Ballard and the story of Lucille Ball vs. Mad Dog. PBS.org.* Retrieved from: http://www.pbs.org/wnet/makeemlaugh/episodes/great-lines/kaye-ballard-and-the-story-of-lucille-ball-vs-mad-dog/?p=102.

Benedictus, L. (2013, September 20). "Comedy Gold: Amy Schumer's Mostly Sex Stuff." *TheGuardian.com.* Retrieved February 17, 2017, from: https://www.theguardian.com/stage/2013/sep/20/comedy-gold-amy-schumer-mostly-sex-stuff.

Bennetts, L. (1987, August 9). "The Pain Behind The Laughter of Moms Mabley." *The New York Times.*

Bruce, L. (2012, August 22). "Joan Rivers on Phyllis Diller: 'She Worked Like a Man'." *The Hollywood Reporter.*

Brumburgh, G. n.d. "ZaSu Pitts: Biography." *IMDB.com.* Retrieved February 7, 2017, from: http://www.imdb.com/name/nm0686032/bio.

Burnett, C. (2003). *One More Time.* New York: Random House Trade Paperbacks.

Cannold, L. (2001). *The Abortion Myth: Feminism, Morality and the Hard Choices Women Make.* New York: Wesleyan University Press.

Centers for Disease Control. (2011, November 27). "Gay and Bisexual Men's Health." *CDC.com.* Retrieved November 27, 2011, from: http://www.cdc.gov/msmhealth/stigma-and-discrimination.htm.

Davis, M. P. (1997, November 24). Archive of American Television. (T. Gilbert, Interviewer).

Davis, P. (1992). *The Way I See It.* New York: Putnam Adult.

DeGeneres, E. (2007). Barbara Walters ABC Special. (B. Walters, Interviewer).

Diehl, C. (1994, March 22). "For the Men Who Still Don't Get It." In M. Algarin, & B. Holman, *Aloud: Voices from the Nuyorican Poets Cafe.* New York, NY: Holt Paperbacks. Retrieved from: http://artvent.blogspot.com/2013/03/for-men-who-still-dont-get-it.html.

Diller, P. (2012, August 21). "Fresh Air Remembers Comedian Phyllis Diller." (T. Gross, Interviewer).

Diller, P., & Bushkin, R. (2005). *Like a Lampshade in a Whorehouse.* New York: Thorndike Press.

Dusenbery, M. (2015). "We Live in a Country Full of Racism, But No Racists: Rape, But No Rapists." *Feministing.com.* Retrieved from: http://feministing.com/2014/12/11/we-live-in-a-country-full-of-racism-but-no-racists-rape-but-no-rapists/.

Editors, B. (2016, January 21). *Moms Mabley Biography.* (A&E Television Networks). *Biography.com.* Retrieved February 7, 2017, from: http://www.biography.com/people/moms-mabley-38691.

Eisenberg, J. (2016, August 10). "As Final Five's popularity soars, America's male gymnasts compete in obscurity." *Yahoo.com.* Retrieved February 14, 2017, from: http://sports.yahoo.com/news/as-final-fives-popularity-soars-americas-male-gymnasts-compete-in-obscurity-011400873.html;_ylt=A0LEV07MJqNYyW8At. JXNyoA;_ylu=X3oDMTEybzQwNWh1BGNvbG8DYmYxBHB vcwMxBHZ0aWQDQjI5NDRfMQRzZWMDc3I-.

Ephron, N. (2006). *I Feel Bad About My Neck.* New York: Alfred A. Knopf.

Fallon, C. (2016, November 16). "'Crazy Ex-Girlfriend' Is a Bad Feminist, Just Like Us." *TheHuffingtonPost.com.* Retrieved from: http://www.huffingtonpost.com/entry/crazy-ex-girlfriend-bad-feminist_us_56464b02e4b060377349016b.

Friedan, B. (1963). *The Feminine Mystique*. New York: W.W. Norton & Co. Ltd.

Friedman, A. (2005). "Unintended Consequences of the Feminist Sex/Gender Distinction." American Sociological Association. Boulder: University of Colorado at Boulder.

Gallup Poll. (2011, November 27). "What Percentage of the Population Is Gay?" *Gallup.com*. Retrieved November 27, 2011, from: http://www.gallup.com/poll/6961/What-Percentage-Population-Gay.aspx.

George Mason University Press. (2011, November 26). "The Historians' Case Against Gay Discrimination." *HistoryNewsNetwork.com*. Retrieved November 26, 2011, from: http://hnn.us/articles/1539.html.

Gilbert, T. (2011, August 7). "The Woman Behind Lucy's Laughs." *NYTimes.com*. Retrieved January 26, 2017, from: http://www.nytimes.com/2011/08/07/arts/television/madelyn-pugh-davis-the-woman-behind-lucys-laughs.html.

Gilreath, S. (2011). *The End of Straight Supremacy: Realizing Gay Liberation*. Cambridge: Cambridge University Press.

Glass, I., & Joffe-Walt, C. (2015, January 23). "Act Two: Freedom Fries." Episode 545. *If You Don't Have Anything Nice to Say, SAY IT IN ALL CAPS*. New York: *This American Life*.

GLTB Project. (2011, November 27). "About the GLTB Project." *GLTBQ.com*. Retrieved November 27, 2011, from: http://www.glbtq.com/social-sciences/elected_officials,2.html.

Goldstein, E. L. (2009, March 1). *Jewish Women: A Comprehensive Historical Encyclopedia*. Retrieved February 7, 2017, from: https://jwa.org/encyclopedia/article/may-elaine.

Gray, J. (2013, July 17). "The Unfair Marginalization of Janeane Garofalo." *Splitsider.com*. Retrieved from: http://splitsider.com/2013/07/the-unfair-marginalization-of-janeane-garofalo/.

Guido, M. (2016). "Mom Tries To Help Daughter Find Period Supplies, Epic Text Exchange Ensues." *ScaryMommy.com*. Retrieved from: http://www.scarymommy.com/mom-daughter-tampon-text-exchange-goes-viral-belinda-hankins/.

Harding, K. (2014, December 9). "We Always Blame the Victim." *Dame Magazine*.

Heimel, C. (1983). *Sex Tips for Girls*. New York: Touchstone.

Ivins, M. (1993). *Nothin' But Good Times Ahead*. New York: Random House.

Jr., C. B. (1999). *A New Birth of Freedom: Human Rights, Named and Unnamed*. New York: Yale University Press.

Kane, M. J. (1996). "Media Coverage of the Post Title IX Female Athlete: A Feminist Analysis of Sport, Gender, and Power." *Duke University Journal of Gender, Law, and Policy*.

Kelley, K. (1991). *Nancy Reagan: The Unauthorized Biography*. New York: Simon & Schuster.

Ladies Home Journal. (1944). "You Can't Have a Career and Be a Good Wife," 91.

Lancefield, R. C. (2004, December). "Hearing orientality in (white) America, 1900–1930." Dissertation in partial fulfilment of the requirements for the degree of Doctor of Philosophy. Middletown, CT: Wesleyan University.

Lang, N. (2017, January 11). "Jeff Sessions Would Be a Disaster for the LGBT Community: Trump's Attorney General Pick Has Spent His Career Opposing Equality at Every Level." *Salon.com*. Retrieved January 27, 2017, from: http://www.salon.com/2017/01/11/jeff-sessions-would-be-a-disaster-for-the-lgbt-community-trumps-attorney-general-pick-has-spent-his-career-opposing-equality-at-every-level/.

Marbella, J. (1992, May 6). "It's time to tell the truth about parents, self, says Patti Davis." *Baltimore Sun*.

Marcotte, A. (2009, May 9). "No Cop-Outs: 37 Years Ago, 'Maude' Got the Abortion Experience Right." *Rewire.com*. Retrieved January 26, 2017, from: https://rewire.news/article/2009/05/05/no-copouts-37-years-ago-maude-got-abortion-experience-right/.

Martin, B. (2003). *A Rich Man's War, A Poor Man's Fight: Desertion of Alabama Troops from the Confederate Army*, 2nd ed. University of Alabama Press.

Maxwell, Z. (2014, March 27). "Rape Culture is Real." *Time*.

McFadden, R. D. (2001, June 3). "Imogene Coca, 92, Is Dead; a Partner in One of TV's Most Successful Comedy Teams." *The New York Times*.

McGlynn, K. (April, 29 2015). "Amy Poehler Thanks Gilda Radner 'For Lighting The Fuse.'" *HuffingtonPost.com*. Retrieved from: http://www.huffingtonpost.com/2015/04/29/amy-poehler-gilda radner_n_7161926.html.

McLellan, D. (2011, April 22). "Madelyn Pugh Davis dies at 90; 'I Love Lucy' writer." *The LA Times*.

Midler, B. (n.d.). "Bette Midler at Divine Madness." *YouTube.com*. Retrieved February 7, 2017, from: https://www.youtube.com/watch?v=eTcFIchjotM.

Murphy, M. (2014, April 25). "Why has drag escaped critique from feminists and the LGBTQ community?" *Feministcurrent.com*. Retrieved February 7, 2017, from: http://www.feministcurrent.com/2014/04/25/why-has-drag-escaped-critique-from-feminists-and-the-lgbtq-community/.

Nancy Snyderman, M. n.d. "Dr. Nancy Snyderman: Communicating Health Issues That People Care About." Retrieved February 13, 2017, from: http://drnancysnyderman.com/bio/.

National Right to Life. n.d. "The Complete Text of the Current Hyde Amendment." *NRLC.org*. Retrieved November 27, 2011, from: http://www.nrlc.org/federal/AHC/HydeAmendmentText/.

NC House of Representatives. (2010). *North Carolina "Woman's Right to Know" Act of 2010.* Legislative Bill, Raleigh.

NC House of Representatives. (2011). *North Carolina House Bill 351.* Legislative Bill, Raleigh.

Nussbaum, E. (2015, February 23). "Last Girl in Larchmont." *The New Yorker.*

Oneill, T. (2016). "This Dear Abby Advice is Insanely Sexist." *TheWeek.com.* Retrieved from: http://theweek.com/articles/635 529/dear-abby-advice-insanely-sexist.

Overbeke, G. K. (2008). "America's Madwomen: Jewish Female Comedians in the Twentieth Century." Honors thesis. Middletown, CT: Wesleyan University.

Pabst, E. S. (2005). "Cold War Insecurity as Women's Opportunity: Sputnik, The National Defense Education Act of 1958, and Shifting Gender Roles in Eisenhower's America." Boston: Boston College, Department of History.

Parker, A. (2017, January 20). "On a largely ceremonial day, Trump revamps the White House website and takes a few executive actions." *WashingtonPost.com.* Retrieved January 27, 2017, from: https://www.washingtonpost.com/news/post-politics/wp/2017/ 01/20/moments-after-taking-the-oath-president-trump-transforms-white-house-website/?utm_term=.a47a2be925ee.

Patterson, N. (2006). "A Womanist Discourse Analysis of the Comedic Discourse of Jackie 'Moms' Mabley." University of Florida, Graduate Department of Communications.

Pollitt, K. (2015, August 5). "How to Really Defend Planned Parenthood." *NYTimes.com.* Retrieved January 26, 2017, from: https:// www.nytimes.com/2015/08/05/opinion/how-to-really-defend-planned-parenthood.html?_r=0.

Poundstone, P. (2006, November 20). *Talk of the Nation.* (N. Conan, Interviewer).

Radner, G. (1983). *The Howard Stern Show.* (H. Stern, Interviewer).

Radner, G. (1989). *It's Always Something*. New York: Simon & Schuster.

Rivers, J. (1975, January 4). *The Carol Burnett Show*. New York, NY.

Rivers, J. (2014, March 27). *The Tonight Show Starring Jimmy Fallon*. (J. Fallon, Interviewer).

Sacks, D., & Thiel, P. n.d. *Stanford University Alumni Magazine*. Retrieved February 14, 2017, from: http://alumni.stanford.edu/get/page/magazine/article/?article_id=43448.

Sedinger, K. (2015, July 10). "WTF Lucy?" Retrieved January 26, 2017, from: https://wtflucy.com/2015/07/10/s01-e19-the-ballet/.

Shales, T., & Miller, J. A. (2008, June 4). "IT'S SATURDAY NIGHT!" *Vanity Fair*.

Sheridan, K. (2016, October 22). "John Banville: 'I have not been a good father. No writer is.'" *Irish Times*.

Silverman, S. (2015, October 22). *Fresh Air*. (T. Gross, Interviewer).

Smith, J. (2014, February 27). "Throwback Thursday: Ellen and Rosie Dance Around the Gay Thing in 1996." *Advocate.com*. Retrieved from: http://www.advocate.com/comedy/2014/02/23/throwback thursday-ellen-and-rosie-dance-around-gay-thing-1996.

Smith, R. L. (1986). *The Stars of Stand-Up Comedy: A Bibliographical Encyclopedia*. New York: Garland Publishing.

Spenser, E. (1845). *The Faerie Queene, Book 5, Canto II. Select Poetry, Chiefly Devotional, of the Reign of Queen Elizabeth*. (E. Farr, Ed.) Cambridge: University Press.

Sprinkle, S. V. (2011). *Unfinished Lives: Reviving the Memories of LGBTQ Hate Crimes*. New York: Wipf & Stock Pub.

Staff, T. H. (2014, September 5). "Camille Paglia Pays Tribute to Joan Rivers: From 'Scorching Candor' to Populist Appeal." *HollywoodReporter.com*. Retrieved from: http://www.hollywoodreporter.com/news/camille-paglia-pays-tribute-joan-730529.

Staff, T. H. (2014, September 10). "The Story of Joan Rivers: 24 Famous Friends From Dick Cavett to Donald Trump Construct

Stunning Oral History for THR." *HollywoodReporter.com*. Retrieved January 26, 2017, from: http://www.hollywood reporter.com/news/story-joan-rivers-24-famous-731383.

Stanley, A. (2008, March 3). "Who Says Women Aren't Funny?" *Vanity Fair*.

Timey, P. (2014, February 24). "Rube Goldberg Butts In." *The Comics Journal*.

Tomlin, L. n.d. *Ms. Sweeny*. (L. Tomlin, Performer). https://www.youtube.com/watch?v=TrgqFVwHf-E, Unknown.

Tucker, S. (1945). *Some of These Days*. Garden City: Doubleday, Doran and Company, Inc.

U.S. Census. n.d. Census Bureau Releases 2011 American Community Survey Estimates. *Census.gov*. Retrieved November 26, 2011, from: https://www.census.gov/newsroom/releases/archives/american_community_survey_acs/cb12-175.html.

U.S. Equal Employment Opportunity Commission. (2017, February 14). "The Equal Pay Act of 1963." *EEOC.gov*. Retrieved February 14, 2017, from: https://www.eeoc.gov/laws/statutes/epa.cfm.

University, Columbia. (2017). Women Film Pioneers Project. Retrieved February 13, 2017, from Columbia.edu: https://wfpp.cdrs.columbia.edu/pioneer/ccp-mabel-normand/.

Vineyard, J. (2014, April 8). "Bette Midler on Soph, Janis Joplin, and Her Early Years in New York City." *Vulture Magazine*.

Wallen, J. n.d. *Jewish Women's Archive—Encyclopedia*. Retrieved from JWA.org: https://jwa.org/encyclopedia/article/barth-belle.

Warton, T. (1870). *The History of English Poetry: From the Eleventh to the Seventeenth Century*. Oxford, England: Trinity College.

West, L. (2015, January 23). "Act One: Ask Not For Whom The Bell Trolls; It Trolls for Thee." Episode 545. *If You Don't Have Anything Nice to Say, SAY IT IN ALL CAPS*. New York: *This American Life*.

Williams, E. (1995). *The Humor of Jackie "Moms" Mabley: An African American Comedy Tradition*. New York: Routledge.

Williams, M. (1922). *The Velveteen Rabbit*. New York: George H. Doran Company.

Williams, P. (1996). *Ain't Nobody's Business If You Do*. New York: Prelude Press.

Women's International Center. (2011, November 27). "Women's History in America." *WIC.org*. Retrieved November 27, 2011, from: http://www.wic.org/misc/history.htm.

Wright, M. (2012, June 27). "Saturday Night's Children: Julia Sweeney (1990–1994)." *Splitsider.com*. Retrieved January 27, 2017, from: http://splitsider.com/2012/06/saturday-nights-children-julia-sweeney-1990-1994/.

Ziegler, M. (2012). "Sexing Harris: The Law and Politics of Defunding Planned Parenthood." Florida State University, College of Law.

endnotes

1. *Roe v. Wade,* 410 U.S. 113, 93 S.Ct. 705, 35 L.Ed.2d 147 (1973).

2. *Whalen v. Roe,* 429 U.S. 811, 97 S.Ct. 50 (Mem), 50 L.Ed.2d 71 (1976). See also *Roe* (recognizing the right of a woman to make certain fundamental decisions affecting her destiny has a substantive dimension of fundamental significance in defining the rights of the person).

3. *Lawrence v. Texas,* 539 U.S. 558, 123 S.Ct. 2472, 156 L.Ed.2d 508 (2003).

4. *Bowers v. Hardwick,* 478 U.S. 186, 106 S.Ct. 2841, 92 L.Ed.2d 140 (1986).

5. *Lawrence* at 572; 106 S.Ct. at 2475.

6. See *The End of Straight Supremacy,* by Shannon Gilreath, quoting *U.S. v. Carolene Products,* 304 U.S.144, 152 n. 4 (1938).

7. See *The End of Straight Supremacy, supra,* note 34, quoting *Regents of Univ. of California v. Bakke,* 438 U.S. 265, 290(1978).

8. *Ibid.*

9. *Harris v. McRae*, 444 U.S. 1069, 100 S.Ct. 1010, 62 L.Ed.2d 750 (1980).

10. *Webster v. Reproductive Health Services*, 488 U.S. 1003, 109 S.Ct. 780 (1989).

11. *Planned Parenthood v. Casey*, 505 U.S. 833, 112 S.Ct. 2791 (1992).

12. J. Scalia, *Casey* at 852, 112 S.Ct. 2813.

13. *Casey,* at 843, 112 S.Ct. 2800.

14. J. Scalia, *Casey* at 851, 112 S.Ct. 2812. See also *Dred Scott v. Sandford*, 19 How. 393, 621 (1857) (Curtis, J., dissenting).

15. *Lawrence* at 573; 106 S.Ct. at 2476.